Rethinking the Life Cycle

Edited by Alan Bryman, Bill Bytheway,
Patricia Allatt and Teresa Keil

M

First published 1987

Published by
THE MACMILLAN PRESS LTD
Houndmills, Basingstoke, Hampshire RG21 2XS
and London
Companies and representatives
throughout the world

Printed in Great Britain by
Anchor Brendon Ltd
Tiptree, Essex

British Library Cataloguing in Publication Data
Rethinking the life cycle.—(Explorations
in sociology).
1. Life cycle, Human—Social aspects
I. Bryman, Alan   II. Series
305.2   HM299
ISBN 0–333–43765–9 (hardcover)
ISBN 0–333–43766–7 (paperback)

EXPLORATIONS IN SOCIOLOGY

British Sociological Association Conference Volume series

Sami Zubaida (editor)	1	*Race and Racism*
Richard Brown (editor)	2	*Knowledge, Education and Cultural Change*
Paul Rock and Mary McIntosh (editors)	3	*Deviance and Social Control*
Emanuel de Kadt and Gavin Williams (editors)	4	*Sociology and Development*
Frank Parkin (editor)	5	*The Social Analysis of Class Structure*
Diana Leonard Barker and Sheila Allen (editors)	6	*Sexual Divisions and Society: Process and Change*
Diana Leonard Barker and Sheila Allen (editors)	7	*Dependence and Exploitation in: Work and Marriage*
Richard Scase (editor)	8	*Industrial Society: Class, Cleavage and Control*
Robert Dingwall, Christian Heath, Margaret Reid and Margaret Stacey (editors)	9	*Health Care and Health Knowledge*
Robert Dingwall, Christian Heath, Margaret Reid and Margaret Stacey (editors)	10	*Health and the Division of Labour*
Gary Littlejohn, Barry Smart, John Wakeford and Nira Yuval-Davis (editors)	11	*Power and the State*
Michèle Barrett, Philip Corrigan, Annette Kuhn and Janet Wolff (editors)	12	*Ideology and Cultural Production*
Bob Fryer, Alan Hunt, Doreen MacBarnet and Bert Moorhouse (editors)	13	*Law, State and Society*
Philip Abrams, Rosemary Deem, Janet Finch and Paul Rock (editors)	14	*Practice and Progress: British Sociology 1950–1980*
Graham Day, Lesley Caldwell, Karen Jones, David Robbins and Hilary Rose (editors)	15	*Diversity and Decomposition in the Labour Market*
David Robbins, Lesley Caldwell, Graham Day, Karen Jones and Hilary Rose (editors)	16	*Rethinking Social Inequality*

Eva Gamarnikow, David Morgan, June Purvis and Daphne Taylorson (editors)	17	*The Public and the Private*
Eva Gamarnikow, David Morgan, June Purvis and Daphne Taylorson (editors)	18	*Gender, Class and Work*
*Gareth Rees, Janet Bujra, Paul Littlewood, Howard Newby and Teresa L. Rees (editors)	19	*Political Action and Social Identity: Class, Locality and Ideology*
*Howard Newby, Janet Bujra, Paul Littlewood, Gareth Rees, Teresa L. Rees (editors)	20	*Restructuring Capital: Recession and Reorganization in Industrial Society*
*Sheila Allen, Kate Purcell, Alan Waton and Stephen Wood (editors)	21	*The Experience of Unemployment*
*Kate Purcell, Stephen Wood, Alan Waton and Sheila Allen (editors)	22	*The Changing Experience of Employmen. Restructuring and Recession*
*Jalna Hanmer and Mary Maynard (editors)	23	*Women, Violence and Social Control*
*Colin Creighton and Martin Shaw (editors)	24	*The Sociology of War and Peace*
*Alan Bryman, Bill Bytheway, Patricia Allatt and Teresa Keil	25	*Rethinking the Life Cycle*
*Patricia Allatt, Teresa Keil, Alan Bryman and Bill Bytheway	26	*Women and the Life Cycle*

*Published by Macmillan

Series Standing Order

If you would like to receive future titles in this series as they are published, you can make use of our standing order facility. To place a standing order please contact your bookseller or, in case of difficulty, write to us at the address below with your name and address and the name of the series. Please state with which title you wish to begin your standing order. (If you live outside the UK we may not have the rights for your area, in which case we will forward your order to the publisher concerned.)

Standing Order Service, Macmillan Distribution Ltd, Houndmills, Basingstoke, Hampshire, RG21 2XS, England.

Contents

Acknowledgements   vii

Notes on the Contributors   viii

Introduction
Alan Bryman, Bill Bytheway, Patricia Allatt and Teresa Keil   1

PART I   THEORETICAL APPROACHES

1   The Individual and Society: A Processual Approach
    Chris Harris   17

2   Measuring the Family Life Cycle: Concepts,
    Data and Methods
    Michael Murphy   30

PART II   POPULAR IDEOLOGIES

3   The Perpetuation of a Folk Model of the Life
    Cycle and Kinship in a Pottery Factory
    Paul Bellaby   53

4   Rethinking the Family Life Cycle: Sexual Divisions,
    Work and Domestic Life in the Post-war Period
    Jacqueline Burgoyne   72

5   Images of Age and Generation Among
    Older Aberdonians
    Rory Williams   88

6   The Social Construction of Babyhood: The
    Definition of Infant Care as a Medical Problem
    Peter Wright   103

v

7   Life: Cycle, Trajectory or Pilgrimage? A Social
Production Approach to Marxism, Metaphor and
Mortality
Ronnie Frankenberg   122

PART III   RESOURCES AND TRANSFERS

8   Intergenerational Transfers and Life Course
Management: Towards a Socio-economic Perspective
David Cheal   141

9   Family Obligations and the Life Course
Janet Finch   155

10   The Effect of Life Cycle on Three Dimensions of
Stratification
Angela Dale   170

11   The Life Cycle and the Labour Market in Hartlepool
Lydia Morris   192

12   The Impact of Mortgage Arrears on the Housing
Careers of Home Owners
Lawrence Took and Janet Ford   207

Bibliography   230

Name Index   248

Subject Index   253

Acknowledgements

The chapters which make up this book were originally presented, along with those in the companion volume, *Women and the Life Cycle*, at the 1986 British Sociological Association Annual Conference on 'Sociology of the Life Cycle', held at Loughborough University of Technology. This very general topic prompted a wide range of stimulating contributions, testifying to the interest it generated. Unfortunately, it is not possible to publish every paper, but we wish to record our thanks to all of those who read papers at the conference and played their part in making the conference so successful. In selecting the chapters for the two volumes we were concerned to maintain some coherence within each book. As a consequence, many extremely good contributions could not be included. We also wish to thank the people who attended the conference but who did not give papers. They, like the paper-givers, contributed to the debate and discussions which are integral components of any conference. We are particularly indebted to the contributors to this volume for their preparedness to respond to matters of revision. We would also like to thank Anne Dix and Mike Milotte of the British Sociological Association for their help and advice in running the conference and assisting in the production of these two volumes.

ALAN BRYMAN
BILL BYTHEWAY
PATRICIA ALLATT
TERESA KEIL

Notes on the Contributors

Patricia Allatt is Principal Lecturer in Social Administration, Teesside Polytechnic. She has previously held posts at the Universities of Keele and Durham and at Newcastle upon Tyne Polytechnic. She has published on the youth service, crime prevention, the family and youth unemployment. Her current researches are on children's perception of other cultures, tenant populations and youth unemployment.

Paul Bellaby teaches sociology and social anthropology, University of Keele, is associate director of the Keele Life Histories Centre and is also active in the Centre for Medical Social Anthropology at Keele. He is author of *The Sociology of Comprehensive Schooling* and has published research on the occupational organisation of both nursing and social work as well as on social control in the school. Recently he has turned to the intersection between the sociologies of health and of industry.

Alan Bryman is Senior Lecturer in the Department of Social Sciences, Loughborough University. He has previously held research posts in the Industrial Administration Research Unit at Aston University and in the Department of Theology at Birmingham University. His main research interests lie in the fields of organization studies, research methodology, and labour market studies. He is co-author of *Clergy, Ministers and Priests* (1977), author of *Leadership and Organizations* (1986), and editor of *Doing Research in Organizations* (1988).

Jacqueline Burgoyne is Reader in Sociology, at Sheffield City Polytechnic. After studying social science at Sheffield University she trained as a teacher. Her apprenticeship as a researcher came through working on a project investigating people's reading habits and then bookselling as an occupation. Her interest in marriage, couple relationships and the connections between people's working and personal lives began with a study of stepfamilies carried out with David Clark, and her recent co-authored book, *Divorce Matters* (1987), is heavily based on this work. She is currently working on a study of managerial careers.

Bill Bytheway is Senior Research Fellow in the Institute of Health Care Studies, University College of Swansea. He has recently completed a research project funded by the Joseph Rowntree Memorial Trust concerning the organisation of care within the families of older redundant steelworkers. He is also involved in a number of studies of health services for elderly people in South West Wales. He has been active in the study of ageing for a number of years, being a founder member of the British Society of Gerontology.

David Cheal is Professor of Sociology, University of Winnipeg, Canada. His current research interests include interpersonal rituals, the sociology of the life cycle, and the sociology of the family. In recent years, he has been involved in a series of studies on gift giving, some of which will be integrated in a forthcoming book on *The Gift Economy*. His newest research project, funded by the Social Sciences and Humanities Research Council of Canada, will deal with the allocation of resources within households.

Angela Dale is Research Fellow in the Department of Sociology, University of Surrey. She is joint author of *Secondary Analysis: A Handbook for Social Researchers* (forthcoming). While most of her research is based on the secondary analysis of large-scale government surveys, particularly in the area of stratification and employment, she is also concerned with the integration of qualitative and quantitative methods in research.

Janet Finch has a background in both sociology and social policy and is Senior Lecturer in Social Administration, Lancaster University. She is currently working on an ESRC-funded research project on family obligations. She has published a number of articles and books in her various fields of interest including *Married To The Job* (1983), *A Labour of Love* (with Dulcie Groves, 1983) and *Research and Policy* (1986).

Janet Ford is Senior Lecturer in the Department of Social Sciences, Loughborough University. Her main research interests are in the areas of housing and household debt.

Ronnie Frankenberg is Emeritus Professor of Sociology and

Social Anthropology, University of Keele. He is currently Professorial Research Fellow and Director, Centre for Medical Social Anthropology at that university. He has done extensive fieldwork in medical sociology and medical social anthropology in Africa and in Britain. Most recently he carried out a two-year study of the dramatisation of sickness in a North Italian Commune. He is International Editor of *Medical Anthropology Quarterly*.

Chris Harris is Professor of Sociology, University College of Swansea. He was co-author of *The Family and Social Change* in 1965 and is author of *The Family* (1969), *The Family and Industrial Society*, (1983), and *Continuity and Change* (forthcoming). He has published in the area of social theory (*Fundamental Concepts and the Sociological Enterprise*, 1980) and directed research into redundancy and the labour market behaviour of redundant steelworkers (C.C. Harris *et al.*, *Redundancy and Recession in South Wales*, 1987). He is currently directing research on the return of women to paid work in mid-life, as part of the ESRC ageing initiative.

Teresa Keil is Senior Lecturer in Sociology in the Department of Social Sciences, Loughborough University of Technology. She has previously held posts at the Universities of Liverpool, Leicester and Aston in Birmingham. She has published on the process of entry into work and, with members of the Work and Employment Group at Loughborough, on labour markets. Her current research interests are in labour market studies and in the social organisation of food preferences.

Lydia Morris has completed research in Puerto Rico, Mexico City, south London, and north-east England. She is a lecturer in Sociology and Social Policy, Durham University, and author of a number of articles concerning the relationship between the household and the labour market.

Michael Murphy is Senior Lecturer in Population Studies and has been at the London School of Economics since 1980, previously working as a researcher at the London School of Hygiene and Tropical Medicine, and a statistician at the Central Statistical Office. His main research interests are in the relationship of socioeconomic factors such as employment and housing experience to each other and to demographic behaviour in household formation, marriage, childbearing and marital breakdown; the mathematical and statistical modelling of life course and household dynamics; and demographic trends in developing countries.

Lawrence Took was Research Officer, Loughborough University, concerned with a project on mortgage arrears. Previously he had conducted research on land tenure and migration in Southern Italy, and acted as research assistant on a project concerned with residential location and family contact in old age.

Rory Williams is with the MRC Medical Sociology Unit, now at Glasgow University, where his interest is in cultural and economic factors in health and health behaviour in the west of Scotland. In the Unit's previous centre at Aberdeen he studied attitudes to illness, ageing and death in the North East. His doctoral thesis and his first post were at Oxford, where his focus was on family and community aspects of housing and health care.

Peter Wright is Head (Academic Development) in the Faculty of Humanities and Social Sciences, Portsmouth Polytechnic. He is a co-editor of *The Problem of Medical Knowledge: Examining the Social Construction of Medicine* (1982), and has published in the field of the sociology of medical and scientific knowledge.

Introduction

Alan Bryman, Bill Bytheway, Patricia Allatt and Teresa Keil

Although the notion of the 'life cycle' has considerable currency within the literature on the family, it has not been a prominent focus for sociologists until relatively recently. Often it has been a taken-for-granted background variable, that is as a residual factor which 'ought' to be taken into account. An example of this tendency can be discerned in the study of work orientations. Thus, in a long footnote in one of the volumes associated with the 1975 BSA Conference, Richard Brown observed that:

> Several writers have argued that the expectations and priorities of women employees must be differentiated with reference to their position in the life cycle. (Brown, 1976, p. 42)

He then quoted extensively a number of these writers but in none of the studies mentioned by Brown does the life cycle seem to have been a primary focus of interest. Rather it seems to have been employed as a variable that is part of the scenery instead of being placed centre stage.

Yet eleven years later, the BSA has supported a conference on precisely this theme. Why should there have been an apparent shift in the level of interest in the life cycle? In part, it can be taken to reflect the changing economic climate of the intervening years which entailed recession biting deep into conventional patterns of family development. Two other recent BSA conference volumes, *Restructuring Capital: Recession and Reorganization in Industrial Society*, and *The Changing Experience of Employment: Restructuring and Recession* reflect a preoccupation with the recession too, as do some of the chapters in this volume. There has also been consider-able interest in the apparent changes in family life associated with developments in the domestic division of labour, the institution of

1

marriage and sexual mores, as well as wider social changes. While studies of the family life cycle have tended to imply a stability to the series of stages associated with it, there is increasing evidence to suggest that there are many changes which may threaten this normative sequence of events (Anderson, 1985; Hogan, 1978, 1980).

However, as students of social change have come to focus upon the circumstances of the individual family, they have found the concept of the life cycle inadequate in coping with the transitions that are involved and, in some quarters, have replaced it with the alternative and more accommodating concept of the life course. The distaste for the concept of life cycle would seem to reflect three different worries. The first is the simple mathematical metaphor – precisely what is it that is returning to its original position? The second is the deterministic implication that life is irreversibly leading something back to where it came from. At one obvious, if coarse, level this is in direct conflict with keeping right on to the end of the road. More subtly, it is neglecting, if not denying, the power of the individual to change the road that is followed. A third worry concerns the failure to settle for a definitive listing of life cycle stages (see Chapter 2). In short, there has been a rejection of the somewhat deterministic style of thinking associated with it, and of the often unsatisfactory treatment of any deviation from the normative pattern. None the less, the life cycle concept is often used as an heuristic as, for example, with James Davis's (1985, p. 13) use of a conventional sequence of stages as a means of teasing out the temporal priority of variables in a cross-sectional correlational study. Thus there may well remain a certain limited utility in this well-established construct.

In recent years, a number of writers, the most prominent of whom are probably Elder and Hareven, have expressed their disenchantment with the emphasis in much sociology upon a fixed sequence of life cycle stages, and have sought to introduce an alternative formulation which promotes the concept of 'life course'. The crux of their approach has been summarised thus:

A life course perspective views the interrelationships between individual and collective family behaviour as they constantly change over people's lives and in the context of historical conditions. The life course approach is concerned with the movement of individuals over their own lives and through historical

time and with the relationship of family members to each other
as they travel through personal and historical time. (Hareven,
1982, p. 6).

Proponents of the life course approach frequently object to the
notion of the life cycle because of its failure to take historical
contexts into account. Further, it is argued that it fails to accommodate adequately the range of variation in the timing of those
events which are constitutive of life cycle stages. As Elder (1978,
p. 56) has put it: 'Families with an identical history, as defined by
a sequence of stages, vary markedly in their respective life course'.
Further, as Morgan (1985) has remarked, apparently marginal or
deviant cases of life course patterns are more easily encapsulated
by this emphasis on variety and variation. The life course perspective tends to be much more appreciative of the way in which early
transitions within the life course have implications for later ones,
an element which is largely missing from the life cycle perspective.

The influence of such thinking can be discerned in Anderson's
(1985) paper on the emergence of the modern life cycle (he uses
life cycle and life course interchangeably) in Britain. He points to
the comparative recency of the structure and timing of many life
cycle transitions. Quite aside from the distinctive timing of many
life cycle transitions associated with the modern family (tending
largely to be earlier in people's lives), there has been a reduction
in the variation in age associated with particular transitions.
Hogan's work (1978, 1980) in the USA has some points of
similarity to that of Anderson. His research is concerned with the
extent to which there is a normative pattern to men's life course
events and their degree of conformity to such a pattern. While
highly redolent of a life cycle approach, Hogan notes that the
ability of a cohort of men to conform to the normative pattern is
dependent upon its reaction to historical processes, in particular
its idiosyncratic experiences of military service and education.
This research also suggests that non-normative patterns have
implications for family disharmony and earnings. It points to the
absorption of the distinctive themes associated with the life course
approach into some recent research, and the same tendencies
underpin some of the contributions to this volume too.

Chapter 1 in particular advocates the life course approach:
Chris Harris proposes a reconsideration of the ageing of the
individual. He notes that age is sometimes used as an indicator of

life stages and at other times is considered a nuisance variable to be controlled in data analysis. In contrasting the significatory practices of society's members with the biological processes associated with age, he notes the potential importance of accumulating experience. In particular he relates age to movement in space-time. Each person is characterised by a unique trajectory – movement over time in social space.

This rethinking of the significance of age leads him to advocate a life course approach as a means of reconciling different sociological perspectives. He distinguishes between societal events and biographical events, and on this basis, rejects the implication in the term 'life cycle' that the individual 'inhabits cyclical time': the life course leads the individual to death not to the completion of a cycle. This approach allows actions to be interpreted in terms of the past actions of the individual and of the wider historical processes. He argues that in the complexity of matching personal time against historical time, sociologists have tended to confine their interests to the broad stages of the life course – constructs that should not be presupposed. The focus should be upon transitions within cohorts, clusters of transitions that characterise the ageing of particular cohorts, and transitions that may be conditioned by the life courses of groups of individuals. In his conclusion, he argues that life course studies provide the means for studying the way in which people both constitute and are constituted by the socio-historical process.

Thus his approach to rethinking the life cycle is to review the ways in which sociologists have previously conceptualised change in the relationships between individuals and societies, to re-examine presumptions in the study of age, and then to advocate the rejection of the concept of life cycle in favour of that of life course.

In Chapter 2, Mike Murphy provides a comprehensive review of the literature relating to this field. This is the longest chapter in the book because we felt that a thorough assessment of the relevant literature would be particularly apposite. The author begins with an overview of a number of classifications of life cycle stages developed by writers as diverse as Shakespeare, Rowntree and Sorokin, but then moves on to a 'received' view of the life cycle as a series of stages through which people inevitably pass. Not only are there many sources of disruption, there is also evidence to suggest that the perception and comprehension of the family life cycle is influenced by historical and cultural specifics. He also points to evidence which suggests that the traditional family cycle model applies to only around half of the population of Britain. In addition, Murphy considers the kinds of data which are required in order to facilitate an empirical elaboration of the life cycle notion. In particular, he emphasises the need for longitudinal data from which generalisations may be drawn.

These two chapters provide a valuable introduction to many of the issues that underlie Parts II and III. The most directly pertinent questions about rethinking the life cycle that were raised in papers presented at the Loughborough conference tended to fall into two groups. There were those concerning the images, knowledge, beliefs and debates that are associated with the idea of life cycle. These are represented by the chapters in Part II. Secondly there were issues raised about resources and transitions. These rather more down-to-earth matters centre upon the organisation of interpersonal and domestic life and raise significant ideas about the relationship between generation and the life cycle. Papers with this orientation are collected in Part III.

Part II seeks to confront the ways in which life cycle constructs are used in different milieux. Notions about the life cycle are not simply inventions of the sociologist; they have widespread currency. The examination of the use of life cycle ideas in everyday contexts does not imply an acceptance of their content and implications, but is a recognition that they constitute an important component of 'common knowledge'. It is, of course, common knowledge which frequently determines the actions and events that tailor and characterise the individual biography.

These themes are dealt with in this section and are related to quite diverse social worlds: pottery workers, older Aberdonians, media pundits on 'the family', Victorian medicine, and Marxist martyrs. Arguably each represents an ideology that is intended to account for the passage through life, albeit at different junctures. While each of the chapters in Part II addresses additional themes, an emphasis upon popular ideologies of the life cycle constitutes a common thread.

In the study of ideology, the concept of everyday life is regularly acknowledged as crucial. It is this concept which is constrained by ideology. However, interest has centred upon the power of ideology while everyday life has frequently been treated purely symbolically. In contrast, there has been little attention given to the ways in which the everyday life of particular, as opposed to typified, people has been affected by (or affects) ideology. These five chapters provide some insight into such interactive effects. They offer evidence that there have been efforts in social worlds other than sociology to rethink the realities and proper constitution of the life cycle.

Chapter 3 is concerned with the mental constructs of the life cycle that people in everyday life employ in the understanding and explanation of behaviour. These preoccupations are illustrated through references to an ethnographic study which Paul Bellaby carried out in a large firm in the Potteries. He is able to draw out the main life cycle stages which make up this 'folk model' from his investigations of both management and workers. In fact, there is a lacuna between the behaviour that is supposed to be associated with each life cycle stage, as implied by the model, and people's actual behaviour. Each juncture of this model is associated with patterns of legitimate behaviour for each of the sexes. He shows how this view of the life cycle which people carry around is deployed as a means of comprehending legitimate behaviour, a point which is illustrated with reference to people's preparedness to accept explanations for absence from work in terms of sickness. Further, Bellaby shows how life cycle constructs are used by personnel managers to facilitate their recruitment of new employees because they 'know' what new recruits will be like because of their life cycle stage. This finding recalls Blackburn and Mann's (1979) research which shows that firms use a variety of rules of thumb as a means of establishing likely 'worker quality' when recruiting. Life cycle stage was relevant to such considerations in that being married with small children was taken to be a potent indicator of a prospectively 'responsible' employee.

This chapter also brings out many interesting findings in connection with relationships between the sexes in the firm. Again, life cycle constructs rear their head, because they are used to legitimate the domination of women by men. In addition, there are some interesting observations about the operation of the labour market. For example, he finds that there is a pronounced tendency for management to seek to recruit family and kin of existing employees, but shows that this is not a tradition within the industry but a response to recent labour market exigencies.

Chapter 4 is primarily concerned with current popular debates about the family. In the post-war period the family has become an important public issue in the United Kingdom. Jacqueline Burgoyne reviews four distinctive elements of the debate: the division of domestic labour, the employment of women, the involvement of fathers in childcare, and trends in marital status and cohabitation. In relation to all of these issues, questions of change are associated with questions of morality. She begins, however, with a brief critique of post-war British contributions to the sociology of the family, suggesting that much of it was essentially reassuring regarding the continuing well-being of the normal family. As a consequence, rising rates of 'deviance' have become a cause for concern both for this sociological tradition and for those engaged in public debate. She discretely points to the wider political implications of the work of sociologists in this area.

In her concluding section, she discusses the dangers of over- and under-estimation of the rate of change in family and household forms, and the temptation to presume there has been an increase in diversity. Her analysis of one example of life at the interface between sociology and the popular media demonstrates well the way in which frameworks designed for analysis can be mobilised within an ideological offensive. She makes it clear that the sociologist, hampered by the 'problem' of personal experience, faces difficult problems in endeavouring to further knowledge about life cycle matters within the public arena.

Chapter 5 relates to later life. Rory Williams's interest is in what is perceived to be the proper approach to ageing. On the basis of open-ended interviews with Aberdonians aged 60 years or over, Williams describes five sets of premises that represent distinctive images of age: early old age as liberation, as a setback, as a repairing of defences, and late old age as resistable, and as a surrender. These notions combine in a number of patterns: ageing as a resurgence, as a siege and as a delayed capitulation.

The contradictions between these images are the basis for personal dilemmas for some of the Aberdonians, but a number of explanations for differing attitudes are possible. First, those images indicative of stigma are primarily associated with late old age, the remaining problem being that of deciding whether the failure, represented by late old age, is within or beyond moral control. Second, explanations based upon group solidarity and the expression of positive attitudes contained certain inconsistencies: optimism was a basis for division within the middle class, for example. In contrast, there was a coherent perception of generational solidarity, although this too was threatened by the continuation of past intra-generational conflict.

In his conclusion, Williams comes to pose questions about the explanation for conflicting attitudes in the experience of different economic circumstances: recession, boom and inequality. The chapter as a whole provides good evidence of how conceptual-isations of, and more particularly explanations for, constructed age statuses concern the ageing, thinking individual. In part these draw upon continuing cultural images of senescence, but it would seem that the experience of historical events and trends can be just as important in determining ways of interpreting the ageing process.

Peter Wright, in Chapter 6, provides a detailed study of the emergence of the notion of babyhood around the turn of the century. He sees this particular life stage to be the construction of medicine and describes how the sociological critique of medicine has culminated in a coherent and comprehensive social construct-ivist view of medical knowledge. He argues strenuously that this does not imply that medical concepts are illusory, only to ground them in the continuing history of human meanings.

He argues that the concept of babyhood was transformed in England during the period 1890 to 1915 as a result of the belief that life in babyhood is a proper subject for medical activity. The metamorphosis has four elements: the realisation that infant mortality can be avoided, the belief that the problem was essen-tially medical, the implementation of infant welfare policies that included preventative home visits, and acceptance of germ patho-gen theory. He sees the transformation as the consequence of a 'generative metaphor' (Schon, 1979) – infant mortality was released from associations with sin and became attached to the newly discovered germ. In discussing the origins of the problem of infant mortality, Wright points to the concerns of Victorian England for the quality of 'the race' and more particularly its potential army recruits.

His chapter provides good evidence of the power of social insti-tutions to tailor popular understandings of the facts of life – a new channel of communication between medicine and the mass was created. Through this and the news about germs, it was possible to legitimate social intervention and more significantly to create a sense of danger. In England the emphasis upon 'the natural relationship between mother and child' implies a further construction of social relations that are intrinsic to the life cycle.

Although primarily addressed to the sociological study of medicine, this paper provides good evidence of how popular ideas about the life cycle emerge. These ideas then come to determine the actual course of life which grant them a certain indisputable reality.

Ronnie Frankenberg, in Chapter 7, emphasises the centrality of death to any account of the experience of life. He criticises past sociology for its death-denying naturalism. Even the contribution of Strauss (1978) to the study of 'deathandying' has failed to escape the bounds of the hospice to relate to the broader study of life. Likewise Marx, despite the evidently social character of suicide, failed to address himself to questions about the production of death. Later Marxist writers have variously evoked the red heroic death, and a rather more silent acceptance of the inevitability of death and the need to use lives to the full.

Frankenberg contrasts the three metaphors of cycle, trajectory and pilgrimage. He addresses himself seriously to the metaphor of cycle with its significant biological implications. Not only is it transparently not cyclical but the metaphor fosters views of society that have strong political overtones. Nevertheless, he argues, we should not neglect that which is cyclical – the daily and the seasonal round in particular. Whilst this is indisputable, it is hardly an argument for the application of cycle to the study of the whole life. He tends to dismiss trajectory in that it both denies the individual any kind of control, and omits the consequences of power, in the management of lifedeath.

Pilgrimage is portrayed as a series of ceremonial events that are separated in space-time. By thinking of lifedeath as the product of social dramatic performance that incorporates play, crisis and ceremony, it is possible to avoid sociological overdetermination. He concludes by suggesting that it is pilgrimage which is the metaphor most relevant to the sociology of life, particularly at a time when mass socially determined death is so threatening and when individuals are being urged to seek their own salvation.

The life pilgrimage (or more specifically the lifedeath pilgrimage) is a provocative alternative to the life cycle. Frankenberg's discussion challenges us to specify more precisely the real character of that which we aspire to study, and to consider more carefully the power and purposes of metaphor.

The contributors to Part III are largely concerned with the linkage between life cycle circumstance and the management of resources within the private multi-person domestic unit.

Chapter 8 is intended to reorientate popular beliefs about the distribution of resources and the significance of government benefits. The presumption that elderly recipients of benefits and services are passive dependants is rejected in favour of viewing them as active participants, wherein they give as well as receive in regard to the transfer of resources. David Cheal sees the popularity of the family life cycle notion as being responsible for the construction of a simplistic model of the cycle of need that is not confirmed by empirical enquiry. An alternative explanation, Cheal proposes, should be structural, historical and based upon theories of action.

His review of the history of Canadian government transfer payments shows that the present elderly have been major beneficiaries: he suggests that those elderly who have benefited most from these forms of universalistic redistribution may make particularistic transfers to their descendants. Cheal argues that the study of the family economy needs to recognise transfers to and from the state, the accumulation of capital, female labour force participation and investments in human capital, as well as the more familiar family life cycle factors. In rethinking the life cycle it is necessary simultaneously to rethink common assumptions about old age and dependency: we have to look more closely at what people do in their everyday lives and the kinds of economic squeezes which they encounter at different points in life.

In Chapter 9 Janet Finch, like Cheal, is interested in the transfer of resources between the generations within the family, but not so much with the actual transfer as with the reasons why it happens, and with the conduct by which transfers are accomplished. Her interest centres upon the contrasts between obligation and responsibility and between norms and negotiated commitments. Her objective is to examine the ways in which solutions come to be seen as obvious. There is a degree to which the application of norms has to be negotiated. She suggests that reciprocity is negotiated through calculation rather than through the power of norms, and likewise that sentiment is influential in the implementation of obligation. Motivation and its expression are important aspects of obligation, as are the particular social and economic structures in which individuals find themselves. Patriarchal power, in particular, is extremely influential at a number of levels.

Moving on, she argues forcefully for the recognition of public morality as a determinant of family obligations, both in the sense of guideline setting and as a resource to be deployed by individuals. Finch then places her approach to the study of family obligations in the context of the life course, rejecting the fairly fixed stages of the life cycle in favour of a perspective that draws upon biographies and transitions. Time is central: norms are associated with timetables, with synchronisation and with historical change. Negotiations are long-term interactions rather than events – both cumulative and reciprocal. In conclusion, Finch reminds us of Mills's goal of understanding the relationship between biography and history. In rethinking the life cycle, like a number of others, she is advocating the life course as a way of reorienting theory towards a less deterministic basis of explanation.

The focus of Chapter 10, by Angela Dale is on the effect of life cycle stages on three dimensions of social stratification. While there is an awareness among sociologists of the implications of life cycle stage for social stratification, this topic has rarely been submitted to such detailed examination as in her contribution. She uses data collected by the UK General Household Survey of 1979 and takes the household rather than the individual as the unit of analysis. Ten life cycle stages, each representing a household type, are distinguished, enabling much finer distinctions to be etched than is normal. As she recognises, there are dangers associated with this approach in that the ten stages may appear to represent the typical life course of a cohort of households. Murphy has already shown how this kind of approach to the analysis of cross-sectional surveys may omit too many individuals and families. Dale, however, is able to encapsulate 90 per cent of the GHS sample within her more refined framework, and on this basis shows how there are striking implications of life cycle circumstance for access to the labour market, for net disposable household income and for household assets – her three dimensions of social stratification. This adds force to doubts about traditional approaches to the study of social stratification which rely wholly or mainly on paid occupation, and indicates that life course considerations cannot be ignored.

Chapter 11 reviews some of the evidence concerning the impact of stage in the life cycle on the labour market involve-

ment of men and women. While recognising that research relating to such issues has born considerable fruit, Lydia Morris
argues that it is important not to view the impact of the life
cycle as conclusive, since historical events and trends moderate
its influence. This view is supported by her study of patterns of
generational progression in the labour market in Hartlepool, a
town which has been hit particularly hard in the 1980s by
economic recession. Not only does a high level of unemployment
disrupt normal life cycle patterns of labour market behaviour, it
has other effects too; for example, it disrupts traditional cross-
generational patterns of job transmission. One major implication
of this cluster of findings is that the typicality of the relationship between life cycle stage and labour market involvement is
heavily influenced by the historical context. As such this contribution adds much to our knowledge of the interaction between
family development and historical change (Hareven, 1978b,
pp. 1–2) which has become the focus for students of the life
course in recent years. Further, Morris's chapter contributes to
our understanding of the meanings of different life course transitions to particular people, a perspective which is absent from
the many studies which rely exclusively on historical data. Along
with the other contributors to this section, Morris invites us to
question the immutability of life cycle transitions from generation
to generation. In addition, she examines an issue of relevance
to the companion to this volume, *Women and the Life Cycle*,
namely the extent to which changes in the pattern of male employment which she adumbrates have any effects on the perception of traditional gender roles.

   Housing is an area in which common sense notions of the life
cycle are particularly entrenched. In Chapter 12, Took and
Ford argue that building societies operate with such ideas to a
very significant extent: couples buy houses on marriage or soon
after; they trade up in the housing market as they earn more;
and so on. Building societies and government policy makers
view families as climbing a housing ladder as their opportunities
and resources improve. In fact, it seems that many of the assumptions which underpin this notion do not hold water. For example,
Took and Ford argue that the image of couples *choosing* to buy
property is particularly difficult to sustain when the contraction
in private rented accommodation is borne in mind. However,
their main focus is on mortgage arrears which, they argue, are

not only increasing but are also under-reported by the building societies. They report findings relating to their study of forty couples who were in arrears. Their evidence suggests that the ideology of owner occupation is deeply ingrained, and that many people drift into owner occupation in spite of inadequate knowledge and resources. They address the often assumed links between marital breakdown and debt, between debt and un-employment, and between the deterioration of properties and the accumulation of arrears. The empirical complexity of such apparent associations strongly implies a more intricate pattern of movements in housing and domestic circumstances than is commonly assumed. This chapter is important to our under-standing of the subject of this book because the notion of a housing ladder, so deeply embedded within public ideologies, is highly interlinked with notions of life cycle: indeed, in many respects it is viewed as dovetailing with the life cycle stages. Yet, in just the same way that Murphy criticises the idea of the life cycle because of the presumption of normality, so too Took and Ford's analysis invites us to question the parallel notion of the typical housing career.

The contributions of Morris and of Took and Ford are highly consistent with some of the ideas associated with the life course approach which were briefly discussed above. These chapters, like Chapter 3, show that essential resources in normal life course patterning can be disrupted by historical circumstance. By contrast, Dale's analysis of social stratification, obliged by the constraints of her data to adopt a more conventional approach to the study of the life cycle, shows that variation between households in resources and constitution (which, as Cheal has shown, is determined by the passage of the family through time) relates significantly to stratification. Finch and Cheal, and to a lesser extent Morris, are concerned with the connections between resources and intergenerational relation-ships. This emphasis is particularly pertinent to one specific implication of the metaphor of the life cycle, namely that of regeneration. It is possible to think of intergenerational transfers, and perhaps more specifically processes of inheritance, as the recycling of resources within the family. This suggests a link between the notion of cycle and the end of life (as opposed to the more usual allusion to reproduction), a link that might serve to distinguish the significance of life cycle from that of life course.

Part I

Theoretical Approaches

1 The Individual and Society: A Processual Approach

Chris Harris

INTRODUCTION

In the dark ages of the sociological past we worked within a dominant paradigm which could be loosely termed that of modernisation. In the terms of this paradigm contemporary society occupied a place between two conceptual poles associated loosely with the past and the future respectively. Past societies were religious, familial and communal; future societies scientific, industrial and associational. Contemporary society was well on the way to the embodiment of the future. In Parsonian terms, past societies were ascriptive and particularistic and modern societies achievement-oriented and universalistic. Ascriptive and particularistic groupings and relationships were on their way out, and of interest only as quaint survivals of the past, and this was reflected by the relative prestige accorded to industrial and urban sociology and to the sociology of stratification as opposed to the sociology of religion, the sociology of the family and the sociology of communities.

Twenty-five years ago it seemed that one of the results of the domination of the modernisation paradigm was the neglect of ascriptive variables by empirical sociology. Today, this neglect has to some extent been remedied. The fields of race relations and gender differences are now accorded prominence within the discipline and there is a growing interest, as the 1960s generation of sociologists advances inexorably into middle age, in ageing. This is not to say that contemporary developments should be welcomed uncritically; on the contrary it is regrettable that the study of social characteristics which are, in Parsonian terminology, *diffuse* in their significance, have become so much *specific* topics of

17

enquiry. While this development is probably historically necessary, it is to be hoped that the discipline will eventually move beyond this particular division of intellectual labour.

AGE

Of particular interest in this regard is the case of age, two conceptions of which have existed side by side in sociological practice: age as an indicator of stages in the life course which constitute substantive specialisms (cf. youth) and age as a face sheet variable, usually regarded as a confounding variable to be gotten rid of by 'controlling' for it in statistical analysis. How many millions of sentences must have been written beginning with the words 'Controlling for age and sex'!

What, however, is age? In itself it has no intrinsic significance and its meaning and importance derives from its being an indication of something else. It is an indirect associative measure. With what culturally or theoretically significant factors is it associated? The answer to this question is complicated by the fact that the connection between age and that with which it is associated is mediated by the practices of society members who themselves use it as an index of other attributes, and it is the fact that age is a sign regularly used in the significatory practices of members that results in its regular association with other social features. The meaning of age is, however, not completely arbitrary, since it is empirically associated with stages in the physiological development of the human animal at the beginning of the human life span, with changes in reproductive capacity and, at the end, with the loss of physiological function, though it must be remembered that the timing and onset of transitions between developmental stages and the severity and timing of loss of function are powerfully influenced by what may, since we are referring to organisms, be termed ecological factors. Given a relatively stable environment it is possible to make inferences about physiological states from knowledge of the organism's age, and such inferences permit further inferences about a person's capacity for different categories of action as culturally defined. Hence there are some purposes for which age is used by both theorists and members, whatever the theoretical allegiance of the former or the cultural membership of the latter.

This observation, important though it is, does not take us very far, any more than the mere observation that gender definitions have a common reference to bodily difference. Indeed it takes us even less far, since over large ranges of the life span variations in chronological age are not associated with physiological changes which can have any social significance which derives from their affecting a person's capacity for different categories of social action.

The mere length of a person's existence does have one implication relevant to the practices of both members and observers however. Short durations preclude the accumulation of large amounts of knowledge and experience. The very young are by definition innocent. Unfortunately the converse is not true. There is no linear relationship between the magnitude of the life duration and the volume of experience acquired: a long life span only makes possible the accumulation of any specific type of experience, it does not necessitate it. It is, however, possible to make inferences about the likelihood of persons experiencing life events on the basis of knowledge about their life duration: in contemporary society the probability of having experienced the death of a closely associated person increases markedly over the life span. Inferences such as these make age a useful datum which informs members' initial orientation to unknown persons and investigators' hypotheses as to the character of sub populations with different age distributions.

Age does correlate perfectly however with the temporal sequence of events in the collective life of the group to which they belong. Hence we know that someone aged 76 today spent his/her childhood during the First World War, because both age and collective events can be plotted on the same timescale. Hence age can be used as an indicator of what might be termed historical experiences. However, this does not take us terribly far either, since what significance being 'brought up during the First World War' has, is likely to vary markedly between, say, the child of a Cumberland hill farmer, and a child resident in south-east England whose father served in that war. To claim that age can be used as an indicator of historical experience is not to claim that age can be used as an unambiguous indicator of generational membership, for *historical* experience varies with *location*, both physically and socially.

SPACE–TIME

The recognition of this fact makes it possible to draw attention
to the distinguishing characteristic of 'ascriptive' variables. The
point I wish to make is that people have bodies and are therefore always located in space–time and since two material objects
cannot occupy the same space–time location, each person is
unique, or if you prefer it, individual. This rather obvious but
not unimportant point is one which Tony Giddens has recently
emphasised (Giddens, 1984; Gregory and Urry, 1985). Although
people may share the same temporal location and hence be
classified together, they never share the same spatial location
and must be classified on the basis of spatial similarity rather
than identity. If, however, one introduces the notion of movement into this static picture, then people may be said to be
characterised by unique space–time trajectories. If one thus
confines one's attention to populations of persons existing at the
same time in a similar location, these trajectories may be plotted,
not in terms merely of an objective space–time grid, but *re-
lationally* in terms of approximations to, and distantiations
from, other members. On this grid may be superimposed another,
by setting up criteria which enable one to categorise population
members, whether these criteria are those of the theorists or
those employed by members or (preferably) theoretical criteria
which take into account criteria employed by members in their
own classificatory practices. Members' trajectories may then be
reconceptualised as movements over time between positions in
social space.

Wilful ignorance of ascriptive variables results in the use of
space–time as a mere analogy of social processes, and this results, in turn, in the substitution of social space and time for
material space–time, so that the history of social life becomes a
dance of social categories to the music of historical time, and
we become concerned with the trajectories of social categories
through social space, as if these categories themselves were
capable of action, and did not have to be embodied in concrete
actors whose distribution in material space–time did not necessarily condition the speed and duration of the movement of social
categories. To claim to have established the trajectory of a
social category through historical time and social space must
have implications for the trajectory of category members, while

category members' trajectories cannot be specified in a sociologically intelligible way unless they are described in terms of
movement in social space and historical time as well as in
material space–time.

Parsons' universalistic societies are societies in which members
respond to others in respect of their common properties which
make them members of a general class, and neglect those particular attributes which individuate them. Such a society may
properly be described as 'scientific' in so far as the categorical
practices of members are isomorphic with the categorical practices of science and are thus rendered knowable by epistemic
canons of natural scientific practice as positivistically understood. Such an outcome is, to say the least, convenient for those
wishing to found a positivistic science of society. The resurgence
of the interest in the study of life histories (Bertaux, 1981, 1982;
Plummer, 1983) is bound up with rejection of both sociology's
natural scientific pretensions and tendencies still persisting in
contemporary sociology to conceptualise individual actions as
mere expressions of structural location and to conceptualise its
field of study as the investigation of the structure of social
objects, rather than the doings of historical subjects. It would,
in my view, be tragic if what I hope will be an increased interest
in the life course were to become a weapon in the armoury of
one of the opposing sides in a battle between some latter-day
version of the 'two sociologies' dispute; for the virtue of life
course studies, is that they provide us not only with a topic but
with a methodology and a dimension to sociological work
which can help us to overcome the sterile opposition between
the recurrent antinomies of sociological discourse.

THE LIFE COURSE

To focus on the life course is to choose a sphere of study in
which two aspects or moments of social life are combined. A
moment is the equivalent, in the case of a process, to an aspect
in the case of a static entity. Under the rubric of a static entity,
I would include an event. Redundancy is an event in the history
of a plant and in the biographies of those made redundant: it
has both individual and collective aspects. The study of the life
course is essentially a study of a sequence of events, that is to

say a process which is both unintended and the result of inten-
tionality and in which earlier events condition later events.
Both the history of a society and the biography of persons are
processes which can analytically be construed as event sequences.
But if the persons whose *biographies* we are considering are
members of the society whose *history* we are also considering,
then (a) societal events will *constitute* biographical events in the
lives of at least some members; (b) the events in the lives of
members will *be constituents* of at least some societal events; and
yet other societal events (c) will *condition* biographical events.
It should, however, be pointed out that biographical events (i.e.
events in the life course of a given individual) will rarely, if
ever, condition societal events. Time forbids the detailed illustration of these points, but an example of (a) societal events
constituting biographical events would be the transition to the
factory system of production or the introduction of rationing;
an example of (b) would be the plurality of decisions to defer
child-bearing constituting a fall in birth rates and resulting in a
changed demand for education and a smaller working population during a future period; while an example of (c), the
conditioning of the biographical by the societal would be a high
unemployment to vacancy ratio leading to decisions to defer or
accelerate child bearing. Biography and history can be seen as
mutually constituting and conditioning processes, but are better
seen as different movements of a total social process which has
both collective and individual moments.

It will, I hope, be fairly obvious by now why I prefer the
term *life course* to that of *the life cycle*, for the latter term is
normally reserved for that period of the life span of an organism
which extends from birth to biological reproduction. A living
species inhabits cyclical time in which the same process, characterised by a regular sequence of stages, recurs until the species
becomes extinct or mutates. As we say when someone dies, 'life
goes on'. But human beings – particular entities, not the general
category – do not. Our lives are not constituted by the endless
repetition of orderly sequences. In so far as our lives constitute
a sequence we move through this sequence once and then stop
at death. Personal time, like historical time, is linear not cyclical.

Death is the final event of the life *course*: only in the case of
those male spiders eaten by the female after intercourse does
death mark the end of the life *cycle*. The distinction between the

life course and life cycle enables us immediately to specify what is, historically, the most distinctive feature of the contemporary life course: the life course is typically considerably longer than the life cycle. As a result the very considerable lapse of time between maturation of a person's children and death has no physiologically-based structuring principle: that is to say there are no transitions which all human beings necessarily face after the demands made upon them by the social organisation of reproduction have ceased. This renders problematic the construction of any framework for the division of the latter half of the life course into stages marked by transitions, yet it is obvious that this part of the life course *is* characterised by change: the pattern of life does not remain the same until senescence commences.

As a result much more attention is being currently devoted to this middle part of the life course; partly because of its extension, and partly as a knock-on effect of the increased concern with old age. Hence developmental psychology which once focused on maturational processes and more recently has concerned itself with old age, has now come to regard the entire life span as its domain (Baltes and Schaie, 1973; Baltes and Brim, 1980). In so doing it has followed the lead of social psychology (Neugarten, 1964; 1968) in paying attention to mid life, which interest derived from the recognition, brought about by the study of old age, of the importance of mid-life events in conditioning the predemise state. As a result, ageing, as understood psychologically, has ceased to be regarded as identical with the process of senescence and come to be regarded as a psychological process characteristic of the whole of the latter half of the life course.

Similar movements have taken place in sociology as is evidenced by the founding of the journal *Ageing and Society* which is explicitly concerned to consider the study of ageing beyond the confines of the predemise state. The absence, however, of clear-cut physiologically-based changes in either bodily functioning (the female climacteric apart) or in personality in mid life has pushed the study of ageing away from physiologically-based models and requires that we produce a theory of ageing which defines that process in social terms. Any such theory must combine an account of what happens *to* people as they age with an account of how that experience is culturally constructed and how these constructs and conceptions affect actions which in turn produce outcomes which affect what happens to the actors and hence their experience of ageing.

THE HISTORICAL CONTEXT

The essence of the life course approach to the understanding of social action is that actions are understood not merely in terms of the synchronic conditions of action, nor in terms of the diachronic experience of the subject, but also in terms of the effects of the past actions of the subject in constituting the context of current action. The context is conditioned also, however, by historical changes. Hence from the subjective standpoint of the actor, the situation is, in part, both the necessary outcome of previous actions and the contingent result of a wider historical process.

Another way of putting this point is to say that the life course of an individual is the point of intersection between two types of time, personal time and historical time. The life course is not, that is to say, a career, as careers have often been conceived in the sociological literature: the orderly progression through a series of locations in a stable structure. When trajectories are conceptualised that way, war immediately breaks out between those who, on the one hand, conceive a career as something *made* by the subject and, on the other, those who see a career as the movement through a predefined set of positions or stages in which the role of the subject is limited to choosing the set and making the effort to move through the sequence. These subjectivist and objectivist accounts of a career are both faulty since what is conceptualised as structure (whether a predetermined sequence or a range of options) is merely a moment in a process of societal change of which the choices of subjects are constituents.

Faced with this complexity it is only natural for sociologists to grab at the notion of broad *stages* of the life course: childhood, youth, adulthood, mid life, and old age; and then investigate the historical emergence of these cultural categories, their definition and the way their use by members influences their conduct throughout the life course. It is in no way to devalue such work to point out that such an approach is extremely partial; indeed one could say of ageing and life course studies that the framework employed in so far as it is historical is not materialistic and in so far as it is materialistic is not historical. Not only does such an approach neglect the investigation of whether the life experience of members of a given population actually exhibit the discontinuity presupposed by the 'stage' notion; at its worst it encourages us to assume the existence of discontinuity when none may exist and then to interpret the subject's *lack* of consciousness of the postulated discontinuity as 'the successful negotiation of the life course'.

Unlike the notion of life cycle, the notion of life course does *not presuppose* the existence of developmental stages: indeed the very notion of sequential stages through which a population's members must all pass is an inherently ideological notion, that is an appearance produced by experience which members then employ in making sense of their biographies, rather than one which can be uncritically employed by the observer. What is central to the notion of the life course is not the notion of *stage* but that of *transition*, that is to say of qualitative changes in at least some aspects of daily living as opposed to gradual and incremental quantitative changes such as those associated with physiological ageing in later life.

The study of the life course involves an examination of what transitions the members of different social categories within a given *cohort* typically experience and puts the question as to whether those transitions are of such a *nature* and so *timed* as to constitute *life* transitions: as to constitute major changes in the whole way of life of the person concerned. While the types of transition experienced during the life course are of course specific to a particular type of social formation at a given historical conjecture, and characteristic of particular cultures, comparative sociological study is none the less possible if only by generating lists of transitions to be investigated in each of two societies and combining them and then examining how typical life histories of category members within the units compared differ in the timing and importance and occurrence of those transitions. Such studies enable us to claim that in different societies (or in societies at different periods) members experience typically different life courses. Such studies may reveal a marked temporal clustering of transitions experienced by the members of social categories belonging to a cohort within a given population such that it is proper to describe the life course of that category as having been composed, at that point in history, of distinct life stages, whether or not its members recognised this at the time, or towards the end of their lives, or not at all. Appendix I lists 26 life course transitions whose timing and character are, it seems to me, worth investigating in our own society.

It is, however, not as simple as that, for two reasons. In the first place each person is the centre of a field of social relationships between him/herself and members of his/her ascendent, own, and descendent generations, and the members of each of these categories are at different points in *their* life courses. In so far as Ego's life is bound up with and affected by their life situations, Ego's life will be periodised not only by his/her own life course transitions but also by those of his/her associates. This is particularly evident in the case of kin group membership, so that events may be located not only in personal time and historical time, but in what Hareven (1978a) has usefully termed 'family time'. But other collectivities and aggregates to which Ego belongs may also undergo their own transitions and 'village' or 'neighbourhood' and 'industrial time' (Hareven, 1975, 1982) immediately suggest themselves as additional chronological series.

More difficult to handle is what I shall term occupational time, but handled it must be because of the importance of what has been termed 'the construction of [social] ageing through work' (Kohli *et al.*, 1983) and of the relation between chronological age and the chances of unemployment (Riddle, 1984). Hence I would suggest the addition of 'local labour market time' since societal events affect persons directly through their embodiment at the level of changes in local social structure, and a local labour market goes through its own transitions whose character and timing are not capable of being inferred from descriptions based on aggregate data.

The mention of the works of Tamara Hareven takes us, however, to the field of family history and the second complication. That is that historical change not only constitutes and conditions biographical events, historical change will involve changes in the timing, clustering, occurrence and significance of life course transitions and hence in the way the life course is periodised. Let us suppose that, as shown in Figure 1.1, given a set of historical conditions (I), the life course typically goes through two major transitions yielding stages A, B, C; that given historical

Figure 1.1　The intersection of personal and historical time

Personal time			LIFE COURSE SEQUENCES				
			1	2	3	4	5
	LIFE STAGE		↓	↓	↓	↓	↓
	1		[A]	[F]	[L]	R	X
	2		B	[G]	[M]	[S]	Y
	3		C	H	[N]	[T]	[Z]
HISTORICAL CONDITIONS			Set I	Set II	Set III	Set IV	Set V

Historical time ⟶

[A]
　[G]
　　[N]　　　　**actual life histories**

conditions (II) it goes through the stages F, G, H and so on.
Let us suppose further that three sets of historical conditions
succeed one another during the life span of a given cohort. It
follows that no individual will, in these circumstances, experience
any of these life course patterns: someone born under conditions
(I) will experience a life course consisting of A, G, N, under
conditions (II) of F, M, T and under conditions (III) of L, S, Z.
In other words the sequence the person experiences will be
made up of components of different life courses. Actual life
histories always differ in structure from the life course associated
with any given set of historical conditions. The life course, i.e.
the structure of a life history, so far from being an orderly
career necessarily exhibits discontinuities even if the plurality of
transitions which constitutes it do not so cluster as to provide
major life transitions which allow us to periodise it into stages.
There is, therefore, a danger in talking about *the* life course, for
a life course is not a progress through a structure but the negotiation of passage through an unpredictably changing social

environment. Moreover, the Past is not merely *past* but a constituent of the Present: it cannot be abolished by merely altering present arrangements and it lives on in the experience of generations, those born between two historical transitions (Mannheim, 1959; Berger, 1961) whose life span extends beyond the second of the pair of transitions which define them.

CONCLUSION

Life course studies provide, therefore, a means for studying the way in which people both constitute and are constituted by the socio-historical process; if their careers through the life course are frequently wild or chequered, this is not because of their passive determination by social factors, nor simply because their actions have unintended consequences. In so far as it *is* so, it is not due merely to lack of adequate knowledge (market imperfection) but because the *context* of their action is, by virtue of those actions when combined with those of others, itself in the process of transformation and change. Life course studies are studies of the point at which what Giddens terms the 'duality of structure' (Giddens, 1984, p. 25) can be observed as process; the structure of life histories (the life course) is both 'the medium and outcome' of a *sequence* of practices.

The study of the life course should not be identified with a particular methodology whether it be the collection of life histories or the construction of demographic models. Nor should it be confused with the study of the private, personal, individual, or particular as opposed to their opposites: it is rather a field where the particularity of individual historical experience is defined in terms of general categories and provides an indispensable practical tool for bridging the gulf between social facts and social acts in a way that does justice to the historicity of both.

APPENDIX 1: INDIVIDUAL TRANSITIONS

1. Home to school
2. Monosex peer group
3. Intersex relationships

4. School to labour market
5. Labour market to continuous employment
6. Stable sexual relationships
7. Residence independent of household of origin
8. Marriage/cohabitation
9. Transition to parenthood
10. Withdrawal from labour market by women
11. Reproductive career of women
12. Return to employment by women
13. Dispersal of children when children reach stage 6
14. Grandparenthood
15. Midlife employment transitions/blockages/unemployment
16. Women's loss of reproductive capacity
17. Care for elderly parents
18. Dispersal of children and grandchildren
19. Withdrawal from economic activity
20. Housing and residence changes related to 13, 17, 18, 19
21. Problems associated with predemise state of parents
22. Death of parents
23. Housing and residence changes related to our predemise state
24. Increased dependence on outside support by social services/neighbours/children
25. Institutional care
26. Death

NOTE Though it is possible to place these transitions in *rough* chronological order, the whole point of life course studies is to establish patterns of timing characteristic of different specific social categories within specific cohorts of engendered subjects.

2 Measuring the Family Life Cycle: Concepts, Data and Methods

Michael Murphy

1 THE DEVELOPMENT OF THE 'FAMILY LIFE CYCLE'

When reviewing the concept of the family life cycle, the words of St Augustine in another context seem appropriate: 'If no one asks me, I know; but if any Person should require me to tell him, I cannot'. The Dictionary of Demography (Wilson, 1985, p. 123) defines the term 'life cycle' as 'the sequence of stages through which individuals or families pass beginning with birth and ending in death (for individuals) or beginning with formation and ending in dissolution (for families)'.

This chapter begins by looking at the development of life cycle concepts and typologies from a demographic viewpoint (Sections 1 and 2) before turning to examine some of the major criticisms that have been advanced of the life cycle approaches (Section 3). Section 4 reviews possible sources of data and finally Section 5 includes a more technical discussion of the methodology necessary for appropriate analyses of the life cycle.

The idea of non-reversible stages through which progression is made with age is not new; Shakespeare used the idea of the seven ages of man: baby; schoolboy; lover; soldier; justice; retired; second childhood. This typology is not inferior to many which have been suggested since but it is distinguished by the fact that it ignores women completely, rather than assigning to them the traditional progression of roles from marriage to motherhood characteristic of later ones. One of the first uses of the life cycle framework in social science was Rowntree's statement that 'the life of a labourer is marked by five alternating periods of want and comparative plenty' (Rowntree, 1902, p. 136). These were:

  i child,
 ii young working adult living with parents,
iii bringing up own children,
 iv children living at home but earning,
  v labourer past work.

Rowntree was not making the point that this was an inevitable pattern, but rather that if other catastrophes were absent (and these were principally demographic ones such as the death of the breadwinner), then this would reflect the typical pattern of production and reproduction of someone living in this class at that time.

Around the same time, Russian rural sociologists were also employing life cycle approaches in the study of peasant families, although this work did not become familiar to Anglophone audiences until the work of Sorokin (for example, Sorokin *et al.*, 1930–32) was published. He defined four stages:

  i married couple just starting independent existence,
 ii couple with dependent children,
iii couple with at least one non-dependent child,
 iv children begin to leave home and all children depart.

Like Rowntree, Sorokin was mainly interested in the effects of change (implicitly demographic change) on the standard of living of the typical family as it grows older.

In 1947, Paul Glick of the US Bureau of the Census produced analyses of the timing of 'major' events in families on the basis of national-level census data. He used a conventional model of family progression starting with marriage, followed by child-bearing and childrearing, and a period when the children have left home. He identified seven key events and indexed them by the median age of occurrence:

  i first marriage,
 ii birth of first child,
iii birth of last child,

   iv marriage of first child,
    v marriage of last child,
   vi death of one spouse,
  vii death of remaining spouse.

Glick's model basically recognises simple demographic changes. However, these family life cycle stages were considered to be of wider importance because they are associated with changes in other social and economic variables such as housing and employment (Glick, 1947, p. 164).

In the 1950s, family life cycle approaches became more widely used. Hammond (1954) included non-demographic but assumed-to-be-important elements such as entering and leaving school into the typology. At this time 'family theorists' such as Hill and Rodgers (see, for example, 1964) began to use even more elaborate formulations. The underlying idea of this school was that there are 'critical role transitions' which mark discontinuities in behaviour. The main focus of such family development analysis has been on changes in the internal organisation and attitudes of married couples especially in relation to bearing and rearing children (Aldous, 1978, p. 83). This chapter is not concerned with such internal interactions, but rather with application of family life cycle approaches in areas where they may be less appropriate.

About this time, anthropologists began to use life cycle concepts under the title 'developmental approach' which focused attention on how families change through time. Fortes (1958) developed a three-fold typology based on phases of expansion (marriage and childbearing), dispersion or fission (children marrying) and replacement (the children take over the family position and property of their parents).

In the 1960s further developments, empirical, theoretical and integrative, occurred. Life cycle typologies proliferated and the importance of cohort analyses came to be recognised. Ryder (1965) stressed the importance of the common experience of a particular cohort (defined, for example, by a common year of birth or of marriage) on subsequent behaviour. Earlier work had been based largely on cross-sectional data. For example, Rowntree had looked at the economic situation of a group of families at different stages at a particular point in time and inferred that the observed pattern would also hold for these families as they progressed through the various stages identified. The recognition of the essentially longitudinal nature of the life cycle approach has clear implications for the sorts of data which should ideally be used for undertaking such analyses (see Section 4).

Edith Duvall (1977, p. 141) stated that 'the life cycles of individual families follow a universal sequence of family development'. This statement is patently incorrect. What she in fact produced was a role model for a home-centred woman living in a contemporary developed society, since the pattern she identifies for a typical American woman involves:

'first two decades of her life growing up and getting ready to have children' (p. 139);
next 25 to 30 years bearing and rearing children;
last 25 to 30 years alone or with husband after children gone.

(This view about the appropriate role for women might seem to be somewhat restricted.)

A good review of the family life cycle literature up to the mid-1970s is given by Young (1977). Indeed around this time, the family life cycle approach reached its pinnacle with the publication of the edited work by Cuisenier (1977). However, criticisms were also becoming more pervasive. It became recognised that patterns of family experience and behaviour are also influenced by the interaction of macro-level social and economic conditions, biological and culturally-determined age-related factors, and by individual 'career-histories', such as in the employment sphere. These factors are incorporated into what has become known as life course analysis, largely developed by family historians (Elder, 1978, pp. 21–2).

While the comprehensive nature of the life course formulation makes it difficult to criticise on grounds of insensitivity or partiality, it does not, of course, give any clear indication about which of the essentially unlimited number of potentially important variables should be included in a particular piece of analysis. Indeed Elder (1981) couples the use of life course analysis with 'the discovery of complexity' in family history studies. Some of these points will be expanded in later sections. However, the next section goes on to consider from a demographic point of view some of the family life cycle classifications which have been widely used or discussed in the literature.

2   LIFE CYCLE CONCEPTS AND TYPOLOGIES

The simplest distinction in the family life cycle is between the expanding and contracting stages. However, this basic distinction has been much elaborated upon. Apart from demographic characteristics, educational system variables have frequently been incorporated since they are assumed to have important effects on the family. Kirkpatrick *et al.* (1934) and Bigelow (1942) disaggregated the child-present phase by the type of school being attended. The major divergence among typologies is whether the stage should be determined by the age of the youngest or of the oldest child in the family: Duvall (1977) uses the oldest, while Lansing and Morgan (1955) and Wells and Gubar (1966), use the youngest child as the index. Typical stages are:

Duvall
Young single person, head aged less than 35, no children.
Families without children, head less than 35.
Childbearing families, oldest child less than 3.
Pre-school phase, oldest child 3–5.
School-age children, oldest child 6–12.
Teenage children, oldest child 13–18.
Launching phase, oldest child leaves home.
Middle age, head over 45, no children.
Ageing family, retirement to death.

Wells and Gubar
Young single person, head aged less than 35, no children.
Families without children, head less than 35.
Full nest I, youngest child less than 6.
Full nest II, youngest child 6 or over, head less than 45.
Full nest III, head over 45; dependent children in household.
Empty nest I, no children at home, head over 45.
Empty nest II, head retires.
Solitary survivor in labour force.
Solitary survivor, retired.

Both classifications presuppose a linear progression through which stereotypical families move. However, the choice of a particular child as the reference individual reflects a view about which event forms the 'natural' transition from one stage to another. For example, it can be argued that the first child starting school is an important event which becomes less significant for the family with succeeding children. Duvall (1977, p. 145) justifies this approach on the grounds that the 'problems' of transition are faced initially by the first child so the oldest child is a primary marker. Alternatively, the event of the last child entering school may mark a significant change in the family's circumstances, such as the child's mother becoming available for paid work outside the home. While the choice between these classifications, or the use of alternative and/or more elaborate ones, reflects a certain arbitrariness in the concept, it does mean that the individual researcher has considerable flexibility in the choice of method. For example, Hill and Rodgers (1964) produced a 24-fold typology based on the ages of youngest *and* oldest children. Stacey (1969) contains a review of alternative classifications.

Another major aspect of family life cycle approaches relates to the statistics which are used to summarise the life cycle stage. Two main procedures have been adopted. The first looks at variations in family size and composition at different stages (in part such an approach is tautological since many of the stages identified are directly related to changes in family size). The other main procedure is concerned with the *timing* of the achievement of certain life cycle stages such as the mother's age at birth of her first or last child. This latter approach has been particularly emphasised by Glick and proponents of the life course concept, for whom a major topic of interest is the way in which period factors affect the timing of key events. The timing and family composition approaches are often considered as alternatives rather than complements: Elder (1977, p. 43) stated that few, if any, major studies have successfully employed the analytic strengths of both approaches simultaneously. Of the various studies considered here, Young's (1977) monograph is probably the most comprehensive and technically competent example.

3   CRITICISMS OF THE FAMILY LIFE CYCLE APPROACH

The family life cycle approach has been criticised on various empirical, theoretical and methodological grounds. A major deficiency lies in the implicit assumption of a single stereo-typical progression through a given number of stages in a pre-determined order. Trost (1977, p. 468) has articulated criticism of the normative constraints imposed by this approach in a particularly powerful way: 'the concept of the life cycle is harm-less *per se*. However, the use made of this concept is not always harmless. The concept might steer the research into wrong channels, or put blinds on the researcher or, when used as an educational tool, act as a conserving agent'. The family life cycle approach emphasises the typical at the expense of the atypical. Thus while much work in this area is concerned with interpreting change in 'family life' by means of indices such as median age at events such as age of mother at first or last birth (Glick, 1977; Norton, 1983) it is difficult to cope within such a framework with family forms differing from that of the 'ideal' form.

There are numerous ways in which individuals and families fail to conform to the typical family life cycle model. These include:

  i the chronology of timing of events may not conform to the ideal model, for example childbearing may start before marriage;
 ii most stages are not reached, for example, by never-married persons;
iii the full set of stages may be truncated by events such as death or marital breakdown;
 iv the implicit isolated nuclear family model is unable to incorporate extensions which may be important in practice, such as the presence of boarders or servants and extended families or other family structures.

The family life cycle model as it is usually elaborated, refers to the family circumstances of white urban middle-class Americans in the 1950s and 1960s – a particularly child-oriented period as Trost has noted. The further one departs from this location, the less appropriate the sorts of classifications discussed earlier are likely to be. Anderson (1983, 1985) has pointed out that the implicit underlying model of a stable nuclear family is located in a rather small period of historical time even for Western societies, being centred around the middle part of the twentieth century. Before that time, events such as death of a spouse would be expected to have dissolved the nuclear family marriage tie before the 'empty nest' phase, a conclusion also emphasised by Wells's (1971) study of Quaker families in colonial America. In recent years, although the mechanism is very different from death, similar proportions of marriages (roughly one third) would be expected to be dissolved by marital breakdown by twenty years' duration. Uhlenberg (1974) has considered four main ways – death in early adulthood; never-marrying; childlessness; and marital breakdown – in which the 'preferred' ideal form of the nuclear family model was broken in historical studies of the population of the United States. (The 'preferred' model is defined as: female arrives at age 50 living with first husband and as a parent of at least one child.)

In other historical studies, Laslett (1983) has emphasised the importance of the institution of service as a typical condition which has effects both on household composition and on the life experience of those concerned. Modell and Hareven (1973) have pointed out the importance of lodgers in the household structure and economy of the urban United States around the turn of the century.

Moving forward in time, the trend in recent years in Western societies has been away from the 'preferred' ideal form. Turner (1969) estimated that it applied to about two thirds of the adult population of Great Britain. Murphy (1983) calculated that under half of women in their 20s in Britain now will progress through the 'preferred' path. Extrapolation of current trends would mean that approximately 10 per cent may never marry, 10 per cent of married women may remain childless; 8 to 10 per cent may have a birth before marrying; and 30 per cent may experience marital breakdown before the age of 50. Among particular sub-groups of the population, the 'preferred' pattern may involve only a small fraction of the population: for example in 1984, half of births in Britain to mothers born in the West Indies were illegitimate, three times the national figure. If one treats cohabitation before marriage as a 'non-preferred' form, then the proportion in the preferred category would be considerably reduced.

Similar increases in 'atypical' behaviour are seen in most other countries. In almost all developed societies, rates of divorce, illegitimacy and cohabitation have risen rapidly. In 1977 Trost drew attention to the fact that in a small-scale survey in Sweden between 37 per cent and 62 per cent (depending on the definition chosen) of women who had been married for five years were not progressing along the 'preferred' path.

Since marital breakdown is the major reason for deviations from the 'preferred' pattern, it has attracted some attention from traditional life cycle analysts. Aldous (1978, p. 93) has formulated a tentative typology for single-parent families of divorced women who do not remarry. However, the utility of this schema is unclear since most divorced women do remarry. Norton (1983, p. 267) stated: 'the fact that premarital birth, separation and divorce, and remarriage are increasingly becoming common life-course events directly affecting one-half of the (United States) population . . . makes it necessary to extend the FLC to include, insofar as is possible, these variations from the "traditional" family development perspective. Without such extensions the FLC is not representative of lifestyles of the past two decades.' Norton (1980) consequently elaborates the family life cycle model by including estimates of median ages of events such as age at marital breakdown and remarriage for various birth cohorts, and also recomputes traditional family life cycle measures for variables such as age at marriage and first birth by whether or not marital breakdown had occurred.

The second major objection to the family life cycle approach concerns the implicit value judgement made about 'acceptable' and 'unacceptable' forms of family organisation. Terminology such as 'empty nest' phase and 'preferred' form suggest that alternative forms of family organisation are considered inferior (and in many cases they are ignored completely). Indeed for some authors, this is a distinctive and welcome feature of the life cycle approach compared to alternative ones. For example, 'The (family life cycle) model should also be normative in the sense that it should reflect marriage and the subsequent sequence of phases which are not only culturally sanctioned but also encouraged by strong social pressures for conformity. Persons born into diverse cultures willingly marry and then remain in the marital union throughout the phases of the family life cycle until death. In other words, traversing the family life cycle is seen as appropriate behaviour for virtually everyone' (Browning and Herberger, 1978, p. 15).

While the difficulties in applying family life cycle approaches to historical and contemporary Western populations are substantial, their use in other societies with different family structures, is even more problematic. In one of the earliest of such studies Collver (1963) compared the family life cycle in the United States and Benares (India). He concluded that 'the concept of stages is inadequate to describe the situation in which early marriage, prolonged childbearing and early death combine to run the stages together' (p. 87). A similar conclusion was arrived at by Morioka (1967) in a comparative analysis of life cycle patterns in the United States, China and Japan. Comparative issues are also considered by Concepción and Landa-Jocano (1975), and in a penetrating and wide-ranging article by Nag (1974): the most comprehensive set of data on international life cycle estimates for both developed and developing societies is in the useful World Health Organisation (1978) publication.

There are two main threads in the justifications for the family life cycle approach. The first stresses the normative (and almost mystical) nature of the approach, in that 'being cyclical by definition, the family life cycle has no beginning and no end. No matter where you stand to study a family by means of its family life cycle, there are always relevant roots in the near and distant past to be considered. Wherever you are at the moment, you have grown out of the stage just before and are heading into the stage ahead' (Duvall, 1977, p. 157). However, other analysts have adopted a more utilitarian attitude to the family life cycle. Sweet (1977, p. 366) considers that 'the fact that there are stages through which individuals normally pass in sequence is of little consequence except that it makes for simpler graphic or tabular presentation. In fact, normal sequencing is frequently of little inherent interest.' If the family life cycle stages are to be regarded as a simple classificatory scheme, then the volume of literature devoted to it would appear to be excessive, particularly since it has not proven to be a very useful empirical classification, a point which will now be considered.

In a widely-cited article investigating the comparative statistical explanatory power of a life cycle approach Lansing and Kish (1957) used a family life cycle classification based on eight categories:

   i young single;
  ii young married, no children;
 iii young married, youngest child under six;
 iv young married, youngest child six or over;
  v older married with children;
 vi older married, no children;
vii older single;
viii others.

They showed that compared to a classification based on age of head of household, the family life cycle explained more variance in a number of socio-economic variables such as: home ownership; amount of debt; whether the wife is working outside the home; income level; and purchase of consumer durables.

However, Elder (1977, p. 43) pointed out that the use of this life cycle classification also partly includes the age of head of household variable, and therefore its apparently greater explanatory power was less impressive than might appear at first sight. Although proponents of the family life cycle approach have claimed that it is a particularly efficient classification, the evidence for this conclusion is surprisingly weak, and Nock (1979, p. 17) has argued that 'while conceptually interesting, family stages have not proved to be powerful as predictors of either family or individual attitudes or behaviors'.

That many social, economic and psychological variables vary with family life cycle stage is not surprising; however, they also vary with a number of other characteristics such as age of the people concerned, the duration of their union, etc. Studies of the explanatory power of family life cycle classifications compared to alternative ones are rare. However, in two recent articles (Nock, 1979; Spanier *et al.*, 1979), family life cycle classifications were compared with alternative classificatory schemes. Nock presented the correlation coefficients (Kendall's tau) of 7 'instrumental' variables (occupation, employment, education, etc.); 13 'expressive' variables (satisfaction with marriage, friends, etc.); and 9 'attitudinal' factors (religiosity, importance of money, etc.) with life cycle stage. He found that the correlations, based on a sample of 1746 adults from the US Quality of American Life Survey, were generally large and statistically significant. However, using a simple dichotomous variable – presence/absence of children – produced the conclusion that 'relationships here are generally stronger than they were with the family life cycle and the same variables' (p. 22). A simple length of marriage variable was also found to be a powerful predictor but less so than presence or absence of children. He then looked at the relationship of the family life cycle with these target variables separately within three different marital duration categories. Of the 29 variables considered, only two retained a consistent relationship with the life cycle variable within the three duration categories, and many variables had a positive correlation with the life cycle in one duration category, and a negative one in another.

The study of Spanier *et al.* (1979) was based on the 1/10 000 1970 US Census Public Use Data file. Three 7-stage classifications were formed; one based on a family life cycle, one on age cohorts, and one on marriage cohorts. They showed how much the distributions of 14 census variables (presence of parents/parents-in-law; number of children; income; socioeconomic status, etc.) vary with the classifications – which is, in fact, rather little. A second analysis showed that there is substantial overlap in the family life cycle and the alternative classifications. A third analysis presented the proportion of variance explained in the 14 target variables by the 3 classifications: the family life cycle and age cohort variables were the most powerful in 6 cases each. 'This comparison . . . indicates that no one stratification method is clearly superior to the others. If anything, these data would suggest that the age cohort method generally would be favored to the family life cycle method, which, in turn, would be superior to the marriage cohort method for developmental research' (p. 34). Finally a log linear analysis of each pair of classifications with 3 'dependent' variables – family income and husband's and wife's socio-economic status – was considered. Age cohort turns out to be the best classification for explaining differences in both income and husband's socio-economic status, and family life cycle for wife's socioeconomic status: however, in all cases, the subsequent inclusion of a second axis of classification leads to a statistically significant change in chi-squared values suggesting that a single classificatory axis is inadequate to account for the observed variability (although this latter result is hardly surprising giving the sample size used). Their speculation that 'husband' variables are best explained by age cohort and 'wife' variables by family life cycle stage is worth emphasising, since it is women's social, economic and demographic states that are heavily affected by the events of child-bearing and child-rearing, while the position of men may be more influenced by age-related factors.

Although a reply to these papers was published (Klein and Aldous, 1979), the authors failed to make any substantial inroads on the points made by Nock and Spanier *et al.* It appears that the main role of the family life cycle approach in future will lie, in Nock's phrase, primarily as a 'conceptual rather than empirical tool'. As the section on methods of data analysis for families will show, in fact very little work on technical statistical analysis of family change now uses the family life cycle approach, since a life course (alternatively entitled event history or life history approach) has both fewer normative connotations and more flexibility for estimation and modelling. It is noteworthy perhaps that life cycle approaches had only very minor roles in two recent major conferences on demographic aspects of households and families organised by the International Union for the Scientific Study of Population (IUSSP) and the European Association for Population Studies (EAPS).

A final criticism of the life cycle as used in practice is its inexactitude. For example, data are often presented on median ages at marriage and at first birth for women. However, not all women who marry will have births and therefore such comparisons may be misleading (for example, only if both data sets refer to mean ages of women with a legitimate birth in first marriage, will the difference between them give the true mean interval between marriage and first birth). This point, which is more to do with the methods of calculation used than the concept itself, is discussed in more detail in Höhn (1983). However, it does emphasise the need to look carefully at the nature of data used, which is the topic of the next section.

4   DATA FOR LIFE CYCLE ANALYSIS

Perhaps the main contribution of the concept of the family life cycle is that, albeit imperfectly, it stresses the fact that families do not remain constant, but rather they change over time. Many authors emphasise that it is essentially a longitudinal concept, whereby earlier experiences are, at least potentially, likely to affect later behaviour. The perceived need for longitudinal data to analyse such processes is not recent. Thomas and Znaniecki (1918–20) used life records to study social change and individual trajectories. Thomas argued that priority be given to the collection of longitudinal data which would give a continuous record of experiences as they occur. These records were seen as being primarily qualitative. However, the main interest of this paper is with quantitative aspects. It is now half a century since Loomis and Hamilton (1936, p. 226) regretted that longitudinal data were not available, so that family circumstances could not be related historically to other social and economic factors, and that life cycle data on families of different ages at a particular point of time have had to be treated as if they came from a true longitudinal sample. Even now, much life cycle analysis is based on cross-sectional data. A related point is that two topics have received only very limited attention so far: one is the differences experienced by various population subgroups (although see, for example, Glick and Parke, 1965) and the second is variability in life cycle measures (although see Spanier and Glick, 1980). In part the reason for this may again be the fact that published cross-sectional census data (which are frequently used to construct such measures) do not permit such disaggregated results to be produced, and this has probably in turn contributed to the lack of interest in models of the family which diverge from a unique 'ideal' one.

For proper analysis of family dynamics, it is necessary to have data about individual families at different times. In historical studies, this may be done by linking records of baptisms, marriages and burials for various groups of individuals (Wrigley and Schofield, 1981). For contemporary populations, however, the main data sources are retrospective surveys and longitudinal (prospective) studies. Examples of three types of such sources will be described briefly.

The OPCS 1 per cent Longitudinal Study (LS) contains information on a one per cent sample of the population of England and Wales, selected from the 1971 Census, and comprising all people born on four selected birth dates. The dates of births and deaths to sample members in the period after 1971 were added to information included in the 1971 Census schedule on the characteristics of sample members, and of others enumerated in the same household as the LS member. 1981 Census information for original sample members, additional members and others enumerated in the same household in 1981 was then added to the study.

Major advantages of the LS for the purposes of this type of analysis include:

The 1971–81 Census matching enables the construction of quite detailed tables showing the proportion of individuals or families who do not progress through the 'normal' stages commonly identified in a life-cycle approach.

The sample size, which is very large by comparison with most surveys, enables the detailed breakdown of population subgroups to be undertaken, for example by ethnicity or class.

The LS is limited in that it only contains information available in census schedules and some information from registration. Data on housing and employment characteristics are consequently rather lacking, and no information on income is collected. Moreover dates of marriages and divorces occurring between 1971 and 1981 have not yet been included in the study, although this is currently under consideration.

An example of a richer, but smaller, source of longitudinal information relevant to the analysis of family change in Britain is the National Child Development Study (NCDS). The sample comprises all those born in a single week in March 1958. To date four attempts have been made to trace all members of the original study, at ages 7, 11, 16 and 23. The 1981 sweep (at age 23) collected information on employment history, family history (including dates of marriage, cohabitation, births and age/status of partners), education, housing, income, health and leisure activities.

The major advantages of this cohort study in the present context are:

It enables the analysis of the influence of a wide range of 'predisposing' factors (attitudinal, socio-economic, etc.) on the subsequent propensity to follow 'unconventional' family paths, including the previous experience of particular family states – for example lone-parenthood.

It allows the linkage of other career trajectories which have been thought to be important to family processes, for example

housing and education/employment careers, to the progression
of stages identified by demographic events (a requirement for
a life course approach).

As with all such studies, a major disadvantage is the very long
period of time for which such a group has to be followed up for
reasonably complete life history data to be available. So far, it
only gives information on individual circumstances up to age
23. A related point is that, since it is itself a cohort study, it is
unable to provide information on cohort influences. As with
most studies of this kind there is also a problem with loss to
follow-up – that is the progressive reduction in sample size
through time.

The detail available in these sources, however, pales into
insignificance when compared with the data available from the
University of Michigan's Panel Study of Income Dynamics
(PSID) which has collected annual information on a sample of
about 5000 families (around 20 000 individuals) since 1968
(Duncan and Morgan, 1985). Both the original sample families
and new families arising from family sample members leaving
their original families ('split-offs'), and/or new families formed
by events such as divorce are included in the sample, so that,
therefore, the sample size tends to grow over time. An interesting
sidelight on family dynamics provided by this source is that
fewer than one seventh of the original families remained intact
in the 14 years of the survey 1968–81.

The data sources described above are different, but have
been constructed and maintained carefully; however, in many
cases this will not be the case (see, for example, comments by
Trost (1977, p. 475) about the difficulties in interpreting a
sample of Reuben Hill's). A particularly important prescription
for analysing change over the family life cycle is that *either* the
data should be truly representative of a well-defined wider
population *or* appropriate techniques should be used to correct
for any unrepresentativeness *or* the non-representativeness of
the sample should be noted explicitly. This is particularly true
when attempting to make comparisons between different populations, where samples are rarely chosen on a comparative basis.

The use of unrepresentative or specially-selected samples can
lead to misinterpretations. For example, Elder (1977) also
points out that the conclusion from Terman's sample of gifted

children – that the incidence of pre-marital sexual activity had
increased for mothers born at successively later periods, and
that therefore pre-marital sex was increasing through time –
was confounded by the fact that these mothers were also younger
at the birth of their child and, in the past, younger mothers
were more likely to be pre-maritally experienced. A representative sample of children will *not* give a representative sample of
the previous generation: mothers of large families will be over-
represented (and childless women, by definition, will not be
included at all). These points are covered by Preston (1976)
and OECD (1979).

Even apparently representative samples need to be treated
carefully. For example, Norton (1983) presents data on median
ages at first marriage and marital breakdown for cohorts born
from 1900–09 to 1950–59. However, these data are not comparable due to selectivity effects – that is, those of the 1950–59
cohort who married and divorced by 1980 must by definition
have done so below age 30, whereas those of the 1900–09 cohort
have had up to 80 years to do so. Thus comparison of ages is
completely invalid in this case. If the median were defined as
the age by which half of *all* women in the cohort were married,
then this value would not change later except for the fact that
the composition of the cohort will change over time due to
differential survival and migration probabilities (remembering
also that the accuracy of responses may change over time).
However, if the median is defined as the age by which half of
the women who are ever-married at the time of the census are
married, then this age will change census-by-census as more
women marry. (Note that the selectivity effect would affect the
computed age at first divorce whichever definition of the median
is used, unless appropriate statistical techniques are used.)

5   METHODS FOR ANALYSING FAMILY LIFE CYCLE DATA

Although the precise form of analysis used in a particular case
will depend on the objectives of the research and the sorts of
data that are available, nevertheless some general guidelines
can be drawn up.

The first point is that the unit of analysis is likely to be the individual rather than the family. A major reason for this is that when analysing change over time, the family is not a well- defined entity. Attention is likely to be given to the movement of individuals through various family states: the main problem is therefore estimating *transitions* between different family states.

By themselves, overall transition rates are of little interest since the likelihood of a transition is usually affected substantially by *duration variables* of various sorts, for example, the probability of death depends on age but not on duration of marriage, whereas the reverse is true, for example, for first legitimate births. The obvious way to combine a series of duration-specific transition rates (such as first marriage rates by age of bride) is by means of a life table survival function. From this it is possible to compute widely-quoted summary statistics such as the median age at first marriage. It is also possible to estimate some statistics directly; for example, distribution of current marital status by age can be used to derive a median age at marriage (but the assumptions needed to produce such estimates should be made explicit). Examples of the use of simple life table models in the analysis of family transitions are given in Murphy (1983), which shows comparisons of marriage and childbearing allowing for censoring of experience by interview of various birth cohorts in Great Britain. Survival functions and other associated life table functions give a full description of the dynamics of the process under study: for example, median and mean ages, the proportions who do not achieve a particular transition and measures of variability can easily be derived.

It is clear that many of these family transitions are affected by the individual's social and economic circumstances. Thus we might want to allow for the effect of such influences in estimating the transition rates. In some cases the relevant variables do not change over time; for example, in studies of marital breakdown, the important variable of age at marriage is fixed for a particular individual over the period of the study. A more complex case, conceptually and computationally, occurs when the variables which are assumed to affect the process are themselves changing through time: for example, the probability of movement (mobility history) interacts with the probability of giving birth (fertility history). An example of the use of models with such *time-varying covariates* is given in Murphy (1984).

Similar methods may be used with data from a cohort study, although, by definition, comparisons between cohorts cannot be made from such a source, other insights not possible with retrospective cross-sectional data may be obtained. Kiernan (1986) used the 1946 Birth Cohort Study, the National Survey of Health and Development, to investigate marital breakdown among teenage brides. She found that variables such as age at marriage, pregnancy history, and housing type were important factors in breakdown, as did Murphy (1985), using a sample of married women of all ages under 50 from the 1976 Family Formation Survey, which collected retrospective marital maternity and housing histories. However, Kiernan was also able to establish that neuroticism at age 16 was an important factor: such data can only be collected in a truly longitudinal study.

The simple linear family cycle model can be incorporated into a series of life tables since each stage is assumed to occur sequentially. However, in practice, family transitions are more complex in that certain states, such as marriage or divorce, may be re-entered. In order for such events to be incorporated into a life table model, a multistate (or increment–decrement) life table model is required. Examples of such models for family transitions are given by Willekens *et al.* (1982) for marriage in Belgium. These models permit not only the estimation of quantities such as the expected time spent in a particular state and transition probabilities to future states, but also, for example, the probability of entering another state in the future and the expected time spent in it. It is clear that this approach is much more comprehensive (and realistic) than the traditional life cycle model. However, there are also deficiencies. In the first place, it requires detailed information on a number of transitions: moreover, it is based on a Markovian model – that is the probability of transition to another state does not depend on individual characteristics or the length of time spent in the particular state – whereas other evidence shows that many family processes display duration dependence and/or heterogeneity. An extended discussion of these statistical concepts and those in the remainder of this section is given in Hobcraft and Murphy (1986).

These recently-developed technical areas which are important for the analysis of family change come under the general heading of hazards models (which is essentially the same as event-history analysis, Tuma and Hannan, 1984). In such models, the effect of individual-level variables on transitions may be incorporated. These models have been used to show the effect of income support on marital stability (Tuma *et al.*, 1979), to demonstrate that earlier work on the relationship between marital break-down and childlessness was incorrect (Murphy, 1985); and to investigate the relationship between family life stage and migration (Courgeau, 1985). It should be noted that the use of such methods does not mean that correctly constructed samples have necessarily been drawn or correct controls made for sample biases.

6   SUMMARY AND CONCLUSIONS

The family life cycle concept is plausible, uses colourful terminology, and emphasises the dynamic aspects of family life which can be overlooked in cross-sectional tabulations. An example of this last point is that even if all couples had two children, there would only be two children present in the household for a relatively short period of time (about a quarter) for the average family. However, the classical life cycle model does not give attention to the age of parents, other factors which might affect family change, or to the effects of earlier experience on the family's current status.

Other criticisms of the life cycle concept have included its normative and ethnocentric nature (involving implicit assumptions about the ideal type of family and the ideal role of women), and the fact that empirically it does not prove to be a particularly powerful classification for discriminating among different families on a number of different axes. For these reasons, alternative classifications based on simpler age cohorts have been proposed. The introduction of life course concepts permits the incorporation of period and cohort factors, as well as the individual 'careers' in influencing the family situation of the individuals who constitute it. The generalised nature of the life course approach makes it less open to criticism, but also gives less clear guidelines for a particular analysis, except that no potentially important factor should be ignored. For this reason, and because the traditional life cycle model does still apply for about half of the British population (with many others involved in at least some stages), the life cycle approach is likely to remain important conceptually even if in a modified and lower profile form.

These conclusions relate mainly to demographic aspects, but similar points also hold in other areas where life cycle approaches have been used. However, this should not disguise the very substantial contributions that even simple life cycle approaches have made to demographic analysis. For example, it has been very useful as a framework for migration research (Rossi, 1980; Speare, 1970). The majority of moves *are* associated with 'mainstream' life cycle events: leaving home, marriage, and adjustments to changes in family sizes. However, such approaches do not incorporate important and growing 'deviant' life course-related mobility such as that associated with marital breakdown (Sullivan, 1986).

Life cycle approaches have been useful in highlighting the need for longitudinal data and hazards models in the quantitative analysis of family change. However, apart from its other deficiencies, the increasing diversity in family forms over the post-war period in developed societies may, on balance, have made the concept of the family life cycle an impediment rather than an aid to understanding demographic aspects of family change.

ACKNOWLEDGEMENT

I would like to thank Oriel Sullivan for her valuable comments on an earlier version of this chapter.

Part II

Popular Ideologies

3 The Perpetuation of a Folk Model of the Life Cycle and Kinship in a Pottery Factory

Paul Bellaby

'Life cycle' is a metaphor drawn from biology. In Western culture, not only the life course but also the variant paths through it of males and females, are viewed as biological: gender is typically construed as sexuality. This is also the construction that pottery workers and their managers place on the growth and ageing of men and women in the workplace.

Work organisation, sickness and absence from work were the focus of the study on which these observations are based. The core of the study was an ethnography of a large firm in Stoke-on-Trent (The Potteries) which mass produces tableware. Data were collected over a two-and-a-half year period, beginning in early 1983. A variety of methods was combined, including a total of one year's participant observation on the shop floor, structured interviews, analysis of sick notes and personnel records and a series of monitored experiments in changing work organisation. A random sample stratified by age and sex of 96 men and 92 women on the shop floor, and 60 directors, managers and supervisors were interviewed; we also collated their sickness and absence records with the interview profiles. The ethnographic work was shared by a female social anthropologist, Judith Sidaway, and the (male) author, as was interpretation of the field notes (Bellaby, 1984a, 1984b, 1985, 1986).

In addition to espousing the biological metaphor, the pottery employees expect individual life courses to conform to the demands of a cycle of social reproduction. These demands are themselves naturalised. Thus, in that portion of a life that is visible at work (between the ages of 16 and retirement – officially 60 for women and 65 for men), are to be found the following stages or statuses:

> The first stage, sixteen to the early twenties, is transitional, spanning childhood dependence and adult independence in relation to family of origin: in keeping with its liminality (van Gennep, 1960; Turner, 1982), this stage is one in which young people have licence (within bounds), but it is 'young lads' not 'girls' who have the greater licence.
>
> The second stage commences with steady courtship but is achieved only after marriage, setting up a neolocal household (whichever comes first) and having the first child. Independence of family of origin is only gradually accomplished and shades into 'responsibility' for spouse and children. Women normally cease work while their children are of pre-school age, returning (part-time more often than full-time) while they are at school.
>
> A third stage is reached when the children themselves enter adolescence, and (normally) become earners, who contribute to the household budget as well as 'having money in their pockets'. Freed from the expenses (for fathers) and the travail (for mothers) of child-rearing and fattened by the contributions of working children, the household attains relative affluence.
>
> However this third is overtaken by a fourth stage in which working children cease to be net contributors and may need assistance, material and otherwise, in establishing their own household and family of procreation. Often simultaneously, one or other, or both spouses' parents become semi-dependent. Women take on the chief burden of their care, and may give up their employment *in extremis*. With the completion of this stage, men and women approach retirement from work.

This model of the life cycle seems to accord with several patterns of sickness and absence from work. For example, married women present self-certificates which give the care of family and kin as their reasons for absence considerably more often than do men and young single women.[1] Again, by their own confidential reports young men with few or no responsibilities take off odd days, even whole weeks when sickness is not their real reason, far more often than others: these are often hedonistic absences (after a night on the tiles, or in order to take a holiday from work).[2] Married men, moreover, tend to have lower absence rates than women and than single men.[3]

At first sight, then, the model of the life cycle seems to be programmed into individual conduct. This impression appears to be confirmed by the unusual (if not unique) degree to which pottery workers and other workers in the Potteries, emphasise links of family and kinship between community and workplace.[4] It may be that the presence of family and kin in the workplace reinforces the requirements of social reproduction in ways considered appropriate for men and women of different ages. Yet further support for such a view seems to come from the fact that migration in and out of the Potteries is and has been exceptionally low.[5] People often say they do not want to move from the Potteries, however much better job prospects may be elsewhere, because their roots are in the area.

'TELLING THE CODE' IN THE WORKPLACE

None of these observations is false. They are, however, partial truths. The model is not only an observer's but also a participant's construct. In anthropologist's terms, it is a 'folk' or 'home-made' model (Lévi-Strauss, 1968, pp. 281–2); much as, for the sociologist, Wieder (1974a), it is a 'code' which is 'told' in accounting for behaviour, not merely one which the sociologist can use to predict behaviour. The gap between predictive and accounting functions of the model is revealed in three ways in the potbank study:

First, interpreted literally, the model overpredicts: for instance young lads are quite often not tearaways; some married women combine full time work with having children under five; and a number of married men have odd-day-off patterns of absenteeism; all these being considered appropriate to other gender/age categories than their own.

Second, the model is invoked colloquially to account for and sanction deviance: for instance, a man who in his late forties continued, so his colleagues thought, to take odd days off without being sick, was considered to be 'childish', not to act his age, and was treated by the manager and fellow workers accordingly (he was relatively isolated).

Third, the model is used by participants to negotiate the unfamiliar: thus, the two ethnographers, male and female, were questioned about their relationship, and, since it seemed unthinkable that two separately married people with children could share their work, were often teased as if breaking the rules – having an affair.

On closer inspection, it transpires that the model of the life cycle is bounded by the workplace. Clearly it builds upon expectations formed in the community outside, but it also makes demands of participants that might contradict practices in their own households and networks. Some data were gathered from the shop floor sample about individuals' household arrangements, such as budgeting and care for dependants. Not a single pattern, as the model requires, but a great variety was typical of contributions of earnings and by gift by the unmarried young to their parents' household budgets: some paid a few pounds only in board, others handed all their earnings to their mothers and received pocket money in return, and a handful had their own flats or lodgings, usually cohabiting. Similarly, there appeared to be no uniformity in the division (for different purposes: basics, extras, savings) of household earnings and expenditure and who controlled this division, husband or wife.[6] The model, however, makes the man breadwinner and the wife the provider of extras, and gives the man control over most of his earnings, apart from what he hands over to his wife for housekeeping. Again, while women are defined in the model as those who take time off when the need arises to care for dependants, many men did so and, without taking time off, contributed heavily to the care of aged parents.

As used in accounting for conduct, the model truncates experience: it permits only certain realities to be treated as genuine (Bellaby, 1984a). Among these are sicknesses. By 'sickness' is meant here symbolic performance which is socially legitimated, of incapacity for work and other responsibilities.[7] To be treated as genuine both by managers and by workers, sickness must conform to the model of the cycle of social reproduction: that is, it must be appropriate to the stage at which a man or woman is expected to be in the life course. Thus a young woman, recently married, was denied validation for her depression, while an older woman in the same work group, who was passing through the change of life, presented an acceptable argument to colleagues for 'suffering with nerves'.[8] Again, a young lad was indulged for taking a Monday off after what he claimed to be a gruelling night of drinking and sex with his girlfriend, while a married man twice his age was identified by both manager and fellow workers as 'having a drink problem', when he turned in late on a similar occasion. Finally, a married man in his early thirties, who confessed on interview that he had long spells of absence through anxiety, made the interviewer swear not to tell anyone else, for his problem was hidden from workmates and managers; indeed, it could be readily concealed because few would believe it of a man of his age who was married. What these (and many other examples from field notes) illustrate, is that individual affliction or absence behaviour might be sharply at variance with the model. The model did not necessarily function as a code, programmed into people's minds before they came to work and reproduced in conduct while at work. Rather, it was frequently used reflexively to account for and sanction conduct within the workplace.

MYTH AND REALITY OF FAMILY AND KINSHIP IN THE WORKPLACE

As we have seen, participants stress ties of family and kinship which not only bind them to the Potteries area, but also link community and workplace. They imply a continuity between their experiences in home, community and work that our analysis has already shown to be lacking in significant ways. There can be no denying the symbolic importance of pottery workers' (and managers') emphasis on family and kin ties between work and community. For instance, several surnames recurred among present and past employees and were a point of note in introductory conversation with those who shared the names. The ethnographers' impression was that the extent of family and kin ties need only be documented: the findings were sure to support the participants' accounts. However, when the shop floor sample were asked whether they had family and relatives working for the firm, it was a surprise to find that less than half had any such ties. More important still, the proportion with ties decreased sharply with age. If the tendency was for workers who settled with the firm to gather their sons and daughters, nephews and nieces around them, the opposite pattern should prevail – the older the employee, the more of them should have ties with others in the workplace (see Table 3.1).

Table 3.1   Ties of family and kinship with other shop floor workers

	Men	Women	% Under 30	30–44	45 + over
Family: Spouse	8.3	11.0	11.8	8.3	8.5
Children	9.4	11.0	16.1	10.0	3.4
Other relations	29.2	18.7	29.4	25.0	17.0
No relations	53.1	59.3	42.7	56.7	71.2
N = (100%)	96	91	68	60	59

Data available for men only in the same sample show that the older the man, the more likely he is to have had relatives working for the company in the past. This suggests that young men have for some years found their first jobs through relatives employed at the potbank, but that labour mobility has later attenuated these ties.

It is notably rare to find husband and wife couples at work in the same firm, even though the workplace is (anecdotally) where marriage partners are found. Since the firm offered twilight shifts, it might be supposed that husbands would work full time in the day and wives part time in the evening, in order to cover for each other with child-care. However, there is no greater tendency for women who work part time in the evenings to have husbands working full time for the firm than for women working full time days to have such husbands. There is nothing to suggest that family and kin plan their employment with this one firm in mind.

Nor were the family and kin who were employed on the same shifts organised in kinship units as they worked. In no case that we observed did relatives work together, though they might be occupied in the same workplace, even the same department. Informal groups ordered around kinship were more common, but not the rule. Sometimes, a wife, daughter or aunt might bring a cup of tea to a man or woman at their work station. Relatives often could not meet in the canteen, because of staggered hours of serving. In most cases where they could, spouses seemed to eat together and travel to work together; however, parents and children, siblings and more distant relatives seldom shared a meal or a car.

The overstatement of kinship ties complements the over-determination of workplace behaviour by the folk model of the life cycle. What then perpetuates these ideas, half-myth, half-reality?

THE EMPLOYER'S STRATEGIC USE OF THE FOLK MODEL OF LIFE CYCLE AND KINSHIP IN THE LABOUR MARKET

That young people should have more ties of family and kinship in the workplace than their elders has taken on new meaning during the recession. Labour turnover fell between 1978 and 1983: for men, from 34.4 per cent to 15.6 per cent; for women, from 53.1 per cent to 19.4 per cent (those leaving as a percentage of those employed on average in each year). By the end of the period a quarter as many men and women were leaving voluntarily to find work elsewhere as had done so immediately before the recession. In total, a third of the firm's jobs were cut. The pattern was similar throughout the pottery industry and in the Potteries generally, where there are several large employers other than ceramics. The personnel department now had a plethora of applicants, especially for unskilled and semi-skilled jobs. It inaugurated a policy of recruiting young people who were (more or less) known to the company, that is who had relatives employed in the firm to speak for them. The policy was advertised prominently on notice boards around the factory.

It is to the firm's advantage to recruit from families of employees, as may be judged from the increase in informal recruitment during the recession, not only in Britain but also in West Germany (Wood, 1985). Because families do not actually form work groups they cannot be a buffer between production manager and worker. Conversely, to pick workers related to the already employed is to provide some insurance against unreliability (most likely to arise, it is felt, with young men). Moreover production managers sometimes use a family relationship between two members of the same department to make enquiries about why one of them is absent: in one such incident, a young manager tried to cajole a daughter into putting pressure on her mother to return early after a period of sick leave.

As for the life cycle model, it can serve to calibrate the differential capacities of labour. In unskilled work especially, capacity for labour is a function of health and of commitment to regular attendance and sustained employment. Through the folk model, personnel managers 'know' that young single men may be enthusiastic, but are disorderly, that women with dependent children take time off when they are sick, that older men in heavy work slow down but are reliable, that older men in middle management have 'missed the boat' and become set in their ways, or, in a particular instance, that a young woman who went about with young men on motorbikes had predictable genito-urinary disorders.

USES OF THE FOLK MODEL OF THE LIFE CYCLE AND KINSHIP IN NATURALISING PATRIARCHY AT WORK

Just as the employer uses the folk model of the life cycle and kinship in labour market policy, so managers and workers use it to give a natural, unnegotiable appearance to male dominance over women in production.

Patriarchy is palpably central to the division of labour in the potbank. Men have a substantial degree of autonomy and control of their work by comparison with women. Men's and women's work is largely segregated, not only by what they do but by where they work. Even so, men imply that women depress their earnings. They also sometimes experience women they work with or manage as a threat to their latent sexual identity. Shop floor work especially has a macho image. As Pollert (1981, ch. 8) has shown, women sometimes accommodate to this. For instance, sexual joking sometimes takes on a subversive form in relations between female workers and male managers, where women may dare managers (in fantasy) to commit sexual acts, rather than (as is the managers' practice) to use the innuendo of male sexuality to cajole women (Bellaby and Sidaway, 1985). This does not make men any less likely to view women as a threat. Instead they adopt a misogynist stance towards work with women, such as marking out all-male territories (the sliphouse, the kilns, the mouldshop) and accusing women co-workers of 'moaning' and 'acting awkward.'

The union in this potbank and nationally is dominated by men, especially by craftsmen. There is no woman representative in the firm. While there are women at representative level in the Ceramic and Allied Trades Union as a whole, none of the permanent officials is a woman. Perhaps as a result, only in 1983 were steps taken to ensure that women received the same screening for respiratory disorders as men, in spite of the fact that they had long, both as clay-end workers and as burnishers, been exposed to similar dust hazards.

The folk model of the life cycle and kinship helps legitimate this precarious dominance of men over women in the potbank. Thus, suitable men were promoted to supervisor in their twenties and progressed to manager by their early thirties. Partly because of their return to work after child-rearing, women seldom reached supervisory grade before their early forties and (with one exception) did not reach managerial level at all. The exception proved the rule that the folk model legitimated preference for males in promotion. She revealed that she had 'put work first and home second' in order to be a manager. Another woman was pursuing promotion to manager from supervisor during our fieldwork. She failed. The personnel office scrupulously avoided suspicion of sex discrimination. However, her fellow women workers complained behind her back of her unrestrained ambition and her alleged use of an affair with a manager to gain preferment. Both women broke the rules for their gender and age. Conversely, of a married couple who worked in the same department, the man was the less skilled (his wife was a trained paintress), but it was he who became a leading hand, she remaining a machine attendant. The relative work statuses of the two were sanctioned by their marriage.

The kinship idea is of value to the employer in another way: it raises the founder-directors above the class struggle between managers and workers. Though this is a public company, the chairman and his deputy are brothers and two other executive members of the board are relatives. The family founded the company, and, even when feelings against management run high, the family are usually exonerated from blame: it is common for workers to say, 'If only the brothers knew what management did, they would be sure to stop it, but managers stand between us and them.' Older workers provide a comparison between the impersonality and inefficiency often thought to characterise management today, and the straight talking with bosses who were not afraid to roll up their sleeves and do the job, thought typical of the past.

The legitimation that the kinship idea might provide for patriarchy is evident, for instance, in the employer's appeal to employees to pull together to meet the customers' needs, or his aloof and alternately benign and stern manner on his Friday walk-about. Similarly shop floor women, who lack much control over their work, may, on interview or when leaving their jobs, say how much they enjoy the (kin-like) company at work. They may also fill roles analogous to that of keeper of kin networks (Firth, 1956), by acting as first aid attendants and collecting for charities and mail catalogues, and (not least) by befriending the ethnographer at the beginning of his or her visit to the workplace.

These are not literal translations of the structure and solidarity of family to the workplace, but a play upon such relations. This is manifest in particular styles of joking, especially ritual insults and sexual joking in the workplace. What Pilcher (1972, pp. 102–9) has shown among longshoremen in Portland, Oregon is also true of pottery workers. Ritual insults (of an understood playful nature) customarily mark the threshold between the age and gender differentiated relations of household and kin, and the start of a working day in the company of peers. Peer groups are basic to the social organisation of work. They have boundaries that must be negotiated symbolically, whether exchanges across the boundary are required by the job or occur informally. One such negotiation is through banter about sex between men and women. Jokes of this kind (we were often told) do not belong in the world outside the workplace: they are 'bad language'. On no account would participants speak as they do in such encounters when in the presence of their families (Bellaby and Sidaway, 1985).

It seems, then, that the model of the life cycle deployed in the potbank has strategic uses for personnel recruitment, for male-dominated shop floor work and for maintaining the aloof authority of the directors. The folk model legitimates, by natur-alising, the inequalities of class, age and gender among the workforce.

THE HISTORICAL MYTH AND REALITY OF FAMILY AND KINSHIP IN THE POTBANKS

The link between community and workplace in the Potteries is a venerated tradition. Hobsbawm and Ranger (1983) have shown that 'tradition' emerges and is sustained not out of inertia, but because of its strategic uses in relations of power. We have begun to uncover the present reality of the myth of family-based work; might something similar prove to be its historical reality?

There are broadly two ways in which family ties could operate in a workplace:

(a) by serving as a means of getting jobs (through relatives 'speaking for' other members of the family seeking work);
(b) by forming the basis on which work is organised on the shop floor (and/or at management or employer levels), that is, by making work itself familial.

Hard evidence of family recruitment and family organisation of work in the pottery industry of the past comes in two principal forms: Census enumeration forms and union membership lists. Methods of analysing the Census returns to date permit us to define kin relations between household members, but not to establish with any confidence kinship networks outside the household.[9] Union membership lists do enable us to infer kin-ship outside the household, at least among people bearing the same surnames. These also provide information on place of work, whereas Census returns state industry/occupation but not workplace. However, unlike the Census household enumer-ation, the union records do not allow us to infer whether potters' households sent wives and children to the potbanks more often than, say, miners' or labourers' households. If it were possible to use both sources for the same historical periods, they would reinforce each other admirably. However, Census returns by household are available only after 1851 and up to 1881 (the hundred-year rule prevents access to later sources). Correspondingly, union membership books having adequate coverage of the pottery workforce are available only from the 1910s. It follows that no definitive answers can be given to the questions we have posed. That is in no way an unusual state of affairs in historical studies. It should not of course prevent us from seeking the most plausible answers on the evidence available.

It is often assumed that industrialisation typically replaced cottage industry with the factory, family work with the collective labourer, whether abruptly or after a transitional period. However, Snell (1985, ch. 7) points out that family work (as found in textiles in seventeenth century Shepshed (Levine, 1977)) was characteristic only of proto-industry where skills were not in short supply and earnings were low. Here women's and children's labour was used to enable the male spinner, weaver or hosier, to produce enough to make a living for his family.

As for the pottery industry of North Staffs, family work may have been typical of its development prior to the eighteenth century, but the industry we know today grew from craft workshops. In the earlier phase, smallholders in the impoverished uplands reverted seasonally to producing butter pots, which were sold in a regional market (Plot, 1686, pp. 108–9, 121–4). The kiln was built in the garden. It is probable that several members of the family took part in making the red-bodied ware. However, the innovators of the white-bodied wares that were the foundation of today's industry were craftsmen, many of them migrants from London, and in the crucial case of the Elers, from Holland. Their workshops, though small, were probably organised on the established pattern of other trades: master, journeymen and apprentices, not family workers.[10]

Before the nineteenth century, workshops rarely reached factory dimensions. Wedgwood's Etruria is the best known, though not the largest contemporary example. The first Josiah Wedgwood built not only a model factory but also a model village to house his workforce. This one-company-town pattern led, if only for geographical reasons, to recruitment of relatives to the same workplace. It was not, however, typical of the pottery industry, and even Etruria by the mid-nineteenth century was the site of competitive employment, especially in the iron industry. Moreover, McKendrick's work on the Wedgwood papers shows that, even if Wedgwood's model village might at first have supplied women's and children's labour as well as that of men to his potbank, he had a rational plan for the division of labour, and for the supervision and reward of his workforce, which probably precluded family work (McKendrick, 1961).

Smelser (1959) suggests that in Lancashire textile mills family recruitment *and* work organisation were common before legislation restricted the use of child labour (see also Lazonick, 1979). The exclusion of child labour in the pottery industry lagged twenty years behind the corresponding legislation for textiles. Children were employed until relatively late, but they were not necessarily the children of potters. Dupree's (1981) work on the enumeration returns of the 1861 and 1881 Censuses reveals employments of household members prior to and after the legislation in question. She suggests that male potters may have *discouraged* their wives and children from finding work in potbanks, for miners and general labourers sent a higher proportion of their women and children into potbanks than did male potters. Nor did wives and mothers work in the potteries to any great extent. While, as the Children's Employment Commission of 1842 suggests, children of pre-apprenticeship age were employed in potbanks until the Factory Acts were extended to the potteries in 1864, married women do not appear to have been employed in significant numbers, unless they had no children.[11] Nor did the child labour legislation cause mothers to find work in potbanks in place of their children. In the latter half of the nineteenth century, then, even the weaker hypothesis that people were recruited to potbanks in family groups receives no support, though it must be stressed that the enumeration by households can (at present) tell us nothing of workplace ties with kin outside the nuclear family. What can be asserted with some confidence is that the stronger hypothesis that work was organised around the nuclear family within the workplace must fall.

It is tempting to conclude that, if the familial pattern of recruitment and organisation was not in place in the pottery industry more than a hundred years ago, it could not have been subsequently. That, however, is to accept the linear-evolution assumptions typical of modernisation theory. Snell (1985) suggests from Poor Law examinations data, that in rural areas, families rarely achieved the stability of settlement, even of co-habitation, necessary for continuity of family recruitment to one employer over generations, until the last quarter of the nineteenth century. Unstable labour markets made it impossible. Might tight-knit urban areas, such as The Potteries, have been founded in the late nineteenth century and held together in spite of rehousing in the post-war period? Whipp (1983) has gathered from union membership records evidence that people were employed in both family and kin groups in the same pot-banks in the first 25 years of this century. We cannot know from this evidence whether relatives in the households of potters were more likely to work for the potbank than their counterparts among miners or labourers; on the other hand, it is clear that families and kin often worked for the same employer. This suggests that there may have been an increase in the tendency of potter's families to seek common employment, beginning in the last decade or two of the nineteenth century.

A contributory factor may have been the rapid increase in the number of women employed in the potteries. For the industry as a whole (i.e. the manufacture of earthenware and china) male employment increased more slowly than population, but female employment went up much more quickly than population: male employment rose from 26 000 in 1861 to 35 000 in 1891 and fell to 34 000 in 1921, while female employment rose from 12 000 in 1861 to 22 000 in 1891 and in 1921 surpassed that of males at 36 000. Female employment was particularly characteristic of the industry in Stoke-on-Trent (The Six Towns). Thus, in 1921, 30 000 females (of the 36 000 in the whole of England and Wales) who were potters lived in The Potteries, as compared with 24 000 of the 34 000 males engaged in the industry.

The influx of women reflects a change in employers' strategies. Those recruited in such rapidly increasing numbers were over-whelmingly single and young. The Census evidence suggests that women were unlikely to return to formal employment after the birth of their first child, unless widowed. Employers sought to displace relatively expensive male with relatively cheap

female labour. They were also attacking the craftsman's autonomy, one aspect of which, as we have seen, was his notion that
his wife and children should not take menial jobs in the potbanks. It was out of the struggles that ensued between craftsmen and employers that the potters' union arose. Master potters,
who often worked on contract, employing their own assistants,
used the union to impose regulations on their underhands
(Warburton, 1939, p. 35; see also Burchill and Ross, 1977). It
would seem that precisely similar circumstances to those which
explain the persistence of the tradition of family work to this
day, also account for its emergence. Perhaps it provided a
rationale for older males' dominance of work groups.

Of course, family and kin recruitment to employment does not
necessarily imply the organisation of work around family and kin
groups. Indeed, the evidence for the twentieth century points
away from the latter. In her historical survey, Sarsby (1985)
shows that both jobs and work areas have long been sex-segregated
in the pottery industry and that cases in which women have
assisted men (whether or not as wives) must have been rare.

The most detailed breakdown of sex and age in relation to
occupation available in the Census is for 1921.[12] It lends support to the hypothesis that even at what may have been the
peak of family recruitment to the workplace, work was in fact
organised by sex and age peer groups. First, in 1921 there was
considerable segregation of the sexes by occupation. Women
were preponderant in painting, printing and decorating and in
the warehouse (not in packing, but presumably in selecting).
Men predominated in management, kilns, maintenance and the
sliphouse. However, and secondly, men were of much higher
median ages than women. The youngest male category were
kiln workers (median 38), the oldest painters (46) (note that
male painters were long the elite of decorators). On the other
hand, the oldest group of women were to be found in warehouses as 'warehouse women' (28), and the youngest as assistants in the warehouses (17). Thirdly, the clay end (where pots
were made) contained both men and women in numbers (rather
more women than men), and since men potters were almost
twice the age of women potters, it is likely that men were of
senior rank. In the clay end, but only here, there is prima facie
evidence that young women (as a peer group) may have assisted
more mature men.

The sociologically most significant difference between 1921 and the 1980s must be that, while in 1921 most women in the industry were of similar age and civil status to domestic servants, most women of today in the industry are married and run their own households. The division of labour between the sexes in our potbank today is in some respects similar, in some respects different to that of 1921. Men still monopolise management, and work on kilns, in the sliphouse or maintenance. Women still monopolise selecting. But men have taken over decorating in numbers. In 1921 men did much of the freehand painting, in the 1980s in mass production they do most of the (semi-mechanised) screen printing, though lithographing (applying transfers) remains women's work and, in the more expensive end of the market, women have become the painters. Conversely, women had all but driven men out of the clay end, until the recession, with casting a partial exception. Pressing (except for flatware) has become women's work. Women have also displaced men in packing. These details apart, segregation of men and women by occupation and usually by the territories they occupy on the shop floor has continued throughout the 60 years we are discussing. Today there is no tendency for women to assist men in their work in any area. Women are as likely to be mature in age and married as men (median age in a simple random sample of shop floor workers was 37, the same for men and women).

Other things being equal, the influx of married women which began in the 1950s should have increased the likelihood that family and kin would work for the same employer, if not in the same work groups. However, the 'return to work' trend was offset by the growth of alternatives to pottery employment, especially for women: in 1921, 60 per cent of the female labour force of Stoke-on-Trent worked in ceramics; in 1981, only 25 per cent of the corresponding group did so.

In summary, the evidence points away from family work in the past, and suggests that recruitment of kin to a common employer may have become more not less common from the turn of this century. The folk model of kinship and the life cycle is not, then, a cultural survival. Much as Littler (1982, ch. 10) has argued that the Japanese system of permanent employment is of recent origin and reflects changing exigencies in capital/labour relations, so we have suggested that the tradition of family involvement in common employment in the North Staffordshire pottery industry developed to meet changed labour market demands in recent times.

CONCLUSION

Marx and Engels (1973, p. 70) believed that the factory system would sweep away traditional production relations:

> The bourgeoisie cannot exist without constantly revolutionising the instruments of production, and thereby the relations of production, and with them the whole relations of society. Conservation of the old modes of production in unaltered form, was, on the contrary, the first condition of existence for all earlier industrial classes.

Family and work were separated and classes arising in employment relations became the chief determinant of the division of labour in society. However, Marx and Engels did not grasp the possibility that patriarchy as substance, and kinship and life cycle as symbols, might continue to dominate the organisation of work, even under capitalism.

Pahl (1984) has tried to reorientate sociology from its focus upon class, to a concern with the household and domestic cycle, suggesting that this is the primary determinant of the social division of labour, and may long have been so, though neglected until now. The point is well made that participation in labour markets is a function of the internal organisation of the household, in particular of the stage it has reached in its life cycle. But in spite of his discovery that opportunities for formal employment contribute crucially to inequalities between households, Pahl tends to treat the household in isolation from capitalist relations of production and distribution.[13]

His attempt to shift the axis from employment relations and class to household division of labour and domestic cycle may be premature. In this paper, we have suggested that a folk model of the life cycle and of kinship, which helps naturalise patriarchy and class relations, has been perpetuated in a pottery firm. This apparently traditional pattern has neither been swept aside by industrialisation nor revived by deindustrialisation. Rather it has been constituted in the historically recent work of legitimating an unequal division of labour in the factory. Might it still be the case, as Dennis, Henriques and Slaughter (1969) found for a coal-mining community in the early 1950s, that formal employment in workplaces where the life cycle and kinship are stereotyped and are used in accounting for and sanctioning conduct, does much to constitute the domestic division of labour? If so we may need to set the argument that Pahl has overturned, back on its feet.

ACKNOWLEDGEMENTS

I owe a particular debt to my close colleague in the study reported here, Judith Sidaway; also to Sheila Cleverly who brought order to scattered sickness and absence records. The firm has extended at all levels cooperation and friendship to a degree no social researcher has a right to expect. At various stages Shirley Dex, Marguerite Dupree, Ronnie Frankenberg, Liz Hart, Jackie Sarsby, Ursula Sharma, David Vincent and Richard Whipp have also contributed personally to my thoughts on this theme, though none of these is to blame for any errors in the paper. My thanks also to Alan Bryman and Bill Bytheway for their thorough and supportive editorial work.

NOTES

1. Certificates from medical practitioners from January 1981 to December 1983, together with self-certificates from their introduction in April 1982 to the end of the same period, were classified by stated reasons for absence. Samples of 106 men and 104 women on the shop floor, stratified by age, had all their certificates collated with separately recorded absences. (Of these, 96 men and 92 women were also interviewed.) Women, it transpired, had 5.8 certified episodes of absence per head and men 12.3, in the three year period: 14.4 per cent of women's certified absences (almost all self-certified) gave illness in the family or among kin as their pretext, compared with 6.2 per cent of men's.
2. On interview, samples of shop floor workers and managers were asked to report their absences over the preceding two weeks and what their cause had been. It was among shop floor workers under 30 years of age (n = 68), especially men, that was found the largest proportion who took time off for non-sickness reasons (21 per cent of both sexes reported sickness, but 35 per cent had been absent on specific days). The older the worker the more likely a report of somewhat incapacitating illness (especially of recurrence of longstanding afflictions), but the less likely an absence (37 per cent of those of both sexes aged 45 and over

(n = 59) reported sickness, but only 15 per cent of them were absent).

3. Married men workers (n = 68) lost an average of 2.99 per cent of working days through absence annually between 1981 and 1983. Single, widowed and divorced men (n = 27) lost an average of 3.91 per cent, married women (n = 79) of 6.02 per cent, and single, widowed and divorced women (n = 22) of 5.57 per cent. (NOTE: we were able to discover the marital status of most of the women in our sample who could not be obtained for interview, but not that of men whom we could not interview.)

4. I am grateful to Elizabeth Hart for sharing similar observations about a china-manufacturing firm in Stoke-on-Trent in which she made an ethnographic study and a film. See 'A Wedding in the Potteries,' (producer, M. Llewellyn Davies) Central Television, 1984.

5. From Census 1981 Small Area Statistics, it appears that about 0.5 per cent of the population in the neighbourhood of the firm that was studied move in or out of the Potteries each year. Life history interview material for the workplace samples corroborates this.

6. This is in spite of closely similar class position and a shared Potteries culture. Compare Pahl, J. (1983).

7. For further discussion of 'sickness' and a rationale for conceptualising it differently from (biological) 'disease' and (experiential) 'illness' see Frankenberg (1980) and Young (1982).

8. 'Menopausal syndrome' is a Western construct, not found, for example, in traditional Japan, though recently imported with Western medicine: see Lock (1986).

9. Michael Anderson is developing methods for using household enumeration returns for this purpose. See Anderson (1985).

10. According to Laslett (1971) it was typical of trades and tenant farmers that apprentices, journeymen and outdoor servants should live in the master's premises and constitute part of his household. Quasi-kin relations obtained between all members of the household (see also Flandrin (1979)). English Common Law, however, distinguished between apprentices and servants and children proper: thus a master was not able to inflict bodily harm on his apprentice; a restriction applied to fathers *vis-à-vis* their children only from the late nineteenth century. Further, neither boys nor girls customarily left their parents until they were around thirteen.

11. Tilly and Scott (1978) show that women's participation in the labour market and type of employment varied greatly from one city to another in Europe and Britain, but that industrialisation reduced rather than enhanced the participation of wives in paid work, since it removed the site of such work from the household.

12. The 1921 Census of Population was the first census in England and Wales to make the modern distinction between 'occupation' and 'industry'.

13. Pahl, R. E. (1984, ch. 12) and Pahl, R. E. and Wallace (1985) emphasise self-provisioning in the household. Unlike Gershuny, Pahl neglects the extent to which this perhaps '800-year old' pattern has only recently become commoditised (by what Gershuny (1985) calls 'socio-technical innovation').

4 Rethinking the Family Life Cycle: Sexual Divisions, Work and Domestic Life in the Post-war Period

Jacqueline Burgoyne

INTRODUCTION

Moral panics about the state of 'The Family' have a long history (Weeks 1981). However, in the decades following the Second World War apparent public disquiet about the social consequences of changing patterns of family and household life has received increasing media attention. As a result 'family life' has emerged as a *public issue* in the sense first described by Wright Mills:

> An issue is a public matter: some value cherished by publics is felt to be threatened. Often there is a debate about what the value really is and about what it is which really threatens it. This debate is often without focus if only because it is in the very nature of an issue that it cannot very well be defined in terms of the immediate and everyday environments of ordinary [women and] men. (Wright Mills, 1959: my addition.)

In this chapter I intend to discuss four interrelated changes in patterns of marriage, employment, and domestic relationships which have generated the kinds of confusions and uncertainties which, in some circles at least, appear to undermine 'cherished' family values. These are the extent to which:

the conventional 'Tarzan: breadwinner, Jane: housewife' domestic partnership based on the family wage and enshrined in the Beveridge social insurance scheme still represents the majority pattern;

changing patterns of employment and, in particular, the increased participation of women in the labour market, has been matched by an increase in husbands' participation in domestic labour;

fathers are taking a more active role in day-to-day childcare; recent increases in divorce, remarriage and – to a lesser extent – unmarried cohabitation have undermined the 'normality', in both the statistical and normative sense, of the conventional nuclear family.

In each of these instances, the question raised about the degree of change is shadowed by another relating to moral and social considerations about whether such changes are a Good Thing.

THE FAMILY AND THE LIFE CYCLE IN POST-WAR BRITISH SOCIOLOGY

In part, for the reasons Morgan delineates so clearly (Morgan, 1985), the sociology of the family has not enjoyed a very high status and has been poorly served by theoretical analysis. This has had particularly unfortunate consequences for the reputation and standing of the discipline more generally as it is an area of considerable potential public interest. In my own case the research on couples to which I refer in this chapter has attracted a good deal of media attention as well as a somewhat intrusive interest in my own domestic circumstances; events for which my own occupational socialisation did little to prepare me.

One of the more acute, yet rarely discussed, problems faced by those who study family relationships and arrangements is uncertainty about how to deal with personal experience and the strong feelings it can generate. Students, teachers and researchers in the 1950s and early 1960s most often responded to the perennial problems surrounding the pursuit of scientific respectability and value freedom by portraying their discipline and its investigations as at least aspiring to scientific purity (see Platt, 1981).

As part of this generation myself, I now recognise that this meant that, once we had donned our scientists' white coats, it would have been improper for us even to admit that we had any particular interest, moral commitment, strong feelings or direct experience of our own chosen areas of research. Unfortunately this has meant that, until recently, we rarely made use of the kinds of opportunities, *de rigueur* within the therapeutic professions, for reflective, self-critical consideration of the ways in which our own values and experiences affect our work. It is for this reason that we also often had profound misgivings about occupying positions where we might be asked to advise others on the basis of our research findings or specialist knowledge.

The textbooks and empirical studies of aspects of family life published during this period suffered accordingly. Morgan has documented the main consequences of their continuing reliance on an outmoded, subterranean version of functionalism and Platt's critique of the work of the Institute of Community Studies illustrates the pitfalls of their approach very clearly (Platt, 1976). However, Young and Wilmott's later work, significantly entitled *The Symmetrical Family* (1973), a series of studies conducted by the Rapoports when directors of the Institute for Family and Environmental Studies (Rapoport *et al.*, 1981) and Fletcher's bestselling *The Family and Marriage in Britain* (1971), whatever the various authors' conscious intentions, served to confirm that, despite evidence of strain, all was well with the post-war family.

These works were widely used by both academics and policy-makers, thus making their own contribution to the stock of 'known facts' and commonsense wisdom about contemporary patterns of family life. They formed an important part of the undergraduate studies of trainee members of personal service occupations, whose ranks grew rapidly during these decades. As such they served to reinforce occupational ideologies which stressed the significance of the division between the healthy and the pathological. These studies offered research-based evidence of rising living standards, home-centred patterns of consumption and the espousal of conventional family norms by the majority of young adults. Such findings were used to support widely-used life cycle schema of the kind first outlined by Rosser and Harris (1965). These images contrasted sharply with the poverty, the 'deviant' family structures and the pathological relationships and behaviour of the minority who would constitute their most difficult pupils, patients and clients, or the object of their therapeutic interventions.

It is not surprising, therefore, that as evidence of change and strain within families has accumulated, including the 'rediscovery' of poverty in the late 1960s, the professional bodies of such occupations and the policy-makers who direct their labours, have sought to draw attention to the extent of family problems. Their analyses of such problems frequently include reference to the erosion of traditional beliefs governing family behaviour and the significance of widespread deviation from the norms of the conventional nuclear family. As such the personal service occupations have played an important part in recent decades in the creation of a climate of public opinion in which the domestic and family lives of individuals, as well as The Family in the institutional sense, has once again become a significant public issue.

Furthermore, in each of the instances discussed below conflicts and disagreements about the degree and significance of change have raised questions about the reliability of the evidence used to support opposing positions as well as, by implication, the professional standing of those of us who collect and present such evidence. As I shall indicate through one specific illustration in the final section of this paper, the apparently 'neutral' stance, with its implicit support for beliefs in the 'naturalness' of the nuclear family (see Plummer, 1975), taken by earlier generations of sociologists of the family does not serve us well in these more controversial times.

TARZAN, JANE AND THE CONTINUING ECONOMIC DEPENDENCE OF MARRIED WOMEN

The lobbying which preceded the passage through Parliament of the Matrimonial and Family Proceedings Act 1984 provides an excellent example of the persuasiveness of the mythological proposition that the legacy of post-war educational, economic and social policy has transformed contemporary marriage into a partnership of equals. From the 1920s onwards therapeutic experts discussing marriage have stressed the importance of closeness, mutual companionship and open communication in marriage (see, for example, Green, 1984). However, in their writing and public pronouncements they rarely distinguish between theories about how marriage *ought* to be conducted and their perceptions, gained principally through direct contact with a 'client' or clinic population, of the extent to which the inner dynamics of married relationships generally conform to this ideal.

The myth of 'equal partners' has also gained currency with increased public awareness of trends in married women's employment outside the home. These parallel trends were, of course, central to Young and Wilmott's much quoted symmetrical family thesis. However, as sociologists of marriage (Hill, 1958) and members of the upper class have long known (Wilson and Lupton, 1959), and as divorcing partners discover to their cost, the foundations of marriage as a domestic partnership have as much, or more, to do with economics as emotion. It is not surprising, therefore, though somewhat ironic, that the mythology of equal partnership has been most widely disseminated in debates about the reform of the laws and procedures surrounding divorce (Burgoyne, Ormrod and Richards, 1987).

At this time, frequent references were made to the 'widespread belief' that the right to maintenance after divorce was now an anachronism. In 1981 David Clark and I carried out a survey of public attitudes towards marriage and divorce which provides some partial confirmation of this view; only 12 per cent of our sample believed that a 'divorced woman who is working and financially independent' should receive financial support from her ex-husband. However more recent survey data from the SCPR *British Social Attitudes Survey* indicates that, when respondents were asked to take into account financial and labour market considerations,

> people found it difficult to hold formally egalitarian beliefs
> .. if it meant penalising women for adhering to the traditional
> domestic division of labour. (Jowell and Witherspoon, 1985)

Although there was generalised opposition to the idea of wives without dependants receiving maintenance after divorce, additional questions which specified the wife's circumstances provoked rather different answers. From their findings the authors conclude that, unlike the powerful minorities represented by the Campaign for Justice in Divorce and the Society of Conservative Lawyers who lobbied the Lord Chancellor in the early 1980s, the representative sample of men and women they questioned,

> seemed aware of the social consequences of the sex-based division of paid work and domestic labour. In other words, women who had performed the role of houseworker and whose employment prospects were low, were accorded entitlements to part of the family wage.

The accuracy of their impression that the majority of women still spend a considerable proportion of their adult lives as the economic dependants of their husbands, because of their domestic and childcare responsibilities, is confirmed in a variety of recent studies. The findings of the *Women and Employment* survey indicate that, although each succeeding cohort of women is likely to have spent a greater proportion of their adult lives in paid employment, marriage continues to shape the working lives of the majority of women to a very significant degree (Martin and Roberts, 1984). In her study of a sample of recently married couples in north London, Mansfield (1985) found that it is still common for newly married women to change their jobs in the early months of marriage in order to work shorter hours or to reduce their travelling time as a way of accommodating their increased domestic responsibilities.

Evidence of this kind suggests that the pace and degree of change is sufficiently limited to challenge both the myth of equal partnership and many of the policy recommendations proposed from it. However, it would be foolish to ignore the potential for change over the life course of current and future marriage cohorts. Recent increases in the proportion of girls gaining O and A level passes and entering further and higher education (Central Statistical Office, 1986, Tables 3.10 and 3.11); the likelihood that, if present trends continue, one in three of first marriages will end in divorce within 15 years (Haskey, 1983); as well as, of course, the continuing decline in traditional areas of male employment, will inevitably affect future patterns of marriage. In addition, we still know relatively little about how older married couples, now in their 40s and 50s, manage their earnings or whether the domestic division of labour is renegotiated in later life. In some instances a wife's relatively secure employment status may enable her husband to opt for voluntary redundancy (Forster, 1987) or may be the main source of their contributions to their children's student grants or the financial help frequently given when adult children marry and set up home themselves (Leonard, 1981).

MEN, WOMEN AND HOUSEWORK: THEORY AND PRACTICE

The study of stepfamilies which David Clark and I began in 1979[1] provides a vivid illustration of the distinction between theory and practice in relation to the domestic division of labour. When we first started this research we rather imagined, generalising perhaps from the increasing number of second partnerships in our own social circles, that they would be characterised by more 'progressive' or egalitarian domestic arrangements than those of first partnerships. Accordingly, we asked each partner questions about household organisation and, in particular, how their second partnership compared with their first in this respect. As we were to understand later, factual responses to such questions were somewhat eclipsed by their desire to portray their present partnership in as favourable a light as possible. As a result, although there was a wide range of responses, with examples of change in both directions, whether they and their partners were now doing more or less, the majority claimed that they greatly preferred their present arrangements (Burgoyne and Clark, 1984).

The material from these interviews provided us with a fiery baptism into the difficulties of analysing and interpreting data on housework and domestic responsibilities. Abstract theoretical discussion of the finer points of the, then flourishing, great Domestic Labour Debate did not seem to help very much. Increasingly we realised that, had we known that these issues were to be so crucial in understanding the study couples' partnerships, as well as contributing to current knowledge about patterns of domestic life generally, we would have questioned them more systematically about these matters as well as approaching the issue in other, more oblique ways.[2]

There are significant parallels between this and a later study of unmarried cohabiting couples which employed a similar methodology.[3] Within this sample were a group of former student couples. Whilst the remarried in our earlier study were anxious to demonstrate that the benefits of their new partnership justified the pain and upheaval their divorce had caused themselves and their children, these former students portrayed themselves as living outside of what they regarded as the constraints of conventional marriage (Burgoyne, 1985a). Both examples draw attention to what Voysey calls the 'public moralities' of marriage and family life which shape our understanding of how we ought to portray our private domestic arrangements in a public world (Voysey, 1975).

This distinction between theory and practice also helps us to understand some of the relevant findings from the *Women and Employment* survey. In the wake of the growing influence of public moralities portraying the ideal marriage as a partnership of equals, it is not surprising that a quarter of the wives and husbands interviewed claimed that they shared housework equally; if wives were working full-time this proportion rose to 44 per cent. As the authors themselves point out, it is difficult to probe such issues in a structured interview. In any event, neither husbands nor wives would be likely to admit – or even consciously to recognise – dissatisfaction with their present arrangements unless they were actively contemplating making some changes.

It is somewhat ironic that one of the unintended consequences of twentieth century feminist campaigns following the achievement of formal emancipation has been to contribute to a climate of consciousness in which the 'equal partners' myth has flourished. As a result, not only do the overwhelming majority of married women still take responsibility for most of the household work over the lifetime of a marriage but, because of the power of this myth, they are increasingly likely to feel guilty for doing so. Like their Victorian sisters from the lower middle-classes, whose limited means prevented reliance on servants, they work in secret while conveying an image of leisured ease (Branca, 1975; Hall, 1979), based on their mythical possession of, not this time servants below stairs, but an apron-clad domesticated husband hovering in the background. In this respect even 'halfway to Paradise' (Wilson, 1980) is an overestimate.

It is also worth considering exceptional cases; the kinds of circumstances and local and occupational communities in which the domestic labour actually performed by husbands significantly exceeds the norm and whether, on occasion, the relationship between theory and practice is reversed. There is a range of historical evidence suggesting that working-class men frequently took over domestic chores in an emergency, such as illness or confinement and that they were accustomed to taking a greater share in household tasks where there was a high proportion of women in paid employment. In addition, autobiographical or oral history material frequently includes descriptions of 'unusual' men who did a great deal of cooking and cleaning but were careful to do so behind the closed doors of their home so that they were not ridiculed by their peers (Roberts, 1971; Dayus, 1985).

Such material suggests that we should remain sceptical about many estimates, past and present, of universally low levels of male participation in domestic work as there are likely to be many instances in which men do more than they 'should' and take pains to hide their activities from the scrutiny of neighbours. It is significant, for example, that one of the tasks unemployed men in Sheffield are least likely to take on is 'pegging out' – hanging out washing – which would provide unequivocal evidence of their new-found involuntary domesticity.

Unemployment and retirement both create the possibility for men to do more domestic work and may also increase their sense of obligation to share household tasks more equitably. However, it is disconcerting for those of us who move in circles where women seem to spend a great deal of time persuading male members of the household to do *more* domestic chores, to discover that male involvement is not always welcomed by wives. Anecdotal evidence about the strains of retirement when wives find that they are unable to 'get on' with their normal household routines because their husbands are in the way, are matched by recent data on the domestic consequences of male unemployment. Both survey (Burgoyne, 1985b and c) and qualitative evidence (Morris, 1985b) illustrate how male unemployment undermines customary gender divisions and taken-for-granted sources of both masculinity *and* femininity in such marriages. Not only are men in traditional working-class communities stigmatised and diminished by their failure to perform their customary roles as breadwinners and by their involvement with 'female' preoccupations such as cleaning and laundry, but their wives also suffer in a parallel fashion. It is not surprising, therefore, that there is now growing clinical evidence of an association between male unemployment and sexual difficulties in marriage affecting both husbands and wives.

MEN AS PARENTS

Evidence about changes in the degree to which men are typically involved in the day-to-day care of their children is, of course, subject to many of the same methodological problems as those discussed in the previous sections. Oakley's (1974) findings are confirmed in the *Women and Employment* survey; wives felt that their husbands were more likely to participate in child care than any other form of household work, and half of this sample considered that their husbands shared equally in daily child care. A realistically lower proportion of husbands felt this to be the case. In this section, however, I want to consider other, more elusive aspects of change as it affects gender and father-hood by exploring changes in the dominant public moralities of parenthood. I want to suggest that parenthood is now ideally regarded as an essential aspect of the contemporary marital partnership, a collaborative venture in which fathers are ex-pected to be more obviously participative than in earlier generations.

In recent decades, at an ideological level at least, fathers have come into their own, taking their place centre-stage in media portrayals of family life. Prince Charles, for example, might be regarded as a model father in this new world. Present at his children's birth, playing with them unselfconsciously in front of the camera in a way which would be hard to imagine his father doing, he makes his – token – involvement in daily decisions about their care quite apparent. Although we must, of course, recognise that such images are carefully and consciously constructed by the Palace press office, they are intended to reflect popular ideals – even fantasies – and as such may point to substantive changes in both beliefs and practice.

As a consequence of recent trends in divorce and remarriage, fathers are also making their presence felt in other ways. As the number of legal disputes about child custody, and more com-monly access to children after divorce has risen, the needs and rights of divorced fathers have become a 'public issue'. The lobbying activities of groups like Campaign for Justice in Divorce and Families Need Fathers have played a significant part in the creation of this new climate of consciousness. In addition several recent popular films offered very sympathetic portrayals of the plight of divorced fathers. Such themes have also had increasing coverage in drama and TV soap operas. This has been matched by a growing volume of social commentary by journalists and social scientists which has helped to foster the impression of a 'trend', a sudden and significant change in beliefs and practices which in reality greatly exceeds the degree and extent of actual changes in the behaviour of fathers. Thus just as public moralities of marriage as a partnership of equals have engendered contradictions for wives over domesticity and household work strategies, so ideologies of parenthood as a collaborative venture create new contradictions for men as fathers. In both cases, these contradictions also affect the other partner as well; traditional gender roles and stereotypes come under challenge as well as taken-for-granted assumptions about what constitutes 'normal' feminine and masculine parental behaviour.

Interest in the changing role of fathers has stimulated several recent studies of, *inter alia*, the experience of becoming a father, including the experience of being present at the birth of their children. The findings suggest that for many this is an occasion at which men are permitted to express unusually strong feelings (Richman, 1982) and that the sense of closeness with their partners at this time gives some temporary substance to images of parenthood as a collaborative experience. However, it is clear that, unlike Prince Charles, once they return to work most new fathers will find it hard to sustain the kind of close day-to-day involvement symbolised in the events of the birth itself. Indeed as Smith and Simms suggest, the birth of a first child often increases a man's commitment to his role as a bread-winner (see also Bell *et al.*, 1983).[4] Whether or not they consciously express regret, it remains true that, even with progressive reductions in working hours, it is still very difficult for men who become fathers in their twenties – 'prime' workers, or on the threshold of demanding careers – to become as involved with the routine care of their children as recent idealised portrayals of the Good Father would suggest.

Furthermore it is not surprising, if their partners have also willingly relinquished paid employment to embark on their real destiny as mothers, that they usually fall into a more rigid and essentially unequal division of childcare responsibilities than that advocated by contemporary popular opinion. Exceptions to this pattern are, therefore, particularly important, given that patterns of employment and the assumptions which underpin them continue to ensure that traditional practices persist in the face of any new orthodoxy.

We need to consider some of the essentially unremarkable changes which take place as part of the life cycle transitions experienced by two-parent families. If fathers become more involved in the care of their children as they grow towards maturity, it is not necessarily part of a conscious plot to avoid the obviously greater stresses associated with the care of very young children, but rather that their own commitment to work levels off or diminishes as they get older. Remarried men are interesting in this respect as they are frequently described as spending more time with the children of their second families than they were with their first. Although there are obviously many different factors at work here, several men in our stepfamily study did comment on the fact that, for work-related reasons, they had more free time when their most recent children were growing up.[5]

Other occupational constraints also contribute to differences in both the level of many men's commitment to collaborative parenthood as well as to their practical involvement on a daily basis. These include: the unusually long hours of work, the high levels of emotional commitment and amount of travel typical of senior managers (Pahl and Pahl, 1971; Evans and Bartolome, 1980); shift-patterns, including extended absences from home found, for example, in the military services and the off-shore oil industry (Clark *et al.*, 1985); and relatively highly paid manual occupations which involve particularly dangerous or stressful working conditions where leisure spent with male peers has long been an institutionalised counterbalance to the perceived demands of their working life (Dennis *et al.*, 1969; Tunstall, 1962).[6]

'DIVERSITY' AND THE SURVIVAL OF THE CONVENTIONAL NUCLEAR FAMILY

Debates about the significance of trends in employment,

household and family formation are liable to become intense and acrimonious. As both observer and participant, I am aware that the sub-text of such arguments often includes an implied question about the acceptability or 'normality' of the various protagonists' own preferred sets of domestic arrangements or household work strategies. Thus the challenge posed to conventional conceptualisations of the life cycle by the changes I have described is not merely intellectual, a matter of academic – in the pejorative sense – debate, but raises very important questions about values, an area of sociological work which Gouldner (1971) some years ago suggested is a particularly difficult one for sociologists. In recent decades British work in this area has been prone to three sorts of dangers. These are:

to overestimate the degree and significance of change by a partial presentation of only those facts which support our perceptions and strengthen our belief in a hoped-for change. Unfortunately some feminist and 'radical' texts in particular have fallen into this trap (see, for example, Segal, 1981);
to underestimate the degree, and particularly significance, of change in the same sort of way, presenting and interpreting evidence in a manner which suggests that, not only is very little changing but that there is widespread popular support for this state of affairs;
to present a reasonably accurate portrayal of the sources of both continuity and change as leading to a diversity of family/ household forms which, regardless of the constraints of continuing gender and class inequalities, may be chosen at will by individuals on a kind of 'supermarket' principle.

In this final section I want to consider a specific example of one of these dangers. It is chosen because it illustrates very clearly what can happen when social analysis, albeit somewhat inappropriately labelled and packaged, falls into the hands of the unashamedly partisan. As such it may offer some warnings to those of us who teach and write in this area.

In 1985 Chester wrote an article in *New Society* about contemporary family life. He did nothing more than present a factual account of recent demographic trends.[7] The article quite correctly emphasised that though the proportion of households which at any one time conforms to the 'Tarzan, Jane and two children' is falling, the majority of people still spend at least some of their childhood and adolescence in such a household and later form another of their own in early adult life. However, the implicit message of the article – including its title 'The rise of the neo-conventional family' and the graphics portraying couples with and without children – was very clear. As such it was a gift to *The Times* columnist, Digby Anderson, who used it as the basis for an article describing the urgent need for a moral majority type pressure group to defend his version of normal family life (Anderson, 1985). Referring to the 'work of Dr Chester' in a way which suggested that he was basing his conclusions on a major piece of primary research, he attacked what he called 'the anti-family lobby'; in his terms, those who attach the label 'family' to anything other than the 'Tarzan, Jane and two children' household. Had Chester included any discussion of the inevitable changes in public consciousness which result from cumulative increases in the proportion of the population who have now experienced divorce and remarriage at first hand or within their own immediate circle; if he had attempted to explain why, as he observes, 'the one-parent family is a vulnerable context for living' (Chester, 1985) he would have rendered himself much less exposed to Anderson's plagiarism.

Writers who fall into my third trap, of implying that household structures and domestic lifestyles and strategies are individually and freely chosen, would not, of course, be very popular with lobbyists who regard any deviation from conventional family norms as suspect and socially damaging, but they enjoyed considerable favour in liberal, policy-making circles in the 1970s. The Rapoports, representing the self-styled British Committee on Family Research based at the Policy Studies Institute, are the most prolific and influential exponents of this approach. Strong on the notion of 'diversity', their language is redolent of the consumer society in which 'lifestyles' and 'options' are freely chosen as an individual act of will. Following the imagery of the symmetrical family study, they portray trend-setting, professional middle-class dual-career couples as blazing a trail for others to follow (see, for example, the conclusions of Rapoport *et al.*, 1981). In this, as in many other respects, their analysis ignores all the evidence of persistent and, as the result of the recession, deepening class divisions which inevitably limit or entirely eliminate the possibility of real choice in this area.

By the same token, the power and continuing saliency of typifi-
cations of the nuclear family as the only normal, natural or
even healthy context in which to live and raise children continues to act as a deterrent to the widespread acceptance of
alternatives to the conventional family.

CONCLUSION

In this paper I have tried to examine some of the most important ways in which social scientific conceptualisations of the
family life cycle interact with popular conceptions and ideologies
of conventional 'family life'. Four major post-war changes affecting what we – misleadingly – shorthand as 'The Family',
illustrate the potential disjunctures between assertions about the
changing character of family life and the continuities in both
beliefs and practice suggested by the available research-based
data.

In each instance an examination of the available evidence,
including both quantitative and qualitative sources, leads us to
the conclusion that assessing the extent and effects of such
changes in Britain as a whole is no easy matter. Further, because many aspects of contemporary family and domestic life
are of considerable public interest and have important policy
implications, those who glibly assert otherwise, basing their
conclusions on very selective evidence or a superficial consideration of the issues involved, do little to improve the already
parlous reputation of academic sociology. The development of
more adequate conceptualisations of typical family and household careers over the life course is, therefore, a critical project
for those working both in the area of family and domestic
relationships *and* on employment related issues.

In a social and political climate in which 'family matters'
generate a good deal of public and individual uncertainty,
learning to take account of 'the personal' – evidence from personal accounts, the effects of the researcher's own motivations,
convictions and experience – must begin to constitute a key
element of such a project. For this reason 'family' researchers
may need to begin to form alliances across traditional disciplin-
ary boundaries, especially with those of a more 'therapeutic'
turn of mind.

NOTES

1. This research was initially financed by Sheffield City Polytechnic and completed with a grant from the, then, Social Science Research Council.
2. An unexpected invitation to write a chapter on food and remarriage provided us with a helpful opportunity to reflect on our material some years on and by then immersed in other work (Burgoyne and Clark, 1983).
3. Paul Wild worked with me on this study which was also financed with the aid of a grant from the, then, Social Science Research Council.
4. When asked to describe their role as stepfathers, those in the Sheffield remarriage study emphasised the importance of being economic providers to their newly acquired family. Their wives also made similar observations.
5. Of course, Nigel Lawson and other remarried members of the present Cabinet are exceptions, as they are unlikely to have experienced any significant reduction in their workloads in the years since they started their second families.
6. This points to the need for a greater integration of research on economic life with its emphasis on work histories with that concerned with domestic, household and family life.
7. In any event this drew very heavily on an earlier paper by the demographer, Katherine Kiernan (1983).

5 Images of Age and Generation among Older Aberdonians

Rory Williams

INTRODUCTION

At a time when not only life expectancy at older ages, but also the proportion of older people in the population has reached unprecedented levels (Smith, 1984), it is especially important to clarify what is considered to be the proper approach to ageing in our culture. In the 1960s, attempts to define popular ideas about ageing tended to assume that there was a single agreed conception; and a good deal of contradictory work resulted, some of which portrayed old age as a time of maintained activity and some as a time of passive disengagement. This work can perhaps best be understood now as an imperfect reflection of several different sets of popular prescriptions and experiences relating to ageing (Hochschild, 1975; Fontana, 1977). And it is this variety and conflict which now poses a challenge to understanding and explanation.

One recent approach to explanation has focused on the stigmatising properties of old age (Matthews, 1979; Russell, 1981). Both active and passive approaches to ageing spring, it is argued, from the continued existence of a devalued stereotype of what it is to be old: in the face of this stereotype some respond resignedly, accepting for themselves the passive and helpless role which it implies; but at the same time others respond with strategies of avoidance, presenting themselves as active, and attributing real old age to others. In this way, both active and passive attitudes to ageing can be seen to spring from the same origin.

A different and more optimistic line of explanation, on the other hand, has focused on situations where there seems to be increased solidarity among the old (Rose, 1965; Rosow, 1967; Hochschild, 1973; Keith-Ross, 1977). Stimulated by the growth of retirement villages in the United States during the 1960s, this argument has suggested that with the increasing independence of generations in the family, some older people are turning to their peers for support, and are beginning to constitute local enclaves and 'subcultures', promoting beliefs and values and a way of living of their own, which are partially distinct from that of other older people and of the population as a whole. Critics of this notion from the more pessimistic tradition have pointed out that since a stigma attaches to old age, membership of a group or community of the old is often regarded with ambivalence and avoided by most of those who are putative candidates for it. Associations of the stigmatised occur, but they are not subcultures, in that the shared values which are peculiar to them are imposed by the world outside. Hence when a subculture of the aged really exists, it must be identified not with a stigmatised image of age, but with some other image suggestive of certain positive shared values generated from within.

Two possible sources of such solidarity deserve exploration in this respect. The first relates to the positive values which may attach to retirement. In some societies, economic roles are set aside in favour of positive tasks of healing, counselling, ritual observance, piety or pilgrimage; but though there have in the past been some indications of such ideas in parts of Europe, they seem to be more strongly expressed in other traditions (Biesele and Howell, 1981; Hiebert, 1981; Amoss, 1981). In the West, retirement, when it is given a positive purpose, seems rather to be prized positively for the power it affords of individual choice in the use of leisure (Phillipson, 1982, ch. 4; Fontana, 1977); but whether this purpose is capable of generating a group consciousness among older people as a whole, especially one which can sustain a supportive subculture with its own partially distinct values, remains in question.

In the light of this doubt the second possibility to be explored may be more promising; for a self-conscious distinctiveness is certainly implicit in the claim that certain groups of the elderly belong to a particular generation. A generation can become a moral or a political force, in which special experiences of youth, and special values and idioms, are preserved as badges of membership (Mannheim, 1952). The theoretical interest has been expressed in generational consciousness among the elderly (Bengston and Cutler, 1976); however, references to it in empirical studies have often remained tantalisingly inexplicit and underdeveloped (Hochschild, 1973; Keith-Ross, 1977) and further investigation is needed.

Finally a third and more comprehensive line of explanation has sought to relate variation in ideas about ageing to historical change. As yet the main attention in this tradition has been concentrated on the ideas expressed in public policy (Macintyre, 1977; Calhoun, 1979; Estes, 1979; Phillipson, 1982; Gaullier, 1982; Means and Smith, 1983; Guillemard, 1983); and the relation of such official notions to popular thinking is uncertain. But there are interesting indications that, while the public image of old age has on the whole benefited from the improvements in life expectancy achieved by capitalism, public attitudes to retirement have nevertheless fluctuated between negative and positive views according to the fluctuating needs of capitalist industry to draw on, or to pension off, its reserve army of labour. How private attitudes, in their turn, relate to biographical experience of slumps and booms, is a question worth pursuing.

All these varying positive and negative images of age and generation are now examined in a Scottish context.

THE DATA

Open-ended interviews were conducted with 70 people aged 60 and over in the city of Aberdeen, focusing initially on health history and attitudes to it, and broadening out to include attitudes people held to the prospect of illness and death as they get older. Thus it was in these contexts that comments on age and ageing usually entered, although some people introduced them as a central topic of concern in their own right. All the people concerned were members of two snowball samples which were built up from age-related clubs in a middle-class area (the West End) and a working-class estate (Mannoch), steered so as to obtain normal proportions by age, sex, marital status, social class, and degree of social isolation; and interviews with these samples were recorded on tape and/or in field notes. All references to age or ageing in this material were indexed and examined to form the basis of this chapter.

CONCEPTIONS OF AGEING

In the space available here, only a very schematic account can be given of the age-related categories used by Aberdonians, but a few central distinctions were apparent. First, the word 'old' and its equivalents, where it had a categoric rather than a merely relative quality, was related to two different sets of events – on the one hand those of early old age (typically retirement, which affected stay-at-home wives as well as those employed), and on the other hand those of late old age (typically chronic illness and the death of others in the same generation). And secondly, to be old in these separate senses often evoked different responses, for each kind of ageing provided its own grounds for optimism or pessimism.

In terms of these primary distinctions, the autobiographical accounts of Aberdonians had a logic which can be expressed in five sets of premises. These are typified by the statements that follow:

1 Early old age as a liberation

'If I am retired, I am free to follow my interests.' In the relatively middle-class view represented here, retirement was extolled as a time for husband and wife to have time together, to see their children, to make loving improvements to house and garden, to practise arts and skills, to travel, see friends and play golf; and the activity was expected to be a matter of preference, so that criticisms were readily made of people who were merely energetic in filling time because there was time now vacant, as in the following comment:

> I've got the feeling within myself that that's an admission of, well, you've got to *do* something, you must *do* something. And I don't want just to do *any*-thing. I want to do something that I like and not just take up an activity because I think I ought to do so ... That to me is an admission of defeat, if I were to do that.

Creativity and spontaneous interests were treated as inner resources, and thus as claims to distinctiveness.

2 Early old age as a setback

'If I am retired, my interests and social connections are reduced', *and/or* 'If I encounter the younger generation, I may have trouble.' This more pessimistic view had a broad range of support in the middle class as well as in the working class. Loss of interests and loss of society was felt in both contexts, giving a negative aspect to retirement; and generational conflict was also a cross-class phenomenon which was already salient in early old age. This was an experience of some importance, which had positive as well as negative implications. A generational pride was quite often spontaneously voiced, laying claim to a thrift and hardiness which were seen as the corollary of having lived through the war and the depression, and invoking a public morality in which neighbourliness was enforced by the authority of parents, police, landlords and those older than oneself. These values were felt to be absent in particular in young people of roughly the generational level of these Aberdonians' grandchildren, and it was clashes with this generation, usually occurring in impersonal contexts, which gave this mixed sense of solidarity and vulnerability to being old.

3 Early old age as a repairing of defences

'If I am retired, I keep my interests going', *and/or* 'If I am retired, I keep up my social connections.' The activist principle in this view of retirement is familiar and needs no comment.

4 Late old age as resistible

'If I keep active, I will always keep real old age at bay.' This carry-over of activism into late old age brought an added implication of moral control over ageing, and thereby gave to those who succumbed to real old age the connotation of moral failure. It was related to prescriptions for fighting against illness.

5 Late old age as a surrender

'If I become really old, I may legitimately give up my activities.'
This, by contrast, represented a charitable view of the very old.
Significantly, it was usually espoused on behalf of others, or, in
so far as it pertained to oneself or those nearest to one, it
outlined a future which had not yet arrived, and might yet be
escaped, one which was seen in a kind of shadow image corresponding to the uncertainties of night thoughts:

> I sometimes – I look at him when he's sleeping, and I think,
> 'Gosh, you're getting old'. Especially with this chest, because
> his mouth's not closed during the night, you see. I sometimes
> stand over him and just look, you know: and his mouth's
> open and he's maybe lying on his back if he's snoring, and
> his hair's grey . . . I just hope he doesn't do the same with
> me . . . [laughing] . . . Because I don't tell him. And I just
> think, 'Oh, Edward', you know, 'What a shame, poor
> Edward' with this breathing. And he's so nice and so gay
> and so good, you know, a lovely kind person. It makes me
> sad. Then in the morning he comes down all dressed up with
> his fancy tie and his nice suit on . . .

Old age proper was thus always in some way external to the
person, and even where it was envisaged as a possible personal
future, views were often held about the management of death –
which provided an alternative possibility of an escape route.

PATTERNS

There were relatively few ways of combining these various
premises into a reliably coherent pattern, and there were certain
combinations which generated contradictions. However, views
about ageing overlapped sufficiently to offer at least one area of
common agreement – concerning premise (3), the importance
of actively repairing defences in early old age – an idea compat-
ible with all coherent perspectives. In this respect everybody
could be an activist; nevertheless, in other respects, three distinct patterns of ideas do emerge.

   The first coherent pattern was the most optimistic, viewing

ageing *as a resurgence.* Early old age was a new stage, a release into fresh interests, a recovery of skills long neglected: a predominately pleasurable time in which habits of activity and social connections could be formed which might protect against the advance of old age proper. The really old, who line the walls of residential institutions, were in this case those who had not established this protective way of life and held to it. This pattern of thinking was thus one which combines premise (1), early old age as a liberation, with premise (3), early old age as a repairing of defences, and/or premise (4), late old age as resistible.

The second coherent pattern viewed ageing, by contrast, as a *siege.* This pattern shared with that just described, the belief that defences could be sufficiently soundly built to keep at bay the advance of old age proper. It differed however in that already in early old age one's social position was under attack, whether because the relationships created by work were not ultimately replaceable, or because generational loyalties and attitudes were bearing one steadily into a position opposed to, or devalued by, the growing generations. The difficulties could be coped with, however, and again the really problematic stage of becoming truly old could still be avoided. This pattern of ideas, then, combines premise (2), early old age as a setback, with premise (3), early old age as a repairing of defences, and/ or premise (4), late old age as resistible.

These two patterns share common ground in (3) repairing defences in retirement, and (4) resisting late old age, and they were not discriminable where people restricted themselves to expressing only these two types of idea; hence any contradiction felt between these two patterns had to centre on the opposition between a liberated and a constrained view of early old age. I have space to give only one case in which such a contradiction was apparent, the man concerned being predictably marginal to the typical middle-class groups who express the liberated view. This man had been shift foreman in a local works, and had relatives in managerial positions. He began on the subject of his retirement with the words, 'But we shoved off to America and really saw life' – and immediately warming to a favourite theme added, 'I'll tell ye some o' the places we were in . . .' Then, after a catalogue of sights worth seeing and places which he 'greatly respected', it emerged that when his wife had visited

America a second time (at a relative's expense), he had chosen to stay at home 'simply because o' that plane'; nevertheless he was 'quite content and happy – I'd always something to do, you know.' And, in fact, he continually set himself tasks in the garden or on the structure of the house, explaining:

> I'm more content when I'm doing something, and I do some jobs you wouldna' believe – and I wisna' qualified to do either – but I do them quite successfully.

He expatiated, for instance, on the wall of massive granite blocks which he had shifted and rebuilt:

> I says, well, this is going to take a long time, but I've got a long time to do it.

Retirement, then, as he presented it in this part of his conversation, had released both time for the jobs he wished to do at home, and time for seeing life (even though seeing it once, it turned out, was enough).

A rather different line of thought appeared, however, when in answer to the question 'Were you looking forward to retiring?' he hesitated, then confessed, 'Well, no. Actually, no' – and asked further whether he missed the works, he replied, 'Yes and no.' He explained that twice since he stopped work they had wanted him back to resolve some problem: 'I dinna' want tae boast or blaw, I winna' tell ye the reason why that man was efter me, but I could easily enough.' This sense of recognised worth which his work had brought him had no counterpart in the activities of his retirement, and his self-respect remained centred in the occupation he had given up:

> I'm proud tae say that our family was really productive – because out o' the six of a family, three was staff . . . We all started off in Steenywood, we landed up in three different works, and every one o' the three is staff.

It was for this reason that he had not been able to look forward to stopping work and could not deny that he missed it; but he also, from another perspective, wished to say that he did not miss it, because he had made good use of his new freedom. The contradiction between the two views of retirement remained, and on the nature of the decision to retire he could only say: 'Ach, it's like a' that thing – it comes and goes.'

An expectation of release in early old age could thus come into conflict with a perception of constraint, but it was also relatively easy to avoid such conflicts while holding elements of both views – and in such cases the flexibility of ideas about ageing was apparent. The obvious resolution which offered itself was to distinguish the particular aspects of early old age for which each view held good. In such resolutions this stage of life was characteristically a release in regard to stopping work and turning to neglected interests – provided suitable resources were available – but a step down in regard to control of conflicts with young people casually encountered, or in regard to the wider acquaintanceship no longer available through work. Thus it was only when one of these aspects on its own was the subject of both these contrary expectations – when work had been both a pride and a burden to the worker – that contradiction was inevitable.

Two patterns of thinking about old age, and the potentiality of conflict between them, have now been discussed; a third pattern, however, was more frequent than either, which viewed ageing *as a delayed capitulation.* This pattern shared with previous patterns the belief in early old age as a time for an active strengthening of defences, and shared also with one of them an acceptance that this stage was inaugurated by various attacks on an accustomed way of life; but it included an ultimate pessimism about late old age, a conviction that in the end, for those who lived long enough, it was necessary and legitimate to lay down one's arms and accept the care of others. The source of this conviction, I have indicated, was primarily an external view of old age, a view derived from caring and seeing people in care, and the idea did not necessarily transfer comfortably from its application to others to an application to one's present self; nevertheless it provided an important image of a possible future. Ageing thus viewed as delayed capitulation, then, combined premise (2), early old age as a setback, and/or premise (3), early old age as a repairing of defences, with premise (5), late old age as a surrender.

A potential for conflict emerged between this view of ageing as a delayed capitulation and both the other views already considered. Specifically, the conflict lay between (5), late age as a legitimate surrender, and both (4), late age as resistible, and (1), retirement as a liberation. The contradiction was evident in the case of Sheila Denny, who had formed her notion of real old age partly from visits to a relative in a denominational home:

> When I first went I was told 'We're only here till the Lord sends for us.' So am I, I suppose, but Heaven help me! – that's not the way to talk.

The unacceptable aspect of this approach lay precisely in the fact that 'to me they're just sitting around waiting to die'; and in this context she plainly would have preferred a more vigorous attitude which could belie the label of 'old folks'. This responsibility for an active attitude was also accepted personally. She chided herself:

> I'm wasting time. On terribly cold days I wouldn't work, I wouldn't do anything, and I kept saying to myself, 'Ah, don't waste time.' Still feel it's sinful.

And this urge to keep doing was of a piece with her remembered sense of liberation in early old age. Retirement had been an opportunity to renew her social life, to entertain her friends, to get to know her neighbours, and occupational demands had been thankfully laid aside. But alongside this activism was an uneasy sense that real old age might eventually be inescapable, that it could be 'awfully sad'; and with this there was an increasing feeling that many of the activities she had taken up in retirement were in any case too troublesome, or too pointless:

> I used to go for long walks, to kind of pass the time. Then I started this voluntary work. And when I stopped it, I never missed it. It was just a time when you needed something. (Entertaining) – that's one thing I've stopped doing. I get so overexcited about it and think things won't be right and things won't be ready and I get worked up and upset . . . You are alone and it can be difficult.

It was of a piece with her sense of the reasonableness and legitimacy of a gradual withdrawal from these former activities, that having expressed a forcible rejection of the passivity of the 'old folks', she shifted abruptly to a contrary position:

> They're well fed, well looked after; of course, they're maybe happy enough – and what are we to judge? (and later) Of course we maybe pity some of these old folkies and they're maybe quite happy.

Then she switched back again: 'Some of them – but not all'; and the dilemma between fighting and giving up was shortly summed up thus:

> I always remember what my friend Sandra said – never wish too hard for anything, because by the time you get it, you don't want it. And it's very, very true.

The dilemma thus portrayed reveals, then, that there could not easily be a legitimate surrender in the last phase for those who put their faith in resistance; and since resistance harmonised with the optimistic view of retirement as a liberation, it is no surprise to find in such cases as Sheila Denny's, that surrender was incompatible with both. If, as occasionally happened, the surrender of the very old was accepted by people with either of these optimistic views, it was only by making a sharp distinction between us and them, in such a way that true old age would never come to us. And this tactic reaffirmed rather than resolved the division of views.

Three distinct schemes of ageing have now been plotted, each internally coherent, which at once supply and limit the stock of ideas on which Aberdonians draw. It is between these possibilities that those searching for coherence have to choose, if they are not to innovate. It now remains to consider this local stock of knowledge in terms of the factors which have shaped it.

CONCLUSION

The Aberdonian attitudes analysed in the preceding section have given substance to the problem with which this chapter started: not only is there a great variety of ideas about age and ageing, but there are important contradictions between some of them which are recognised and felt, in certain situations, as personal dilemmas. Indeed the ideas which are consistent with most points of view – essentially the obligation to repair defences and maintain activity in early old age – are less numerous than those which are disputed; and to that extent there is little basis for viewing older Aberdonians as an age 'stratum' subject to expectations which are culturally agreed (Riley *et al.*, 1972).

Earlier a number of explanations were rehearsed, each of which has been addressed to some aspect of this variety and conflict. These explanations are in some respects supported, and in other respects limited and qualified, by the picture which has emerged of Aberdonian culture; and at the same time it is possible to see ways in which themes from all three types of account connect together.

Explanations of attitudes to ageing which are related to the stigma of being old need first to address the way in which different stages of ageing are implicitly distinguished in common talk. Such explanations have greater force in regard to the late rather than the early stage of ageing, as Aberdonians distinguished them. Late age was certainly stigmatised by many older people themselves, in the sense that it was seen as a passive, pitied state, the outcome of living beyond the normal time to die. And the way in which it was viewed from an external point of view, attributed to others and denied for oneself, 'they' being passive and 'I' being still active, also reflects a general characteristic of stigma. To this extent, late age was indeed viewed as the kind of discreditable identity which is regarded as abnormal and suitable for a degree of segregation and special treatment. But this segregation does not itself make clear why late age was sometimes viewed as an unlucky outcome which could not be helped, and sometimes in an opposed fashion as a moral failure, a symptom of insufficient self-discipline in preventive activity. The question raised by this opposition was whether late age was within or beyond moral control, and the origin of this dispute lies in factors outside the stigmatising process, which declares only what is normal and abnormal.

The second way, mentioned earlier, of understanding the clash between optimistic and pessimistic views of ageing was one which drew attention to evidence of increasing solidarity amongst some groups of older people, and to positive notions of age which went with this. And indeed positive notions of retirement, and a degree of generational solidarity, were apparent in Aberdeen. However these two positive themes were in no way related.

Optimistic notions of retirement certainly did conflict with more defensive notions, creating felt contradictions; and it is also true that this optimism was mainly characteristic of a limited group of people with a particular middle-class style of life, and that the interests and skills from which the optimism derived were shared with others of a like background. But this was no age-based subculture: those with whom interests were shared were not necessarily of the same age, and the basis of acquaintanceship was very individualistic. Other acquaintances of the same age and background remained unconvinced about the liberating effects of retirement, and became the unrepentant butts of the optimists' disapproval. Optimism about retirement was in fact a basis for division rather than for solidarity amongst older members of the middle class; there was an element of individual distinctiveness, even of one-upmanship, about it. And while this way of looking at retirement certainly brought with it an element of that conflict and disagreement about the proper way of growing old which is at issue, its effect was again limited to its part in disagreements about one phase of ageing – the early phase – and the sources of these attitudes to early old age seemed to reside more in individual biographies than in present membership of an age-related group or subculture.

By contrast, the other positive notion which characterised people by age – that of generation – was in essence a unifying one. Although generational differences were brought to the forefront by only a proportion of older Aberdonians, they were defined in such a way as to include attributes common to all, and they were expressed in a similar form and with similar frequency across classes. In that sense this generation had the basis for a unified consciousness of certain distinctive values – respect for neighbourliness, for authority, for perseverance and thrift; and it was this positive generational consciousness, more than the stigmatising character of age, which, in their own accounts, lay behind the conflicts and defeats which this generation had experienced with the young. Entitled now themselves, within this perspective, to respect, and to the exercise of authority in defence of these values, they found their claims to control overturned, especially by the young adolescent and by the adult generation with whom their ties were weakest. It was the struggle for control, then, in which the stigmatising value of the term 'old' was only one possible weapon, and one matched by discrediting counter-offensives against the 'young', that had inflicted many of the wounds of age; and it was this same struggle which had engendered a sense of generational unity. But although this generational consciousness was quite often expressed, and expressed in terms applicable to everyone whether or not everyone expressed it, it was not to the forefront of most people's minds, and it did not banish the moral divisions which were based on success in ageing. It was a consciousness which added to the variety of connotations given to age, but which did not add to, or subtract from, disagreements about the proper way of ageing. And to the extent that it reflected a certain solidarity among older people, the origins of that solidarity still remain to be considered.

Though ideas of a generational difference were formulated by Aberdonians in the course of struggles to control the values of the young, such struggles are in some ways perennial, for adolescents seeking control in the present time, as in Shakespeare's, may make a speciality of 'wronging the ancientry', as the most vulnerable of those who hold the existing control over them. But the degree of conflict is also affected by historical experience. It is not necessary to suppose, with Karl Mannheim (1952), that this now ageing generation has always emphasised its present distinctive values since the formative period of youth. Other divisions of ideology may in their youth have seemed more salient, and there may have been a greater diversity in their responses, splitting them into a multiplicity of factions based on other loyalties besides age. The bitterness of the mid-war period in the North East of Scotland, and the aftermath of the General Strike, portrayed in the trilogy of Lewis Grassic Gibbon (1973), should not be underestimated; but it was echoed, in 1980, only in the conversations of a few hardened campaigners, and these felt, in regard to the younger generation, like the rest. It seems, therefore, that it was only as this new antagonist arose after them, that some consciousness of unity was formed around the particular pattern of values which is now emphasised, and its formation reflects a relative impoverishment, since the war, of those above retirement age compared with those below – an impoverishment which has recently been documented from public statistics (Thomson, 1984). This countervailing character of generational conflict, muting class divisions between contemporaries, has been noted elsewhere (Foner, 1974); but the British experience may have been somewhat special in Europe, for among the old in France the experience of wartime occupation has continued to bequeath divisions between former collaborators and former members of the Resistance, despite the explosion of generational conflict in 1968 (Keith-Ross, 1977).

If the solidarity of the present older generation thus reflects to some degree the shift during their lifetime from economic recession to economic boom, do the moral divisions between them on the subject of ageing also reflect, as has been claimed, other aspects of the same economic process? This is a complex question which there is no space to consider here. I have indicated one obvious aspect in which the logic of political and economic change does indeed affect views of ageing; but while this may serve to underline the interest of this approach, it will be necessary, in accounting for the wider conflict between positive and negative views of ageing, also to consider cultural continuities in moral arguments about old age. But this is a topic for another occasion.

6 The Social Construction of Babyhood: The Definition of Infant Care as a Medical Problem

Peter Wright

THE PROBLEMATISATION OF MEDICINE

During the period in which sociologists have been engaged in studying topics concerned with health and medicine one tendency in particular has persistently emerged: that of problematisation. Typically, sociologists have been unwilling to accept the common-sense, intuitive assumptions of medical practice at their face value and have, instead, analysed them as social constructs – as the conventional products of particular forms of social relationship.

This tendency is of long standing and can be traced back to such classics of the sociology of medicine as Zborowski's studies of pain or Roth's analysis of the treatment of tuberculosis as a bargaining process. (Zborowski, 1969; Roth, 1962). Over the last fifteen years it has become more pronounced and has been developed by the work of a number of sociologists (Freidson, 1970; Jewson, 1976; Waddington, 1977; Johnson, 1972).

It has also been stimulated by writers outside sociology. The work of Philippe Aries and others on conceptions of childhood and of death; that of Michel Foucault on madness, the clinic and sexuality; the extension of the work of medical anthropology into the study of industrialised societies; even the theories of Kuhn and the debate they have engendered; the new sociology of science: all have acted as further stimulants to the problematising approach (Ariès, 1973, 1983; Foucault, 1970, 1976, 1979; Kleinman, 1980; Kuhn, 1962).

As the years have passed, so the range of what has been problematised has tended to extend. At first, the analysis was directed towards subjective meanings of various kinds – such as perceptions of pain, then it gradually began to embrace also the categories that are used to organise the experience of our bodies, including technical medical knowledge itself. This tendency has, perhaps, been most strongly expressed by the contributors to the Wright and Treacher collection (1982) who advocate a social constructivist view of medical knowledge.

Although there are few self-conscious social constructivists at work within the sociology of medicine, I would argue that most medical sociologists in practice share the concern of social constructivism to render problematic medical meanings – and, even, the categories of medical knowledge. Indeed, it can be argued that the process of problematisation is central to the whole endeavour of sociology. Where social constructivists tend to differ from others is not, then, in their desire to problematise, but in the extent that they do so, and in the fact that they are unwilling to accept the existence of any social knowledge, immune from the formative effects of society.

What does it involve to look at babyhood as a social construct? Firstly, it certainly does not cause us to doubt the material existence of our own bodies, or of diseases, or of such stages in the life cycle as babyhood: social constructivists share the general view that diseases should be dealt with in the most effective way possible. Far from social constructivism regarding the objects that it studies as illusory, it grounds them yet more firmly in reality, by basing them on the foundation of all human meaning: the lived, and shared, experience of human societies.

Social constructivist analysis starts from the basis that all human knowledge, including medicine, is the product of human social activity and is used by human beings to bring into existence their own lives and experience. Clifford Geertz put this well (writing of Max Weber) when he wrote: 'Man is an animal suspended in webs of significance he himself has spun' (Geertz, 1973, p. 5).

Scientific and medical knowledge are important strands within these 'webs' despite the obvious features that distinguish them from other aspects of culture. Even the characteristics that appear to distinguish science – and to a lesser extent medicine – from the rest of culture (the transformation of the material world, privileged epistemological status, technicality, etc.) do not negate their cultural role; indeed they are precisely the features that give them such force as repertoires of symbolic meanings.

This is not to say, however, that medicine is subject to exactly the same forces, or is shaped in exactly the same way, as are other elements of culture: different cultural discourses must be expected to have varying degrees of independence from each other and from outside forces bearing upon them. The form and nature of these differences is something to be determined by analysis: not to be assumed in advance.

The essence of the social constructivist approach to medicine is the precept that medical knowledge is to be regarded as a distinctive social product that is constituted and actualised in social practice and which must, therefore, be examined with the tools of social and cultural analysis.

This chapter attempts to apply a social constructivist approach to one particular aspect of the life cycle in modern Britain: the establishment of a certain dominant definition of the baby – as a creature whose life, feeding and activity were the proper subjects of medical activity, and concerning whom the only true experts were professionals trained in, or under the aegis of, medicine.

It looks at the transformation of the concept of babyhood in England – which, I contend, took place roughly during the twenty-five years between 1890 and 1915 – and suggests that it was the over-determined consequence of several different clusters of factors: changes in medical science; the development of new kinds of health practice; ideological and cultural shifts; the political redefinition of the position of the working class, and so on.

THE SOCIAL CONSTRUCTION OF INFANCY

The new conception of infancy comprised four elements, none totally new in itself, but which served, when brought together, to metamorphose the social and cultural significance of the baby in English life – above all, to render it into an object governed and controlled by medicine.

The first was that the death of the newly-born ceased to be

seen as an inescapable fact of nature and was recognised, instead, as a problem about which something should be done.

The second was that the problem came to be understood as essentially medical in nature. That is to say, infant rearing was constituted as a medico-technical field rather than as it had been until then: an application of a moral discourse in which actions were judged against accepted moral values and sanctions applied against those who transgressed them. Medicalised child-rearing became a domain where actions were regarded as attempts to assert instrumental control over the natural world and in which deviance was reconceptualised as inadequacy and incompetence.

The process by which child-rearing was transformed into a technical field was neither smooth nor without reverses: there was a persistent tendency for discussions of the subject to slip into moralism. None the less, by the end of the period one can detect a major change of emphasis. By this time, the campaign to reduce infant mortality is intended to be practical and is anchored in the medical science of its day. It does not seek to make a change in morality a precondition for reducing infant deaths; it takes the attitudes of working-class families as given and seeks to change limited aspects of them and of the baby's environment.

The third element was the distinctive way in which infant welfare policy was put into practice. What happened was that a largely new pattern of institutions and practitioners was brought into existence which, even though it was legitimated by medical science, was usually quite separate from existing medical provision and almost unconcerned with therapy. It was also distinctive in that it involved a form of practice in which preventative home visits played a central part.

The final element of the new baby care was its incorporation of the germ pathogen theory. This both endowed it with scientific force and enabled it to harmonise with many ideological concerns of the period such as the lurking fears of invasion, aliens and degeneration that are so characteristic of the pre-First World War years.

The argument of this paper is that, in combination, these elements caused the condition of babyhood to be re-defined, and brought into being a situation where quite new kinds of thought and practical actions became possible in relation to it.

Schon (1979) has coined the term 'generative metaphor' to refer to occasions when a radically new way of conceptualising a problem enables those concerned to approach it freshly and more productively. One of his examples is of the difficulties faced by those trying to develop paint brushes with synthetic bristles who, he tells us, found it very´hard to understand why their products – unlike traditional natural bristle brushes – delivered paint discontinuously, in a 'gloppy' way. They only became able to conceive of the resolution to their problem when one of them succeeded in thinking of the familiar paintbrush in a novel manner – as a kind of pump. Only when this had happened were they able to see the physical problems affecting the functioning in a way that enabled them to solve the problems associated with the use of synthetic bristles.

The conception of infancy that took shape in the years around 1900 can also be seen as such a 'generative metaphor' as it threw a quite new light on the position of babies in English society and changed the ways in which it was normal to regard the causes of infant mortality. The deaths of babies were gradually taken out of a context of meaning and explanation in which they were associated with such concepts as sin, natural wastage and seasonal rhythm and established in another where the key points of orientation were such things as the germ theory of disease, sanitary engineering and nutritional research. Like a gestalt shift, the change utterly transformed babyhood and made it hard indeed for those who had shifted to understand how others might see things differently.

INFANT MORTALITY AS A SOCIAL PROBLEM

The first signs of public concern over the high incidence of death among babies becomes visible in the 1850s and 1860s. Martineau (1859), for example, played a major part in arguing that the rate of mortality (which she estimated at 40 per cent of all under-fives) was needlessly high and could be reduced by abandoning bottle feeding for breast feeding. Such advice was not new in itself, however, having been a common ingredient of homilies addressed to married women for the previous two centuries at the very least; what was new was the fact that increasingly it was supported – not by a rhetoric of 'naturalness' and 'duty' – but by recourse to statistical evidence that showed bottle feeding to be associated with an above-average rate of infant mortality.

None the less, this concern was not to become generalised until much later. As Armstrong has shown, in the mid-century, for instance, an infant mortality rate as such was not even calculated by the authorities: the crude numbers of deaths of children less than one year old was included in the Registrar General's *Annual Reports* from 1857, but it was only in 1877 that these began to be presented as a rate, a proportion of all births (Armstrong, forthcoming). Until this had occurred it was very hard to perceive geographical or social variations. What is more, the rate of infant death was unlikely to appear as a problem until there was generally accepted evidence that public health measures could be effective against death among other, less seemingly fragile, members of the population. This was not clearly the case until the 1880s when a steady and apparently irreversible decline became evident in the death rate of all age groups except infants.

The difficulties of isolating the infant death rate statistically interacted with the ways in which its causes were conceptualised. There seems to have been a powerful predisposition to see infant death as normal and to assimilate it to natural processes of decay. Thus, for instance, when the Registrar General redistributed in 1855 the statistical remainder category of 'deaths of uncertain seat', it was only to replace part of it by a new category which grouped together infant deaths from congenital malformation, prematurity and debility, atrophy and wasting, and old age. The new sub-classification was entitled 'diseases of growth, nutrition and decay'!

But how was this apparently unproblematic naturalness called into question and eventually eroded? How was it that much later, in the 1950s, the rejection had become so great, so irresistible, that even the remaining unexplained (and probably heterogeneous) cases of infant death were grouped together under the heading of 'sudden infant death'?

Although Armstrong hints at several answers to this question and to parallels elsewhere – in education, in welfare and so on – it is not easy to find an explicit explanation. It is difficult to resist the feeling that the implication of his work, like that of much influenced by Michel Foucault, is that medical discourse evolved as it did as one of a series of related, unspecified and, it seems, immanent forces. Foucauldian analysis has certainly played an important part in stimulating a new kind of socio-historical study of medicine. None the less, if not taken further, it tends to become self-validating and to close off the examination of what appear, *prima facie*, to be interesting issues. In the case of infant death, for instance, the Foucauldian approach gives us no appreciation of process; no awareness of the contingencies and loose ends that shaped the particular way in which babyhood took form in Britain. To be aware that there might have been other outcomes is not just idle conjectural history. It would be interesting, for example, to investigate whether what Armstrong takes as essential aspects of the 'medical gaze' might simply be contingent factors incorporated into it from other cultural and social spheres such as the ideological and the political.

In fact the historical material itself encourages one to focus on just this sort of issue. Not only is there evidence of controversy within the medical profession as to the main causes of infant death, there is also much to support the view that its public salience in Edwardian England was connected with the political and ideological climate of that society (Davin, 1978; Wright, 1978).

There are obviously parallels between the changing attitude towards infant mortality and the shifts that were taking place in late nineteenth-century English social policy, which have been charted by writers such as Gilbert (1966), Searle (1971), Semmel (1960) and Stedman Jones (1971). That is to say, with an approach that saw the social evils of the time not as primarily the consequence of moral failings, but as the working-out of deep-seated structural forces within the economy and society. Semmel in particular has argued that this shift was closely linked to the rise of imperialist politics and the re-evaluation of the position of the home working class that tended to accompany it (Semmel, 1960).

Just as poverty came to be seen as a technical problem associated with casual labour, or some other structural aspects of the economy, rather than as the outcome of drunkenness or indolence, so too the attitudes of working-class mothers towards their children came also to be presented in a positive light, and their shortcomings regarded as the remedial consequences of technical ignorance, not evil intention. This new conception was rather patronisingly displayed by one speaker in 1902:

> our English mothers of the working classes . . . are, with all their ignorance, stupidity and superstition, affectionate to their children, jealous to promote their comfort and enjoyment, tenderly solicitous for them in sickness, anxious to make them honest, polite and considerate for the weak and suffering. It is to our English mothers, I suggest, that we mainly owe the admirable conduct of our soldiers in South Africa. (International Congress, 1902, p. 18)

Here, as in many other documents of the period, the Boer War serves as a lens to gather and focus a range of concerns related to health and family welfare. These include: the quality of the workforce and potential army recruits, eugenics, the position of women, the integration of the working class and, of course, the notion of decline, which is embodied in the very title of the well-known enquiry of the time, the Inter-departmental Committee on Physical Deterioration of 1904. 'National Efficiency' becomes the small change of political speeches (Searle, 1971).

It was the common assumption of most writers on infant and child death that it could be reduced by inducing married women not to work, although, as Dyhouse (1981) has shown, there were a few statisticians who questioned the existence of a strong causal relationship between the two.

Perhaps the most recurrent theme, however, was of the supposed link between infant welfare and 'quality'. The realisation that the birth rate was falling among higher social groups at just the time that the rest of the population was thought to be facing degeneration bred alarm. It was feared that the outcome must be a weakening in what was often described as the 'quality of the race' and that this would undermine Britain's position in the world.

Davin, quoting Arthur Newsholme, one of the most vocal advocates of the infant welfare movement in those years commented that: 'For many doctors and medical officers in the 1900s the saving of infant life seems to have become "a matter of imperial importance" ' (Davin, 1978, p. 14). Later in her paper she writes that:

Healthier babies were required not only for the maintenance of empire but also for production under the changing conditions made necessary by imperialist competition. The old system of capitalist production (which itself had nourished imperialist expansion), with its mobile superabundant workforce of people who were underpaid, underfed, untrained and infinitely replaceable, was passing. In its place, with the introduction of capital-intensive methods, was needed a stable workforce of people trained to do particular jobs and reasonably likely to stay in them, neither moving on, nor losing too much time through ill health. (Davin, 1978, p. 49).

THE MEDICALISATION OF INFANT CARE

But why was it that infant care was dominated by a technical model drawn from medicine rather than from some other technical field? In the medical handbooks of the mid-nineteenth century, and later, doctors seemed to have nothing special to say on the subject and to be laying claim to no particular expertise. For many years comments on child-rearing by medical men simply echo the moralistic exhortations to the poor that were uttered by all who saw themselves as moral leaders of the society: clergymen, politicians, lawyers, well-bred ladies engaged in visiting the poor, and so on. It was not surprising that one author of a book on child care addressed to young schoolmistresses cited as authority for her views, 'the best old nurse I ever knew' (Lonsdale, 1885, p. 12), nor that an anonymous mother could write that she had,

> known physicians who made infants and children an especial study, and who were very clever as regards the ailments of children, quite at a loss as regards the feeding of a young infant, and obliged to rely more or less on the knowledge of an old nurse. (A Mother, 1884, p. 35)

By around 1900, in contrast, the tone of the advice has begun to change noticeably and the grounds proposed to legitimate it typically begin to take a scientific form. It has become precise, specific and authoritative, where previously it had been vague, general and open to question. Increasingly it incorporated aspects of the germ pathogen theory. In 1886, for instance, the medical author of a pamphlet on infant feeding acknowledged that the topic had frequently been neglected by the medical profession and distances himself from the old style of writing. 'The proper feeding of infants,' he wrote, 'is based on scientific principles to understand which a medical training is absolutely necessary' (A Physician, 1895, p. 5). The annexation of infant welfare to medicine was a complex process which necessarily had to involve more than the simple extension of some existing sphere of practice. Hitherto, doctors had had almost no contact with healthy infants and probably not as much with the sick as might have seemed likely from the prevalence of infant death.

What happened was that a new system of practice came into being that was primarily concerned with the health and survival of infants and new practitioners were trained to work in it. In the two decades before the First World War health visiting was routinised and expanded, domiciliary visiting by trained midwives organised, schools for mothers and infant welfare clinics set up, schoolgirls taught about baby care and so on.

The creation of this field of practice opened up a new channel of contact between medicine and the mass of the population. All the evidence suggests that, previously, general practitioners had had little to do with infants and probably only saw a proportion even of those who subsequently died – and then probably when their deaths were imminent and unavoidable.

Within the medical profession, the issue of infant death was central only to the work of the Medical Officers of Health. From the mid-nineteenth century many had assembled statistics on it with the result that, by 1900, a considerable body of epidemiological evidence was in existence. This demonstrated that a high rate of infant mortality was strongly associated with cramped housing, poverty, bottle-feeding of babies, unpaved streets, hot summers and a lack of mains drainage. Such findings were interesting – if unsurprising – but gave the MOHs little additional leverage: they had been advocating paving and drainage for decades. The difficulty was that not simply did there seem little that could be done at the local level about many of the causative factors, because of ignorance of the exact causal mechanisms involved, it was impossible to determine which measures would be most effective or what the priorities should be.

What changed this was the incorporation of the germ pathogen theory into the infant welfare debate: this provided a model of causation that was to dominate discussion and to be used to legitimate the advice given to mothers.

MOHs were not quick to take up the germ theory: it served, as Jean Raymond has pointed out, during most of the 1870s as, 'a sort of intellectual top-dressing to reinforce doctors' claims to public power and prestige' (Raymond, 1985, p. 4). Bacteriological knowledge only became a routine part of public health work about 1895 and then primarily in connection with anthrax and food poisoning. Only after 1900 were bacteriological techniques generally used to investigate summer diarrhoea and other major categories of infant death.

There were many reasons for this, but without doubt the biggest hindrances to the assimilation of infant death to germ pathogeny were cognitive. MOHs, especially, found it difficult to break from two intuitively powerful principles that they had long used to organise their experience: that of a connection between dirt and disease and of the influence of seasonal and meteorological factors on disease.

Thus, Newsholme, who had begun his career in the 1880s in the belief that high temperature was the primary cause of summer diarrhoea, but had later accepted germ causation, still expressed himself in 1911 in ways that echoed his earlier position:

The fundamental condition favouring epidemic diarrhoea is an unclean soil, the particular poison from which infects the air, and is swallowed, most commonly with food, especially milk. (Newsholme, 1935, p. 357)

'Soil', 'poison' and 'air' had all been key components of the earlier discourse.

Again, the fact that the main category of infant death was classified at that time as 'summer diarrhoea' was another problem, as the term diarrhoea was more usually employed to denote a symptom – not a disease in itself. This meant, as the Royal College of Physicians noted, that many doctors were hesitant to certify a death from this condition because it seemed too trivial to be an acceptable cause of death, and, if used, could cause the dead baby's parents to question the professional competence of their doctor. As a solution the RCP proposed that the condition be re-classified as 'epidemic enteritis' or 'zymotic enteritis' (Waldo, 1900, p. 1344). In other words, the condition should be presented in a way that emphasised its likeness to typhoid rather than to what was regarded as a minor symptom.

None the less, during the Edwardian period the emphasis on summer diarrhoea and the role of microbial agents in its causation grew persistently until a point was reached where it became the paradigm for understanding infant mortality, and encouraged the neglect, as Dyhouse points out, of other causes of death – even 'wasting diseases' – which had been the biggest single category during the 1890s (Dyhouse, 1981, p. 91).

The rise of the germ pathogen model was a complex phenomenon, and is certainly not to be accounted for simply by the claim that it was true and instrumentally powerful science. To begin with, it is both unclear how far it really threw a new light on the causes of infant death or, of itself, made possible more effective action to combat it. It is not impossible that it may even have hindered improvement by drawing attention away from nutritional factors and made too much of parallels between infant death and epidemic diseases of adults and older children.

Certainly, Smith, writing about the decline in the infant mortality rate that occurred in England in the Edwardian years writes:

> I know of no advance sanitation which could explain the sudden change after 1902, nor of any major innovation in medicine which affected infant lives in those years. (Smith, 1979, p. 113)

His conclusion, like that of others studying the decline, is that it was probably brought about by a combination of factors some at least of which – like general nutrition – had no connection with the infant welfare movement or the germ pathogen theory.

THE NEW INFANT WELFARE PRACTICE

The thesis of this paper is that the principal explanation for the predominance of the germ pathogen model in the Edwardian infant welfare movement lies in its social uses: above all, in the fact that it provided a rationale for social intervention and a metaphor for social danger.

Intervention by government in the lives of the working class was increasing rapidly in these years, especially in the field of health, and local initiatives were being taken up nationally and often put on a professional footing. This can be seen, for example, from the case of health visiting – an activity which had been born in various provincial cities, but which was generalised in 1905–6 into a national service to which only those were admitted who had successfully completed a course of medically-based training. What provided the occasion for the health visitor's work was also the direct government intervention: the Notification of Births Act, which meant that the authorities were alerted quickly to each birth that took place and health visitors were able to influence infant care from the very first days of life onwards.

The establishment of health visiting was paralleled by many other developments in these years including the conversion of midwifery to a trained occupation under medical scrutiny, the foundation of numerous infant welfare clinics (there were 195 in 1916), schools for mothers, baby competitions, depots for sterilised milk, payments to mothers whose babies survived the first year of life, the publication of pamphlets on infant care and much else besides.

The new practice created new audiences and a need for new kinds of explanatory and teaching material. The new health visitors, midwives and instructresses had to be armed with arguments strong enough to convince their working-class clientele of the need to follow the precepts of the new child-rearing, even if this meant – as it often did – abandoning practices deeply rooted in family and local culture.

Although the infant welfare movement made some use of existing institutions such as schools and hospitals, its distinctive feature was that it established a new channel of communication directly into the working-class home – to the mother. What is more, its agent, the health visitor or midwife, differed from the doctors, clergymen and charitable ladies who had sometimes previously visited, in being far closer to her client in background and experience. A new kind of dialogue thus became possible, relatively free from mediation from husbands, neighbours or the local community. The process seems to resemble that which Jacques Donzelot has in mind when he refers to the creation of the new sphere of the 'social' (Donzelot, 1979, pp. xix-xxvii).

Unlike France, where the infant welfare movement did not involve home visiting and led to the expansion of nursery schools, in England the emphasis was very much upon the home and upon keeping the mother and child together in it (Boltanski, 1969). As Dyhouse has shown, one of the central themes of the movement was the belief that there should be a reduction in the proportion of married women in employment. In 1908 the Consultative Committee on the School Attendance of Children commented on the great importance of 'the natural relationship between mother and child' and went on to stress that, together with the influence of a 'good home' it was, 'a moral and educational power which it is of high national importance to preserve and strengthen' (Consultative Committee . . . , 1908, p. 16). Such a concern was reflected in changes in school attendance: it fell from a peak of 43.52 per cent in the 3–5 age group in 1899 to 33.76 per cent in 1906.

The significance of domiciliary visiting may easily be overlooked unless an effort is made to see it in the context of its time: a period when there were relatively few channels of communication into the working-class home, especially to women. For many, the only contact would have come through the school, and perhaps to a limited extent through poster advertising. The popular press had scarcely been born, and anyway was most likely to reach men. Nor, of course, did women share the homogenising experiences of army or navy life that some of their male kin were exposed to. Although women were more likely to be involved in religious practice than men, religious practice in towns was not great, particularly among the unskilled.

But it was not only the channels of communication of the new infant welfare that were distinctive, so also were the tone and authority of the messages that it conveyed. They were cast in what Habermas (1969) has referred to as a purposive-rational mode. That is to say, they were not presented as social norms that mothers should follow because they derived from desirable values (what Habermas calls 'communicative action') but as instrumental instructions deriving from technical rules. Breast-feeding, for example, was urged not as previously – because it was natural, divinely-ordained or a proper expression of the mother's role – but as a successful way of avoiding the death of the baby. Similarly, the consequences of disregarding such advice were presented as material failure – the working out of scientific laws leading to the death of the child – not as social nonconformity that ought to be stigmatised.

In this, the notion of germ pathogeny played a key part: it was an exemplar of the scientificity of medicine and spread a cloak of authority over the new infant welfare workers which served to validate the stern advice that they gave on a wide range of topics: their opposition to 'the excessive kissing of infants' (Local Government, 1914, p. 2); demand feeding and 'dummies' (Porter, 1906); masturbation (Coolidge, 1905, p. 20) and, even, the dangers of a baby sleeping on its right side – 'to avoid the pressure of a full stomach on the heart' (Maynard, 1906).

Although germs and sterilisation are central themes in the infant care literature of these years the advice given extended, as we have seen, into many other areas too, and often involved an emphasis on the need for general qualities such as regularity, abstinence and order. One example can be found in a penny pamphlet written in 1906 and probably aimed at the mothers themselves:

> Regularity is the first of the baby's education ... (the mother) will find it easier to train it in *clean habits*, for if the child is fed at odd times the bowels will fail to act regularly. (Maynard, 1906, p. 19)

As Douglas has pointed out, anxiety about germs and infection coheres easily with a framework of values that gives pride of place to such values as order, obedience, regularity and so on (Douglas, 1966).

THE CULTURAL POWER OF GERM PATHOGENY

If the germ pathogen theory did, as I claim, act as a major source of legitimacy for the infant welfare movement, wherein lay its power? So far, very little has been written on the cultural resonances of medical knowledge (except Sontag, 1978).

None the less, perhaps two types of explanation may, tentatively, be put forward.

The first is that germ pathogeny represented for the lay public an object lesson in the benefits of applying scientific knowledge to medicine. There is certainly some evidence for this: Koch, Pasteur, Lister and Semmelweis are celebrated repeatedly in popular writings; and there can be no doubt that the identification of the microbial agents transmitting diseases such as tuberculosis, anthrax, gangrene and puerperal fever were events that caught the imagination of large sections of the public. Although this may only be one facet of the generally rising prestige of science at that time, the campaign against infectious diseases concentrated the issues in a particularly potent way – so potent, indeed, that in popular writings the prestige of these medical scientists assumed almost hagiographic proportions. For example in 1916, one English hygiene textbook intended for older schoolchildren wrote:

> Truly after the Great Healer of Mankind, no man has done more to banish disease and death than Louis Pasteur. It cost him much – at one time almost his own life . . . he showed mankind its most merciless foe, its most powerful enemy . . . (Hood, 1916, pp. 179–80)

Seen from this standpoint, germ pathogeny derived its cultural power from the authority of science in general; it can be explained only to the extent that the cultural ascent of science as a whole can be explained.

But the appeal of germ pathogeny had another side too – the metaphorical: its power to act as an image that could endow human affairs with meanings that appeared authentic and convincing. This is not easy to demonstrate since it involves making retrospective judgements about the relative plausibility of various frames of reference. None the less, there is much evidence to suggest that Edwardian England was a culture that placed considerable importance on categories related to purity and boundary maintenance and was sensitive to many of the related distinctions to which Douglas's work (1966; 1970) has made us alert. Such emphases were especially evident in the language of politics and social policy. The political speeches and journalism of the period were replete with words and phrases such as 'social purity', 'mothers of the race', 'the imperial race', 'British Stock', 'degeneration', 'purification' and many more (examples quoted in Davin, 1978, pp. 13–19).

Two main concerns seem to inform all this imagery. The first is the critical importance placed on the boundary between inside and out: between the 'Imperial Race' and aliens; the nation and its enemies. The second is the dread of internal pollution: the danger of degeneration, internal decay, dissent, 'race suicide'. The terminology of the germ pathogen model of disease obviously did not produce this kind of thinking but it fell into easy harmony with such imagery, strengthening it and endowing it vicariously with some of the force of science. Germ pathogeny came to serve as a trope for society and social affairs as a model with which to make sense of disease.

These points are well illustrated by some excerpts from the hygiene textbook already cited, *Fighting Dirt: the World's Greatest Warfare*, by E. Hood (1916):

While the boy and girl yearn to handle a sword and go to the wars, deadly enemies surround them, lurk in their clothes, cling to their flesh, penetrate into their mouths, and only wait a favourable moment to attack their bodies in force, as soldiers have attempted the capture of some great fortress, such as Gibraltar. (pp. 16–17)

Your body is a great fortress, and contains yards of trenches in which are ranged countless invisible soldiers to defend it . . . (p. 18)

. . . while the comparatively small submarine can destroy huge vessels, so the tiny germ of disease can lay low the strongest of men. (p. 28)

Thousands of babies die quite needlessly every year from summer diarrhoea. Where the infant draws its food straight from the mother's breast there is no danger of the milk becoming contaminated by flies or filth, but with cows' milk there are scores of opportunities in carelessly kept dairies and homes for the enemy to enter the milk and so be carried into the delicate stomach of the baby. There the usual plan of campaign is adopted – poisons are produced by every member of the invisible invaders, and unless the doctor is at once summoned to check their ravages, the baby soon surrenders its weak little body into the hands of the foe. (pp. 154–5)

CONCLUSION

The aim of this paper has been to consider the establishment of medicalised childrearing as a social construction. In its creation, it is argued, many different social forces were involved that happened to come together into one particular set of contingent relationships.

Four groups of processes have been considered in varying degrees of detail. The first are those that contributed to child mortality and health becoming issues of social importance and high political visibility in Edwardian England. These are examined in considerable depth by Davin (1978), Dyhouse (1981) and Lewis (1980) and are touched on only briefly in this paper. The second group consists of the changes that were taking place in professional, medical ideas at that time. Some writers including Armstrong (forthcoming) have discussed these in terms of the internal evolution of medical knowledge. I, in contrast, have tended to give greater weight to the impact on medical attitudes to infancy of factors such as the changes in the organisational forms within which practice took place. In addition, I have also tried to suggest how differences in the day-to-day experience of doctors may have encouraged shifts in the judgements that they made about the relative plausibility of different ways of conceptualising infant death.

The main emphasis of my approach, however, has been on two remaining groups of processes: the creation of a new sphere of professional activity directed towards infant welfare, in which a new kind of knowledge would come into being and be practised; and, the association of infant welfare with the germ pathogen model of disease which led to the establishment of a vocabulary of powerful imagery through which infancy could be apprehended and understood.

Inevitably, this paper does no more than scratch the surface of these last two groups of processes. Both merit sustained research, particularly the question of the cultural and ideological power of medical ideas.

How we may ask, returning to Schon's notion of 'generative metaphor', mentioned earlier, does it happen that a new social situation may suddenly provide a space in which new forms of medical knowledge may rapidly constitute themselves? Or again, how should it be that an element of seemingly esoteric medical knowledge may suddenly serve as the prism through which groups within a society succeed in making sense of what is occurring around them?

These, I believe, are some of the central problems of the social and historical study of medicine; but they are essentially cognitive, not instrumental. They must not be confused with issues of whether medicine 'works' in some unproblematic, pragmatic sense. Take, for instance, what John Harley Warner writes about the weakness of the history of medicine in his recent survey of writing on the history of American medicine:

> there is virtually nothing that analyses the meaning of science from the patient's point of view . . . it is plainly necessary to consider why Americans bought what many plainly believed that laboratory science gave them to sell. Even if the ideal of experimental science won the hearts and minds of physicians, the questions of to what extent and why it did the same for the lay man and woman remains unclear especially given the doubtful ability of scientific medicine in the late nineteenth century to deliver the goods in terms of a demonstrably elevated power to care. (Warner, 1985)

Having rightly drawn attention to the neglect of the important question of why patients support a particular form of medical practice, he then writes as if he simply assumes that this neglect is made more serious because medicine in the period in question was 'demonstrably' unable to 'cure'.

But surely those involved in the cultural and historical study of meanings can never allow themselves to make such assumptions? A social constructivist, for example, must always examine how a particular sphere of knowledge is successful – or not – in asserting its claims to cultural credibility. The question should never be begged simply by assuming that the 'rightness' or 'effectiveness' of knowledge is its own justification (Bloor, 1976). In trying to explain why medicalised child-rearing was successful in establishing its claim to credibility I have argued that it is necessary to give close attention to the part played by medical practice and ideas in the constitution and reproduction of ideology.

7 Life: Cycle, Trajectory or Pilgrimage? A Social Production Approach to Marxism, Metaphor and Mortality

Ronnie Frankenberg

Life is a terminal illness for all of us. It is just that some know the end before others.

Bluebond-Langer (1978)

It has sometimes seemed to me that our subject is not always held in such high esteem or taken with that seriousness which as a practitioner I feel it deserves. There may be many reasons for this ranging from inelegance of language to a fear of that radicalism it has hardly ever expressed. There may be technological and stylistic as well as sociological reasons why even such best sellers as the 'Bethnal Green' studies (Young and Wilmott, 1957) fail to reach the mass audiences of 'East Enders' or the Adrian Mole books.

However, I wish to argue a more fundamental problem which is that, on the whole, sociology is dogged by naturalism rather than realism: that compared, for example, with the writers of soap opera, sociologists appear to be a romantic crew. There are few adulteries in the Bethnal Green of the sociologists. Similarly sociological writings on the life cycle often contain little reference to the fact that dominates the real phenomenon, its inevitable end. Whatever the truth in the modern capitalist industrial world of the sociological notion – with Anna Freudian overtones – of the death-denying society, it is, by and large, a fair description of much sociological work (Kellaher, 1984).

My discussion of the rival claims of cycle, trajectory and pilgrimage as organising concepts in the study of lifedeath and its sociologically significant moments, seeks in both senses to depart from this point. In order to do so I shall also depart from the sociologists' usual concept of deathandying and introduce instead (as permanent mnemonics) two compounds, lifedeath and deathlife (compare Heidegger's 'Being-towards-Death' – Heidegger, 1962, pp. 279 *et seq.*) These are intended to indicate the finite nature and the two possible emphases in considering life processes. I am in fact adopting the proleptic view adopted in the fifteenth century by Sir Thomas Malory when he used the title 'The Death of Arthur' to describe his account not only of the life of Arthur but of many others as well.

My starting point may be, at least partially, attributed to feminist influence since, both physically and spiritually, death, or at least dying has, like so much else, been accorded a feminine nature, whether seen as the sphere of female nurses rather than male doctors; or of mothers, daughters or wives; or the catholicity of Mary to whom it is prayed that she should be present now and at the hour of death (Bloch, 1982).

Deathandying, on the other hand, has come to provide an excuse, even for sociologists brave enough to break the taboo, to escape from the lifelong implications of the fact of death into the albeit useful social technology of helping to ensure a smooth passage to the other side. In so doing they avoid discussion of the implications of knowledge and acceptance of death on the nature of life.

The deathandying approach isolates and localises death in space and time and leaves it to hospice staff, hospital nurses and family to reverse the socialising experience of a lifetime and to convince the incumbent of the dying role that death is after all a natural, indeed social phenomenon. I am not, of course, arguing against such an activity, merely pointing out the relationship between undoubtedly useful social reform and undoubtedly necessary social revolution in a different and perhaps unusual context.

There is no doubt either that both to Marx and to Durkheim the death of an individual was a social act. The irony of demonstrating the importance of social facts and the social nature of death by an analysis of individual self destruction was recognised by Durkheim (1952) just as it has been by sub-sequent commentators. Marx, too, more outspoken even than Phillipson (1982), did not hesitate to attribute not only the pains of old age but also the timing and causes of proletarian deaths (including suicides) to the workings of capitalism. Like Durkheim, he appreciated the paradox that suicide was the most social form of death. He did not, however, perhaps fol-lowing his own principle that mankind only sets itself problems it can solve, devote more than five lines to death as a more general social problem (Marx, 1959, pp. 104–5).

His failure to take death sufficiently seriously as a more general sociological problem and to enquire as to how men and women produced their own personal and social consciousness of the meaning of lifedeath, led him also to neglect the possible relations of such production. This was not the least important cause of perhaps his greatest intellectual, and his followers' greatest political, error, namely the facile assumption that the desire for ritual, and its power to make possible the more in-strumental aspects of social life, would disappear at the same time as organised religion (Lash, 1981, p. 192).

MARXIST APPROACHES

Marx was curiously silent on the philosophical implications of death for what I have chosen to call the lifedeath pilgrimage. He has further been harshly criticised for his apparent indif-ference to Engels's feelings on the death of his lover, especially harsh in the light of Engels' later suggestion that Marx's own death was hastened by grief and hopelessness engendered by the death of his wife and daughter (Foner, 1973, pp. 27–8; Kapp, 1972, p. 247).

Marx's followers have, by and large, taken one of two views according to circumstances. One, in times of violent struggle, has been called the idea of red heroic death, in which resur-rection, or at least continuity, has been assured by the example to surviving revolutionaries of dying for the cause. This is symbolised by the press report of Mikhail Koltsov during the Spanish Civil War, that dead republican combatants were carried upright in their coffins to the grave. Remaining on their feet, they were an invitation to the survivors to continue the struggle (Giovannini, 1984, p. 58). Republican and Second World War Partisan songs emphasise this view in contrast to the rival Fascist culture of glorifying death for its own sake. This last can be seen as uncomfortably close to the less orthodox variant of Red Heroism namely, the courting of death, more or less deliberately, either by attempting suicide or by acting so recklessly as to make death for the cause inevitable.

This has proved as sharp a cause of controversy in revolutionary movements as it was for the early Christian Church. The second most common line is that of silent acceptance and endurance of death's inevitability which seems to have been the position adopted by Gramsci in prison (Giovannini, 1984, p. 86). Both Bloch and Trotsky pushed the problem into the future although in slightly different ways. The former saw the development of socialism and ultimately communism as creating a society in which alienation would be overcome. Each individual would feel so much a part of each other individual that one would not experience one's own death as at all threatening. However, it has been pointed out that such a situation might paradoxically make the death of others even more poignant in a way reminiscent of some of Donne's writing on the subject.[1] Trotsky, with characteristic robust bluntness, saw socialism as making possible the development of healthy minds and bodies which would reduce the fear of death and turn absurd fantasies of an afterlife into a rational caution in the face of danger.

Feuerbach, a precursor of Marx, suggested that the significance of death was its indication to us that we should use our lives to the full (Feuerbach, 1980). A funeral oration, often repeated for London-based communists at Golders Green Crematorium, expresses this value clearly:

Man's [sic] dearest possession is life, and since it is given to him to live but once, he must so live as not to be seared with the shame of a cowardly and trivial past; so live as to have no torturing regrets for years without purpose; so live that, dying, he can say 'All my life and all my strength were given to the finest cause in the world, the liberation of mankind' (Mahon, 1976, p. 496 – attributed to an unnamed Soviet source).

It is clear that Marxist thought, however imperfectly developed it may be, presents death as a collectively social experience. This has produced a clash with Christian thinking about death as individual, although even Marxists place responsibility on the individual for the proper achievement of societal aims, just as a good Christian dies in communion with the church if not with society at large.

CYCLES

Few sociologists seem to be aware of, or concerned about, the biological and other implications of the life cycle metaphor. An exception is Turner who describes himself as transcending it in a way we shall explore in more detail below. He writes:

> In the social process – meaning by 'process' here merely the general course of social action – in which I found myself among the Ndembu of Zambia, it was quite useful to think 'biologically' about 'village life-cycles' and 'domestic life-cycles', the 'origin', 'growth' and 'decay' of villages, families and lineages, but not too helpful to think about change as *immanent* in the structure of Ndembu society. (Turner, 1974, pp. 31–2)

He goes on to argue that the winds of change were blowing from outside the village, and that the dynamic nature of social relations in general led him away from thinking of change as cyclical and repetitive and of time as structural rather than social, and towards a view of drama in social relations which enabled him to see the social in terms of a metaphor drawn from culture rather than from nature, and therefore as being more appropriate.

Thus the application of the life cycle concept (if concept is not too grand a term) to the analysis of social life clearly has its dangers. Used uncritically, perhaps used at all, it implies views of society which are overdeterminist, overbiological and perhaps even over-moralised. There is an implication that the stages postulated are normal, necessary and functional. In the same way as feminists have pointed to the concepts of the family and the family wage as determining expectations and imposing self-fulfilling prophecies on individual life, the requirements of research methodology may, in effect, label the unmarried, the childless and the gainfully-employed seventy-year-old as abnormal and ill-adapted (Bernardes, 1985, 1986). In advanced industrial society, the stages and stability of the life cycle are socially constructed artefacts to be empirically established rather than assumed. Furthermore, except for imperfect Buddhists, Hindus, Pythagoreans and perfect geneticists, it is not cyclical either for the individual or for the society. Given the ability of human beings to think about and act upon their social and natural environment, it is only in the narrowest sense that it is cyclical even for the species.

Perhaps the cycle still remains, not unusefully, in the text of the beholder and in the development of the discipline. Amongst the first social analyses to which I was subjected and which I in turn reiterated, was Arensberg and Kimball's (1968) celebrated functionalist analysis of the Irish countryside of County Clare. In my presentation, one was invited to see wheels within wheels. Women, as was later more graphically revealed in the works of Edna O'Brien, were caught with young children in an unchanging daily round of activity throughout the year, a daily, genuinely repetitive, life cycle. (Significantly the novelist, unlike the ethnographers, points to the possibility and even the actuality of rebellion and of breaking out of the, literally magically sanctioned, circle – O'Brien, 1963.) The men, with their tasks outside the home, have a cycle operating on a larger timescale, the year and its seasons. Overlying these cycles of daily and seasonal rounds are the intersecting life cycles of birth, first communion, marriage, and two kinds of, at least partial, social death: emigration and retirement. Biological death (or failure to give birth) may lead to incomplete farm families which cannot complete the cycles successfully, and so fail to continue the Great Cycle in which, blessed by Church and State, son succeeds father and father breeds son, and the name stays on the land.

Pahl (1984), in his recent analysis of John Bull's third island, the Isle of Sheppey, points out that incomplete power-drill households are as disastrous an interruption in the family life cycle there as incomplete farm families were in County Clare. Although Pahl is, as one would expect, more sophisticated, both analyses emphasise the nature of household work and the divisions of labour within it. In the former Irish case, the results of the analysis suggest (probably over-optimistically) a life cycle continuity. In the latter, the divisions of labour themselves represent a break in the cycle's continuity with the past and portend further breaks in the future.

A very different set of studies, Strauss's analyses of work in the modern hospital (Strauss *et al.*, 1985), brings me to the second metaphor for the analysis of moments of lifedeath, trajectory.

TRAJECTORY

Pahl focuses his study of the community on the way that *work* is organised and divided. Many years ago I myself suggested that the study of communities could be equated with the industrial sociology of child rearing, the last of the great cottage industries. Goods and services, in modern urban industrial society are produced in factories but also, as Pahl details, in households. Socially situated adults are produced in households but also in institutions (equivalent to factories). Lifedeath, together with its attendant ritual and ceremonial, is produced as a byproduct to these socially rather than biologically productive activities. It is appropriate then that we should accept the challenge of Strauss's team of hospital researchers and use their theoretical concepts of trajectory and arc of work to replace the purely biological (and especially anti-interactionist) theorisation of cycles:

> We suggest that studies of work, done from whatever disciplinary perspective, should include *any enterprise*, even when those engaged in the enterprise do not think of it as involving work. We have in mind not only enterprises like some touched on in this book (dying with grace, living as decently as possible despite an intrusive illness), but the thousand and one lines of action as lines of *work*: escape from a prisoner of war camp, a political campaign, a fund-raising campaign by unpaid volunteers . . . ,

or further out on the margins of what seems at first blush non-work (they might have added from a male viewpoint): going through therapy, keeping a marriage going, raising a child properly, making a quilt or doing a puzzle, learning to ski or skate,

> any or all of these activities may be fun (one's paid work can be fun too), but they also involve some, even tremendous, amounts of work. Each can usefully be conceived of as a trajectory, with its arc of work and implicated tasks. (Strauss *et al.*, 1985, p. 290)

Strauss and his associates first introduced the concept of trajectory as long ago as 1967 in their book on grounded theory. However their pragmatic choice, in *Awareness of Dying* (Glaser and Strauss, 1965), of confining themselves to the labelled terminal phase of dying in hospital, meant that the concept is only fully developed in the much more recent *Social Organisation of Medical Work* (Strauss *et al.*, 1985). In that work it is used to mean not only the physical unfolding of the course of a patient's disease, but also the impact on those involved with that work and its organisation. It is perhaps necessary to say that they find it useful in the study of the modern American hospital because, they contend, the characteristic of the hospital is high technology and the complicated interlocking work organisations that are associated with it. The characteristic diseases now treated therein are acute, recurrent episodes of chronic disorders, and the characteristic patients are necessarily at least as conscious and conversant with their own problems as are the many other members of the work team (nurses, porters, relatives, doctors, mechanics, auxiliaries, etc.).

They see trajectories as divided into particular phases each involving a set of work requirements which they call an arc of work. This involves different teams doing different kinds of work severally and together. The arc can be analysed in terms of physical tasks: moving the patient around, surgery, consolation, connecting to terminals and so on; by type of activity; by the nature of the team involved; or by the status of the work. The common thread in almost all these tasks is their inclusion of bodywork. Activity on the body is a characteristic which unites the work of, for example, hospital porters, ambulancemen, parents collecting children from school, taxi drivers and airline pilots as well as, perhaps in more penetrating ways, surgeons, hairdressers, prostitutes, dentists, lovers, chiropractors and football coaches.

I think it is not unreasonable to suggest that lifedeath is in this sense the chronic dis-ease *par excellence*, one which is also dominated for much of the time by various forms of bodywork. Seeing it in this way also has many analytical advantages. Not least it enables a critical sociological approach to be applied to what are more often seen as life cycle stages, receiving by default a biological definition.

Two major emphases imposed upon the analyst by the work orientation of Strauss' concept of trajectory are consciousness of the existence of the work teams and of socially determined temporal limits or boundaries. This last is central to our deathly concerns. The definition of the terminal patient is, of course, entirely of this kind. Orthodox Jews say the shema regularly and certainly before retiring for the night, insuring thereby their readiness for death. I understand that girls in convent boarding schools arrange their bodies for sleep according to similar principles. I was delighted to be told by an Italian Parish Priest of unusual sensitivity and perhaps liturgical heterodoxy, that he administered the church's last rites to men and women as they passed their sixtieth birthday so that religious preparation for, and discussion of, death could be achieved without undue rush or last minute panic.

It does not follow, however, that all workers in such a team are working to the same timescale, and Strauss here suggests the terms: temporal matrix, intersections, nodes and images. These are conceptualisations which, in the present context, enable one to distinguish between, say, a widow of 20 years standing with a 70-year-old married daughter, and another widow of 50, widowed two years ago with a single son of 18. The intersections of one biography with another, complicated by other time measurements like: the length of residence, the history of the occupation being carried out and the length of time a status itself has existed or been widely recognised (for example, compare: lawful wedded wife, commonlaw wife, mistress and homosexual or heterosexual live-in lover), may all be relevant factors to an enquiry concealed behind the orthodox pseudo-biological 'married without children' or 'single'.

For suggestive examples of other ways in which Strauss's ideas can be developed I must refer you to the cited work. I will suggest two difficulties in the approach. The first lies in the metaphor itself with the image it arouses of ball, bullet or spaceship propelled through the air or space and, even, if out of the control of the prime mover, still at the mercy of other forces of impact or interference. As in other interactionist approaches, the determinism of structure has been replaced by an almost patternless, because over-patterned, anarchy of interacting, ever multiplying, differentially viewed and experienced experience. The individual lacks control not merely of the conclusion of the lifedeath trajectory but of every step along the way. Perhaps this is true, and certainly, from time to time, we all partake of such a view.

Sociologists, however, like human beings in general seek to generate meanings. The analysis of the hospital, and of the process of dying before it, does not necessarily suffer from this theoretical confusion (although cataloguing does sometimes seem to have taken over from analytic exposition) because, although Strauss and his colleagues draw theoretical conclusions, their aims were rather practical; how to run more efficient and pleasant hospitals, and how to facilitate deathandying for all participants.

Their aim is radical reform within a conservative framework which explains the second difficulty. While the differential distribution of power is apparent in passing, it is not analysed in detail, nor is its redistribution suggested in any serious way. The facts that the chronic patient, and even her nurse, knows the details of the disease better than the doctor, and that the technician understands the machine better, are in no way used to suggest that the medical director of the hospital should be replaced by patient or technician.

Applied to lifedeath, Strauss's theoretical approach lacks Feuerbach's cutting edge or even Durkheim's. It does not suggest as did Feuerbach's and Durkheim's that God as director of the drama should be replaced, either by the individual captain of his/her own fate or by society or relevant social group. I suggest that the concept, work, as it is used by both Pahl and Strauss, despite their best intentions, tends to lead them towards analysing the relationship between people and things, or even teams of people or houses full of people and things. The concept, production, might have served them better whether applied to health, wealth, meaning or a good lifedeath.

PILGRIMAGE

At first sight perhaps, pilgrimage seems out of place as a concept placed alongside cycle and trajectory, given their shared
air of science whether ballistic or biochemical. Thompson
(1963) pointed out to us long ago that the two texts of social
analysis of those who were first in English Capitalism to seek to
change society through analysing it, were Paine's *The Rights of
Man* and Bunyan's *The Pilgrim's Progress*, the latter an allegori-
cal account of what I have called lifedeath. Indeed, even earlier,
Chaucer found in pilgrimage a frame in which to represent his
social criticism to the first English speaking audience. Pilgrimage remains a powerful symbol to left and to right as many
examples could testify. Pilgrimages or journeys to places where
others have died or are buried, Lenin's tomb or Mao's; Haworth
Churchyard or Poet's Corner; are symbolic parallels to seeing
lifedeath as a journey of achievement and conquest. Shrines
represent a kind of immortality, a triumphal transcending of
the inevitable end, achieved by the social individual over
biological extinction.

My own use of pilgrimage in this context is derived from the
anthropologists, Victor and Edith Turner (1978) who, as
Catholics, engaged in a rare exercise in *real* participant observation and studied Marian pilgrimage. They point out that
pilgrimage of this kind consists of a series of ceremonial events
which are separated from one another not only in time but also
in space. It can profitably be seen as an alteration of structural
relationships – organised travel, fixed stages, scripted liturgy –
with relations of anti-structure, which Victor Turner sometimes
calls communitas. In the latter, people relate to each other as
people rather than in terms of previously structured roles and
as incumbents of bodies rather than as incumbents of social
positions.[2] So-called life crises including succession to position,
marriage, giving birth, sickness, recurrent festivals and many
more, are moments of communitas in a sea of structure, even if
it often requires intoxicants to persuade us to leave our social
positions for our bodies (see Young and Wilmott's brilliant
description of a Bethnal Green wedding). In relation to Christian
pilgrimage, the Turners draw attention to the paradox that the
highly structured church provides a framework and a formal
hierarchical organisation which enables pilgrims to step outside

their normal social environment. A parallel to this is to be found in the honeymoon, the office Christmas party, the conference disco, and even in the structuring of statutory and school holidays and tourism.

Turner (1974) calls such intervals between structural positions 'liminal' if they occur in the course of ritual and, for the more secular form we have been discussing, he uses the term 'liminoid'. In particular, this approach helps us to overcome the intractability of the detail thrown up by the applications of Strauss, by drawing attention to the unity of expression and action. Lifedeath is not only lived; it is simultaneously performed. This is not an incidental but an essential part of the ascription of meaning to the essentially ephemeral. The stages of life, the points on the trajectory, are stops on the way to the terminus and all human societies mark them accordingly. Judaeo–Christianity usually sets *its* terminus beyond the grave which gives it the ambivalence in the face of social policy that is symbolised personally for us by Enoch Powell, Franco and Digby Anderson on the one hand, and Camillo Torres, the Bishop of Durham and Donald Soper on the other. Marxism, as I have suggested, has somehow to come to terms with the full stop.

The idea of lifedeath as pilgrimage can also help us to conceptualise in a way that can overcome the bogey of sociological overdetermination which, as I have already hinted, dogs the advocates both of structure and of interactionism itself. For if the dramas in which incumbents of roles are involved, are themselves part of a sequence that is influenced not only by the history of their own past and the antecedent biographies of the actors, but also by the conscious and unconscious foreshadowing of the shape of things to come – Sartrean protentions in contrast to retentions (Sartre, 1956, p. 109, fn.) – then men and women can still be seen as making their own biography within the framework of past and future mortality. The alternation of long periods of more or less accepted structure (marriage, work, school, family) with phased dramatic crises that are partly structured to produce antistructure, is what lifedeath (as cultural performance) and pilgrimage have in common.

Performance is interestingly enough the term used by nurses to enquire about bowel movement, midwives to praise the achievements of recent mothers in the labour ward, and sex therapists to register their clients' successes. In each case they are concerned with a flow across or through body boundaries, with a consequent symbolic recognition of transition from persona to individual, mask to body. As Turner implies and as I shall develop below, the non-work or play overtones of performance are of major importance.

Social drama is to pilgrimage what arc of work is to trajectory. A breach of existing structured social relations, the parameters of which may have been moving towards crisis for some time, finally shows as a crisis disturbing the even flow of social life. Redressive machinery is brought into *play* leading either to reconciliation or to the emergence of new social groupings. Such dramatic crises may, so to speak, be casual incidents (sickness, an accident, a quarrel) and, in modern urban industrial society, although accompanied by some ceremonial, may be unritualised and apparently random.

Crises may, however, be recurring and structured. One form of these is made up of the changes in social relationships engendered by life crises, like birth, sexual maturity and death, which are accompanied by compulsory ritual practices that are more or less socially imposed and sanctioned. Van Gennep suggested that such rituals could be seen as including, in order, rites of separation, transition and incorporation or re-aggregation. Turner's achievement was to map the ritual relations upon the social relations and to analyse the consequences, theoretically and empirically. He pays most attention to the characteristic transition period in ritual; ceremonial and events where structure is least defined. He calls this the stage of liminality. During liminality, the unity of culture breaks down and its elements are freely combined in 'ludic' playlike patterns. The paradox of pre-industrial society is that on the one hand play and work are not rigorously bounded in space or time, and on the other that the ludic is an obligatory part of rituals. It is the contrast of this with modern urban industrial society which leads to the initial distinction Turner makes between liminal and liminoid: 'optation pervades the liminoid phenomenon, obligation the liminal' (Turner, 1982, p. 43). Using these ideas, I have suggested elsewhere (Frankenberg, 1986) that acute sickness amongst Italian children that is not life threatening can be conceptualised as a battle between Carnival (liminoid indulgence) and Lent (liminal deprivation).

I now want to suggest that ludic elements in the social ascription of meaning to death are part of life at various moments of history and morphological change. I follow here the analogy of the industrial sociology of childbirth, and pick up on the methodological suggestions of both Strauss and Pahl. The key question I shall merely begin to answer is: 'How is the production of lifedeath organised in different societies and fragments of society, at different times and in different places?'. I wish to suggest that this is the key question that has to be tackled in order to understand the other questions raised by the study of the so-called life cycle. Only then can sociology earn the designation of realism and comparison with lasting literature, as against that of naturalism and comparison with worthy, but ephemeral, journalism.

Obviously a good starting point is the work of Ariès (1974) with his clear but, as Elias (1985, pp. 12–13) points out, unconvincing claim that in mediaeval times, the mass production of death was accidental and natural rather than socially willed and cultural. Monasteries and priests, writers, architects and painters produced mass meanings for lifedeath but the efforts of crusaders and others were limited to decimating populations. The total destruction of populations was left to black rats and plague bacilli. Social interventions in the major disasters were essentially negative. There were inadequately organised water supplies, housing provisions and quarantine systems. Alongside the system of mass destruction, personal lifedeath was a cottage industry (or at best as in Boccaccio and the Masque of the Red Death, a mansion or castle one). People died in their homes comforted, or hastened joyfully on their way, by relatives and by the comforts of Mary and mother church. The ludic element in the castle was provided by jesters with symbolic skulls and the concept of the dance of death. For certain groups of churchmen and for the commons, the public comedy of lifedeath was played out in the annual carnival, in which in times of peace death was mocked, and in times of unrest planned and executed. It is significant but not original to point out that festivals of fools were placed in liminal, liminoid periods of the calendar, the liturgical pause between birth, lifedeath, deathlife, death and life everlasting, and between solar and lunar feasts, as well as in the secular threshold between death in life in winter and the life in death of summer (Bristol, 1985). We should not be surprised that Ariès romanticises a cottage industry of death-life, since once it is seen in that way it lends itself to the general sociological, social history tendency of modern mass urban industrial society to which we all occasionally succumb.

Such romanticism is, of course, not wholly reactionary in the strict sense. In the light of 'small is beautiful' and the achievements of socialist local government and co-operatives at home and abroad and faced with the power of massive technology to destroy massively as well as to create, we are more careful about accepting Marx and Engels' loving (?) criticisms of the Chartists' harking backwards to three acres and a cow. In the same way we may find the appeal of the hospice movement and of Aldous Huxley's *Island* (1964) more attractive. An intermediate, often equally romanticised, stage and one often confused with proletarian reality, *tout court*, is represented in our subject by the syndrome of Bethnal Green and *Coal is our Life* (Dennis *et al.*, 1969) and possibly, in the view of some, *Communities in Britain* (Frankenberg, 1966). The stable shared community meanings built upon and around a shared interest in work, in which men are united with their employers by their struggles against them and women, similarly, for and against their menfolk.

To me the ludic deathlife spirit of the Artisan mode of death production is crystallised with personal poignancy in the novels and occasional writings, perhaps almost forgotten, of Gwyn Thomas (1953), whose comic evocations of the Rhondda, where he was a classmate of Will Paynter, the miners' leader, were popular in the late 1950s and early 1960s. To him, miners travelled from the black pit to the black meadow on their way to the black nothing. He told a famous story at an Oxford Union broadcast debate of a disastrous funeral which ends with the casket and cadaver, ill attended by well-oiled pall bearers, sliding from the back of the hearse at the entrance to the Black Meadow on the mountain top and parting company at the bottom of the lane where the mining village begins. The box sails on through the village street but the body goes through the swing door of the village chemist and as its feet strike the counter is projected upright. The corpse then asks the startled pharmacist 'Can you give me something to stop my coffin?' I hope the resonances of this punning joke about the lifedeath/deathlife of Welsh miners are too obvious to require semiotic analysis.

In the present situation of capitalism in crisis, we are faced with two, at first sight, contradictory aspects of the meaning of deathlife. In the first place we are in an era of the mass production of death, one where current plagues are socially willed even when this is concealed by a sickness metaphor. The holocaust, the Second World War, Dresden, Hiroshima and Nagasaki, death camps in east and west Europe and the Far East, and mass genocide in Amazonian jungles are now part of history; third world famine and poverty-induced disease are part of the present, and socially preventable mass production of death by weapons of mass destruction or ecological disaster does not seem, if unprevented, to be far in the future. There is a worldwide widespread putting-out system whereby the mass production of patriarchal social systems is achieved at the expense of the lives of women and children.

At the same time, the nineteenth-century belief of the parents of social preventive medicine in the power of social action to delay death and to enhance lifedeath, has been watered down. The prevailing message of bookshop and television station in the industrialised west is to the individual to save her/himself as a biological entity by consuming more durables but less fat, more artificial health foods, but fewer cigarettes, and so on.

However much sociologists of the life cycle may shy away from it and anthropologists of medicine may exoticise it, and important though the individual easing of deathandying certainly is, consciousness of lifedeath is always a central feature of any culture. A critical approach to the sociology of life must take note of the fact that at the very moment when the social prevention of mass socially determined death should be their most major concern, prevalent ideology successfully maintains that, just as the unemployed can work themselves as individuals out of poverty, so individuals can work themselves out of death.

Pilgrimage as a concept fruitfully combines individual choice with awareness of the necessity of structure, the instrumental with the expressive, the passage of time with passage through space, and the symbolic with the merely signifying. It reminds us of death in life as well as life in death and can for all these reasons provide a counter to those reductionist concepts which lead sociologists blindly to re-present, rather than critically to analyse the real and imagined problems of society.

NOTES

1. But see Bloch (1986), especially page 1172 *et seq*.
2. Elias (1985) echoes more elegantly the earlier description of death as an unscheduled status passage of Glaser and Strauss (1971) when he mourns that, since there is no longer a structure in which to relate to the dying, people cease to relate to them at all.

Part III

Resources and Transfers

8 Intergenerational Transfers and Life Course Management: Towards a Socio-economic Perspective

David Cheal

Intergenerational transfers are usually thought to take the form of a redistribution of resources that is carried out through state taxation and social security programmes. Government benefits to children and the elderly have therefore received a great deal of attention, and have been the subjects of a number of official studies. A major weakness in most of these studies has been that the recipients of government transfers are implicitly treated as passive dependants (Cheal, 1985). In the following discussion an alternative point of view will be presented, and the elderly will be portrayed as active participants in the process of intergenerational redistribution. The principal theme will be the existence of a system of family transfers that predates, and which is largely independent of, the system of government transfers. Within the system of family transfers the elderly are not solely, or even largely, the recipients of economic resources. Recent American research shows that they are, in fact, often notable providers of resources for others (Chen and Chu, 1982; McConnel and Del-javan, 1983). It is the propensity of the elderly to give, rather than their necessity to receive, that requires sociological explanation at this time.

Traditionally, sociological discussions of intergenerational family transfers have located them within a model of the individual life course defined as a cycle of dependency. The thesis to be presented here is that this view of the life cycle can no longer be considered to provide a satisfactory account of resource distribution processes within modern families.[1] It will therefore be necessary to develop an alternative account, derived from a different conceptual framework. In order to see what is involved here, we must first say something about the evolution of life cycle models of the family economy, and why they have been so important.

THE FAMILY LIFE CYCLE

The dominant view of the family life cycle has been that of a cycle of expanding and contracting needs. The idea of a cycle of needs originated in early British social research into the problems of the industrial working class. In his pioneering study of poverty in York in 1899, Seebohm Rowntree concluded that the life of a labourer was marked by five alternating periods of want and relative plenty (1902, pp. 133–7). Childhood, early middle age, and old age were times of need, whereas youth and young adulthood, and late middle age were times of comparative ease. Rowntree showed that at the end of the nineteenth century the wages paid for unskilled labour in England were insufficient to provide food, shelter, and clothing 'adequate to maintain a family of moderate size in a state of bare physical efficiency'. Most of the children of labourers therefore spent their childhood in poverty, and most working class parents were poor during their child-rearing years. Old age was also a time of poverty for labourers, Rowntree concluded, because the male household head was too old to earn a wage, and because 'his income has never permitted his saving enough for him and his wife to live upon for more than a very short time'.

Rowntree's work has had a great influence on models of the life cycle, because he showed that alternating periods of need and ease were a predictable feature of the normal life course. Nevertheless, it is essential to recognise the focused, and therefore limited, nature of his enquiries. Rowntree's main purpose was to describe working-class poverty as a social problem. His principal legacy to the sociology of the life course has therefore been a distinctive structure of interests. The moral link that he assumed between the problem of poverty and the idea of progress (Rowntree, 1941) has had a profound influence upon social policy formation. As a result, the conceptual links that he established between poverty, working class life and the life cycle defined the questions that were to be explored by sociologists such as Peter Townsend after the Second World War. In Townsend's work there was in fact a subtle shift of emphasis. The main focus of attention became the conjunction between poverty, working class family life and old age (Townsend, 1957).

According to Townsend, there has been an enduring pattern of inequality between the elderly and the young in the United Kingdom. Viewed as a problem in the social organisation of income distribution, the incidence of poverty in old age was described by Townsend as 'a function of low levels of resources, and restricted access to resources, relative to younger people' (1979, p. 785). That situation was seen as being largely due to the continuing struggle of those who are well off to preserve and enhance their class interests through actions of the state and other institutions.

In his early research on family life in the working class community of Bethnal Green, Townsend showed that the standard of living of the elderly was often subsidised by transfers of income within the extended family. Those transfers included money and gifts from relatives (usually married children) living in separate households. One of the more influential conclusions to emerge from that study was that most of an individual's needs are met by the exchange of goods and services within the three-generation extended family (Townsend, 1957, pp. 108–12). At the same time that Townsend was making that point, its implications were already emerging as a major focus for sociological studies on ageing and family life in the USA (Sussman, 1965).

As we have seen, Rowntree had demonstrated that adults' financial needs fluctuated over the life course as a function of their responsibilities for children and their earning capacities. His views on the life cycle were introduced into the United States by Hunter (1904, pp. 56–8) during the Progressive Era of reform. American interest in financial need and the life cycle was renewed in the period of social reconstruction after the Second World War, when it was given a characteristically

optimistic tone. The challenges that are imposed upon individuals and families during times of need came to be defined by
American sociologists as 'developmental tasks' in the family life
cycle. The notion of developmental needs and tasks had been
borrowed from psychology (Hill and Rodgers, 1964). In the
work of child psychologists such as Havighurst (1973), individuals were seen as facing a predictable series of problems of
adjustment, due to biological changes and related changes in
social expectations (Datan and Ginsberg, 1975). The social
tasks in this developmental process were described by Rhona
Rapoport as setting 'the critical transition points in the normal,
expectable development of the family life cycle' (1963, p. 69).
In the social-psychological models elaborated by family sociologists such as Evelyn Duvall (1977) and Joan Aldous (1978),
these normal and normative transition crises became defined as
the turning points for developmental stages in the family life
cycle.

Much of the work that has been carried out from a developmental family life cycle perspective has been concerned with
the quality of personal relationships. However, that approach
did also provide the conceptual framework for Reuben Hill's
investigation of the changing economic circumstances of households in Minneapolis-St. Paul in the late 1950s. Hill's abiding
interest in the family as an adaptive system committed him to
seeking 'an improved family development theory of the economic
and social achievement of families' (Hill and Mettessich, 1979).
As Townsend had done, he conceived of those achievements as
being affected by social position within a three-generation
system of familial transactions.

Hill's research on intergenerational family transactions was
heavily influenced by the functionalist theory of the modified
extended family. According to this point of view, the members
of independent nuclear families are thought to meet the needs
of others through the provision of mutual assistance within extended family networks. Like Rowntree, Hill maintained that
there was a cycle of need during the life course. Young married
adults, and the elderly, were described as being more in need of
economic support than the middle aged. According to Hill:

By linking three generations into one functioning network,
the modified extended family, through its middle generation,

is able to help the very vulnerable married child generation get started while also meeting the grandparent generation at its level of need. (Hill, 1970, p. 79)

In this functionalist theory of intergenerational resource flows, transfers are thought to take the principal form of 'intergenerational aid'. The largest providers of aid are held to be the middle generation, since they support both their married children and their elderly parents. Hill referred to this middle generation as 'the lineage bridge across the generations' (Hill, 1970, p. 78).

Hill's findings from the three-generations study have provided the basis for much theorising about how the family life cycle influences the direction of intergenerational aid. Wesley Burr (1973, p. 221) has hypothesised that there is a curvilinear relationship between age and net aid flows, in which the early adult years are characterised by balanced reciprocity, the middle years by giving more than receiving, and the later years by receiving more than giving.

I have shown elsewhere (Cheal, 1983) that data from the 1978 Family Expenditure Survey in Canada do not support Burr's conclusion. Although comprehensive measures of net transfers do show some curvilinearity, the predominant flow of resources between families and unattached individuals appears to be from older to younger age groups, at all age levels. The elderly give less as they get older, but they also receive less. Similar results have emerged from an independent study of Christmas transactions, conducted as part of the 1984 Winnipeg Area Study (Cheal, forthcoming a).

It seems that we know less about the nature of intergenerational family transfers than we had once supposed. This is a rather important conclusion, because it must throw some doubt upon traditional models of the family life cycle. Established views on the life cycle therefore need to be rethought, and the latest research findings need to be integrated with recent developments in social theory.

THE FAMILY ECONOMY AND THE LIFE COURSE

One possible method for moving beyond the standard theory of the family life cycle is to explore the various alternative paradigms from which relevant hypotheses might be developed (Cheal, forthcoming). However, the available models turn out to be based upon simplifying assumptions that are often severe, and which are all questionable to some degree. A different approach will therefore be attempted here. We will see what happens when the simplifying assumptions of the standard theory of the family life cycle are relaxed. The results of this method will be more complex, and perhaps more confusing, but they are also likely to be more realistic.

The conventional wisdom on intergenerational family relationships has its origins in the standard sociological theory of the extended family (Cheal, forthcoming b). It therefore has the characteristic weaknesses of that approach. Standard theory models have tended to be essentialist (i.e. monolithic), functionalist, and a-historical. If the theory of intergenerational transfers is to overcome the limitations of such modes of theorising, then we must try to develop models that are structural, historical, and based on theories of action. We shall consider each of those requirements in turn.

Structuration of gift behaviour

Standard sociological theories of ageing and society usually include the assumption that the elderly comprise a distinct category in an age-graded social system. In the advanced industrial societies, the image defined by the conjunction of poverty, working class life and old age has meant that old age is usually seen as being in essence a period of socio-economic marginality. Such monolithic notions of the social status of the elderly must be replaced by structural models of economic relations, and of the variations in, or transformations of, those relations (Cheal, 1983). In particular, it is necessary to keep in mind that in a class society the elderly are in reality a very diverse group of people, containing some of the very poorest and the most affluent of individuals. In this regard, it is worth remembering that Rowntree's model of the family life cycle was class-specific. He was concerned with the nature of poverty among 'the working classes', and he therefore studied the families of wage-earners. A study of the property owning classes at the same point in time might well have produced a rather different model of the life cycle.

In recent years it has become increasingly clear that a knowledge of the patterns of ownership of personal assets is important for understanding variations in individual life courses (Henretta and Campbell, 1978; Pahl, 1984). Although most of the elderly do not own much in the way of income-earning assets, many of them do benefit from the possession of expenditure-reducing assets, such as houses. The level of home ownership, and in particular the ownership of homes whose mortgages have been paid off, is an important qualification to the usual pattern of inequality between elderly and non-elderly households. In this respect, old age is often a time of relative wealth rather than relative poverty (Townsend, 1979, pp. 793–4; Harris, 1981, p. 76).

The behavioural consequences of different kinds of economic resources need to be studied in a more systematic way than has usually been the case in the sociology of the life cycle. I have shown elsewhere (Cheal, forthcoming a) that the level of expenditure on valuable Christmas gifts in Winnipeg is related not only to the amounts of personal income and household income, but also to the proportion of household income absorbed by accommodation expenses. In future analyses of intergenerational transfers it would clearly be desirable to separate income effects from asset effects, and to show their comparative importance for the gift behaviour of the elderly.

Changing fortunes

The relative economic well-being of different age groups is a variable condition that is affected by a number of factors (Pampel, 1981; Clark *et al.*, 1984). Changes in those factors can be expected to have a variety of consequences for family relationships, and an historical perspective on the life course and the family economy is therefore necessary (Elder, 1977). As Mitterauer and Sieder have observed, 'Research into the history of the family cycle may lead one to appreciate that models of family sociology, and their interpretation, cannot be seen as absolute' (1982, p. 49).

The changing economic fortunes of different cohorts, and of different age groups, must be taken into account in any contemporary analysis of intergenerational family transfers. To begin with, it is probable that the ownership of domestic property has a more widespread significance in the modern industrial societies than it did in the early industrial societies. The proportion of households in England owning their own homes, for example, has increased considerably since Rowntree's study of York at the end of the nineteenth century (Townsend, 1979, p. 794).

The distance between Rowntree's day and ours is particularly evident from the fact that he added to the second edition of his report some calculations on the number of people whose poverty would be relieved if a scheme of universal old age pensions were to be introduced. In the 87 years since Rowntree's survey, the financial well-being of the elderly in the western societies has indeed been improved by the expanded activities of the welfare state, particularly in the areas of medical services and social security payments. Insofar as much of the money for those programmes has come from the income taxes paid by wage-earners, some intergenerational redistribution of wealth in favour of the retired elderly must have occurred in recent decades. At the same time, younger age groups, and in particular youths and children, have been adversely affected by rising levels of unemployment and by the growth in single parent families.

The most recent intergenerational comparisons for the United States indicate that by the early 1980s the elderly had made quite substantial relative economic gains (Clark *et al.*, 1984, p. 47; Chen, 1985, pp. 646–7). Poverty rates among Americans living alone are still somewhat higher for the elderly than they are for the non-elderly; but elderly families now have lower poverty rates than do non-elderly families (Government of the United States, 1985, pp. 160–9). The changing economic fortunes of different age groups in Canada have been very similar. Poverty rates among non-elderly Canadians have risen in recent years, while poverty rates among the elderly have continued to decline. Families with elderly heads are now under-represented in Canada's low income population, although the unattached elderly are still highly over-represented (National Council of Welfare, 1984, p. 29). Elderly unattached individuals have a higher rate of poverty than any group of non-elderly. However, the difference is not large for those who are under 25 or who are approaching retirement (age 55–64). Among families, the rate of poverty for the elderly is now lowest equal (with the 45–54 age group), and it is far below the rate for families whose heads are under age 25 (National Council of Welfare, 1985, pp. 23–9).

The elderly have been major beneficiaries of government transfer payments in Canada (Beach, 1981, pp. 173–5), and it is therefore appropriate to ask about the effects that those payments may have had on economic behaviour. From a sociological point of view, it is necessary for us to begin to see those payments, as Marcel Mauss did (1954, pp. 65–6 espec.), as moments in a *total* system of prestations. The elderly, who have received transfers from younger age groups through the universalistic redistribution programmes of governments, may in turn be more inclined to make particularistic gift transfers to their descendants, thus bringing about an intergenerational circulation of resources (Cheal, 1985).

Adaptive strategies

The active participation of the elderly in social worlds of various kinds has received growing attention in the field of social gerontology. Action theorists, such as symbolic interactionists, have sought to account for the social involvements of old people in terms of their goals and strategies, rather than in terms of the functioning of social systems (Marshall, 1986). If we are to have an adequate understanding of the connections between the life course and the family economy, then we clearly need to know more about the different kinds of strategies that families use in adapting to their life cycle squeezes (Moen, Kain and Elder, 1983). One strategy for coping with the pressure of familial demands upon personal resources is to raise family income. That can be done by working extra hours, or by increasing the number of family members in paid employment. In the latter part of the nineteenth century, the most effective means for achieving the latter was to send children out to work at an early age. In the second half of the twentieth century, the increased utilisation of family labour power has usually taken the form of wives entering the labour market.

Oppenheimer (1974; 1982) has conducted detailed investigations of the relationships between men's life cycle squeezes, the family's need for an additional income, and the pressure on wives to take up paid employment. From a family life cycle

point of view, one of the more interesting features of her work
has been the claim that in the contemporary United States men
in their forties and fifties who work in moderate-to-low-paying
occupations are often under severe economic pressure. That is
because they are increasingly responsible for maintaining and
educating their adolescent and young adult children, at a time
in life when their career cycle earnings have often peaked. In
the past, those children would have been working full-time.
Under modern conditions that is becoming less feasible, due to
the practical necessity for them to remain in the educational
system for longer and longer periods of time.

Oppenheimer refers to the modern middle age squeeze as the
second of three common life cycle squeezes. The first occurs in
early adulthood, when young couples are attempting to set up
independent households, and when young men's earnings are
usually very low and are frequently unstable. The third occurs
in old age, when the loss of earnings due to retirement from
market employment often means that incomes decline precipi-
tously. The first and the third squeezes are familiar features of
intergenerational family transfers theorising. But if Oppenheimer is correct, middle age may be a time of greater financial
pressure than the standard family life cycle models assume. As
she has remarked:

> in considering three-generation families, the ability of the
> middle generation to provide aid (monetary or otherwise) to
> an older generation in the third squeeze period may be re-
> duced if the middle generation is experiencing a particularly
> severe second squeeze at the same time. (Oppenheimer, 1981,
> p. 50)

The 'piling up' of the second and third life cycle squeezes in
the contemporary western societies might, indeed, account for
some of the political pressure to expand government services to
the elderly. If the middle generation finds it increasingly difficult to transfer resources privately to the elderly, the long run
result may have been a greater reliance of working class three-
generation families upon the system of public transfers (Oppenheimer, 1981, pp. 72–3).

Oppenheimer has shown that one adaptation to the second
life cycle squeeze has been increased participation by married

women in the labour force. Wives' employment can augment
the financial ability of middle aged couples to support aged
kin. It can also help increase the resources that couples build
up in order to cope with their own post-retirement squeeze
(Oppenheimer, 1981, pp. 74–5).

The strategy of increased utilisation of family labour power
is not often followed in old age, where the reverse process of
withdrawal from the labour market is the normal pattern
today. Retirement is clearly a more common experience for
men now than it used to be (Palmore, 1981, pp. 32–3).
Preparation for retirement may therefore have become a
quite widespread feature of life course management, with its
own distinctive strategies. One such strategy is the accumulation of personal assets through savings from earnings
(Haines, 1985).

Economists have recognised for some time that a life cycle
model of saving has a useful contribution to make to the
theory of household consumption (Clark and Spengler,
1980). The planning of future consumption, and therefore of
present resource allocation, is assumed to be a general characteristic of economic action. Individuals are thus hypothesised
to stabilise consumption levels by distributing their life-time
earnings over the life cycle. This involves saving during peak
earning periods, and dissaving in low earning periods such as
old age.

The availability of privately held resources in old age, particularly in the form of liquid assets, may be an important
facilitating condition for the generosity of the elderly in
Canada and the USA (Cheal, 1983, p. 808). Studies of the
social distribution of assets have confirmed the existence of a
life cycle pattern of resource accumulation. Net financial
worth has been shown to increase from one age group to the
next until age 64, after which it declines somewhat (Weisbrod
and Hansen, 1968). According to the life cycle consumption
model, the lower level of net financial worth among the
elderly should be due to them drawing down their assets for
consumption purposes, including transfers to others. That
possibility needs to be treated with some caution, as we shall
see in a moment. Before discussing that issue, however, it will
be useful to summarise the main points that have emerged
from the above discussion.

ISSUES IN SOCIO-ECONOMIC THEORY

The system of intergenerational family transfers in industrial societies has been widely studied by sociologists, particularly where voluntary transfers involving the elderly have been concerned. Nevertheless, that system is still not well understood. The standard sociological theory of intergenerational transfers has held that they are expected outcomes of the functioning of extended families. According to this view, the elderly in general are thought to be supported by their kin. We have seen here that predictions from this theory about the intergenerational direction of net transfers flows have not been upheld by recent research employing large data sets and comprehensive measures. Several considerations have therefore been presented that must be included in a more satisfactory account of the determinants of familial transfers.

The main point to emerge from the above discussion is that flows of intergenerational transfers are likely to be influenced by a number of features of the family economy that vary over the life cycle. In addition to the well known family life cycle factors of childbirth, school attendance, marriage, and retirement, we must recognise the importance of: 1) life cycle transfers to and from the state; 2) the life cycle accumulation of domestic capital and financial capital; 3) life cycle female labour force participation; 4) extended life cycle investments in human capital (i.e. further education). Taking all of those factors into account will require a complex, and dynamic, theory. Existing models of the family life cycle, with their fixed timetables of developmental stages, are not well suited to dealing with these issues, and new approaches will therefore be necessary.

Considerable importance has been attached in the above discussion to economic variables, and it is clear that a rapprochement between sociology and economics is needed here, as elsewhere. A socio-economic perspective that draws on both disciplines is required, since on present showing neither seems likely to provide a satisfactory analysis on its own. The difficulties with much economic theorising in this area are well illustrated from the recent history of the life cycle consumption model. While it has proven to be a useful guide to understanding the accumulation of domestic capital and financial capital in households, the evidence provided by studies of the distribution of wealth is more convincing for a life cycle saving hypothesis than it is for a life cycle dissaving hypothesis (Mirer, 1979). The average net financial worth of those age 65 and over in Canada is comparatively high, and is often found to be only slightly below that for the 55–64 age group (Beach, 1981, p. 187) Furthermore, it is well known that cross-sectional data on age groups confound age effects with period effects. The somewhat lower level of financial net worth among the elderly may be due more to the historically lower incomes during the period of their peak earning years than to any erosion of assets in old age.

In order to evaluate the relevance of the life cycle consumption model for the economic behaviour of the aged, it is necessary to have data on the resource flows of consumer units. Fortunately, several kinds of data have become available in recent years. In Canada and the United States, it is clear that savings and earnings from investments are more important sources of income in old age than they are at earlier stages of the life cycle (Beach, 1981, pp. 173–5; Harris, 1981, p. 86). It is therefore interesting to find, from a major national survey, that elderly Americans were less likely than the non-elderly to have drawn upon their savings to meet financial emergencies in 1980/81 (Harris, 1981, p. 84). Even more disturbing, from the point of view of the life cycle consumption model, is the finding (from the same survey) that 42 per cent of elderly Americans had actually *saved or invested* a portion of their income during the previous year (Harris, 1981, pp. 79–82). They were, it is true, less likely to have done that than non-elderly Americans (50–53 per cent), but the difference in the relative frequency of savers is considerably less than we might have expected. Furthermore, although there was an apparent overall decline in the amounts saved or invested with increasing age, the modal response of the elderly when asked to compare their current level of saving with that two to three years before was 'about the same'.

A variety of evidence has emerged which indicates that the dissaving behaviour of the aged does not conform to the classical life cycle model (Mirer, 1980). Indeed, it may well be that one of the principal economic characteristics of old age is wealth-holding. If that is in fact the case, it would require substantial revisions, not only to the prevailing micro-economic models, but also to the standard sociological accounts of the family economy and the life cycle.

CONCLUSION

The concept of dependency, upon the state and upon the extended family, has dominated both public and social scientific discussions of the place of the elderly in the modern western societies (Walker, 1982). It has been at the centre of the definition of old age as a 'problem' for which policy solutions are sought. And it has been the core notion in the sociological description of old age as a 'stage' in the life cycle. We have seen here that in the process of rethinking sociological models of the family life cycle it is also necessary to begin to rethink some common assumptions about old age and dependency.

One of the problems with the concept of dependency, as it has been applied to the elderly, is its implicit assumption of passivity. That assumption has taken a particularly mystifying form in those social theories which regard the elderly as the hapless victims of the class system (Myles, 1980). If the idea that actors participate in shaping their own lives through their actions in relation to others is to be taken at all seriously, then it is necessary for us to look more closely at what people do in their everyday lives. As Glen Elder has reminded us, that means studying 'the family economy of consumption, production, and life course management' (Elder, 1984, p. 128).

NOTE

1. Presentation of this paper at the British Sociological Association's Conference on the Sociology of the Life Cycle was assisted by a travel grant from the Social Sciences and Humanities Research Council of Canada. I would like to thank Victor Marshall for his useful comments on an earlier version of this paper.

9 Family Obligations and the Life Course

Janet Finch

INTRODUCTION

The topic of this chapter is support, aid and assistance, of both practical and material kinds, between adult kin in contemporary British society. My concern is not so much with documenting the actual support which passes between kin, but to explore concepts of 'obligation' and 'responsibility' to assist one's relatives, the circumstances in which these come into play, and the processes whereby they get translated into actions. A particular focus is upon how much processes operate over time, using the concept of the life course as a means for illuminating this aspect.

My discussion represents both a critical review of the study of family obligations, and an argument for a specific theoretical framework as the basis of such study. This framework is being tested out in an empirical study which was under way at the time of writing.[1]

A FRAMEWORK FOR STUDYING FAMILY OBLIGATIONS

I shall begin with a discussion of the main features of a theoretical framework for studying family obligations[2] before moving on to consider how a life course perspective should be incorporated in this. My main argument in this section is that such a framework can be built on a contrast between two different ways of conceptualising obligations: as moral norms and as negotiated commitments. On the one hand, family obligations can be seen as part of normative rules which operate within a particular society, and which simply get applied in appropriate situations. On the other hand, they can be seen as agreements which operate between specific individuals, and are arrived at through a process of negotiation which may be explicit, but which is probably more likely to be covert; that is, using the concept of 'negotiation' very much in an interactionist sense (Strauss, 1978). I would argue that a full understanding of what family obligations mean and how they operate almost certainly contains elements of both.

This can be illustrated initially by a hypothetical, although not an unusual, example. This hypothetical case concerns an elderly couple who will eventually need some form of personal care and who have children. If we understand obligations (in this case, filial obligations) simply to be a matter of normative rules, then all three children are in precisely the same position with respect to their parents, each of them being subject to a normative rule which, in British society, says something like 'Children should be responsible for the care of their parents if that becomes necessary'. This norm is of course expressed at a very general level which admits a number of different ways of fulfilling it, and this immediately opens up the possibility of negotiation. However, it is unlikely in my view that the three siblings will wait until the time comes when their parents actually need care, then open up round-the-table talks to decide precisely how each will fulfil her or his responsibilities. Probably such overt negotiations will never be necessary, because over a period of time – probably covering many years – it will gradually become 'obvious' to all concerned that when the time comes, one particular sibling (almost certainly a daughter) will actually be the one to provide daily care, another will perhaps provide some financial support, and the third will take the parents for a month every summer. In this instance, concrete obligations between specified individuals have been arrived at in some way through a process of negotiation, but those negotiations themselves are shaped by the general normative prescription about children taking responsibility for their elderly parents. I see it as a central task of any empirical work in this field to explore the relationship between moral norms and negotiation of obligations, and to understand the processes through which such arrangements as I have described above become 'obvious'.

Having explained the contrast between norms and negotiations by use of a single illustration, I shall now set out more formally the reasons for conceptualising family obligations in each of these ways.

Obligations as normative rules

The argument that family obligations can be seen as normative rules immediately raises the question of what I mean by 'rules' in this context. The example just given should make it clear that I do not mean that these are rules which offer clear, unambiguous directions for action. Rather, they represent much more general guidelines for 'proper' or 'correct' behaviour towards one's relatives, which then have to be interpreted in specific situations. Defined in this way, what is the case for seeing family obligations as normative rules?

This case rests partly on empirical evidence from existing studies of kinship in Britain. For example, in one of the best known and thorough pieces of work on British kinship, the study of Firth and his colleagues of middle-class kin relations in North London, concepts of 'responsibility' and 'obligation' played a prominent part in people's accounts of their relationships with relatives, although there was often room for flexibility about when and to whom these concepts should be applied (Firth, Hubert and Forge, 1969, pp. 385–97). More recent supporting evidence of the importance of moral norms can be found, for example, in Cornwell's excellent study of a small number of kin groups in Bethnal Green, where it is apparent that regular and substantial aid between mothers and daughters can be sustained over a long period of time, despite the fact that all parties resent it, because giving practical support to one's elderly mother is felt to be 'the right thing to do' (Cornwell, 1984, pp. 86–8). There is of course an important issue about precisely to whom such obligations refer, with the clearest cases of anything which looks like a fixed structure of obligations applying to primary rather than to secondary kin and especially to relationships between parents and children, although this is not invariably so (Morgan, 1975; Allan, 1983).

One possible analytical approach to understanding obligations

between kin in terms of normative rules is to see kin relations as
a special category of social relations which have an intrinsic,
specific quality. In anthropological literature, this reflects the
view (not universally accepted, of course) that kin relations
have a special 'moral character' which is perhaps most graphically expressed in the phrase 'sharing without reckoning'
(Bloch, 1973). If we take this idea of the moral character of
kinship as a starting-point, we can then generate a range of
questions which require empirical answers: Do kin relationships in contemporary Britain have this moral character which
distinguishes them from other social relations? To which relationship does this refer? What is the nature of the normative
rules implied by these relationships? In what circumstances do
such norms apply or not?

Obligations as negotiated commitments

A variety of arguments can be made to support the view that
obligations can be seen as negotiated commitments between
specific indivduals. The very fact that the norms themselves are
frequently expressed in very generalised terms which need to be
applied to specific situations almost requires an element of
negotiation. This feature is characteristic of British kin relations,
especially relations between secondary kin, which are 'permissive'
rather than 'obligatory' in character (Allan, 1979); or, as Firth
and his colleagues put it, there are standards of conduct but no
detailed rules for putting into effect notions of responsibility, and
therefore an individual has to make choices about how to respond
when a relative needs assistance (Firth, Hubert and Forge,
1969, pp. 451–2).

   Further, the notion of reciprocity, which is a central feature
of many classic discussions of kinship, itself suggests a negotiated
element. There is of course a sense in which reciprocal rights
and duties are themselves part of the 'moral character' of kinship, part of the inherent obligation to share. On the other
hand, historical evidence of kin relations in Britain, especially
the work of Michael Anderson (1971) suggests that kin relations
in the past at least have been much more calculative than the
concept of 'sharing without reckoning' would imply. Evidence
from the more recent past also suggests that performance of
obligations is at least partly related to the past conduct of the

person requiring assistance (Firth, Hubert and Forge, 1969, p. 110).

A further dimension of kin relationships, which again points to the negotiated character of obligations, is their emotional content. The closeness and intimacy which kin relations allow, but do not necessarily promote, is very likely to have some bearing upon whether obligations are honoured or not although precisely how this operates is a complex issue which sociologists often have not addressed very effectively. I would be inclined to the same view as Harris on this difficult and important issue, namely that obligations cannot be explained solely *by* sentiment, nor can they be adequately explained *without reference* to it (Harris, 1983, p. 13). It seems prudent to acknowledge that the negotiated character of obligations derives partly from the quality of relationships between specific individuals, even if it is difficult to find research strategies for studying how that operates.

Linking the two accounts

I would argue that these two alternative ways of conceptualising family obligations – as moral norms and as negotiated agreements – offer a useful basic framework within which to develop an empirical study of such obligations. However, I would not in any way regard them as mutually exclusive or competing explanations. Indeed, it seems to me that some of the most interesting and important questions for empirical study derive from considering the relationship *between* norms and negotiations. I shall indicate briefly some of the ways in which the two accounts need to be linked together and contextualised in order to develop a coherent framework for understanding family obligations.

First, it is important to focus on the way in which moral rules are put to use in concrete situations (rather than simply to consider their normative content) and this includes importantly the use of rules in negotiations between specific individuals. In what ways do people make use of normative statements to develop or to explain their conduct (including anticipated conduct) towards their relatives?

The emphasis here on explaining conduct, as well as the actions themselves, is important. Indeed I see the process of reaching negotiated commitments over time as a process which is centrally concerned with each individual developing an account of his or her own conduct which is coherent in terms of relevant normative rules, and therefore acceptable as a public account of conduct. In focusing in this way on the use of rules and especially upon their use in constructing accounts of action, I am drawing on an underlying set of ideas in which moral rules are seen as part of the repertoire of resources which human beings can make use of in constructing social meanings. This draws upon an intellectual tradition which rejects the idea that normative rules can be used as an explanation of human conduct (conceiving of such conduct as rule-governed behaviour) in favour of the study of the rules themselves and how they operate in social life, using normative rules as a topic of study rather than a resource (e.g. Douglas, 1971; Wieder, 1974b; Cunningham-Burley, 1985).

Second, this way of conceptualising obligations can be seen as an exercise in the sociology of motivation, which also focuses upon how moral norms are put to use. This perspective draws upon Wright Mills' work on 'vocabularies of motive' and especially his argument that, when a person confesses motives for a particular act (past, present or future), she or he is using a vocabulary which provides an acceptable justification for that conduct (Wright Mills, 1940; Gerth and Wright Mills, 1954). That justification has to be developed by using the particular vocabulary of motives which is acceptable in a given social context and regarded as relevant to the situation in question. The importance of being able to present one's actions in these terms may be such that, in Wright Mills's view, the action itself is determined by them. Thus the question 'If I did this, what would I say?' looms very large and 'Decisions to perform or not to perform a given act may be wholly or in part set by the socially available answers to such queries' (Gerth and Wright Mills, 1954, p. 116).

Third, any rounded account of obligations or responsibilities and how they operate between kin in practice must place the relevant individuals within the context of social and economic structures. In particular, it must include an understanding of power and how it operates at both an interpersonal and at a structural level. It is of course a classic criticism of the interactionist concept of 'negotiation' of social meanings that this fails to take into account questions of power (Strauss, 1978), and in studying the negotiaton of family obligations one clearly cannot operate on the assumption that all parties to the negotiation begin from a position of equality. In particular I see the operation of patriarchal power in families as significant here, making the position of women and men very different in negotiation about family obligations. This is a matter both of the position of each within social and economic structures and of interpersonal power. For example, while women are either out of the labour market, or in a disadvantaged labour market position by comparison with men, economic considerations will continue to make them look like the obvious people to take on the unpaid work of caring for others, as I have argued elsewhere (Finch, 1984). At the same time at an interpersonal level the nature of patriarchal relations enables, for example, men to delegate certain kinds of tasks to women, especially tasks which involve taking care of other people (Rose, 1981; Stacey, 1981).

Fourth, an understanding of moral norms themselves needs to be socially contextualised since these are not simply a matter of personal preference or arrived at solely by processes of independent reasoning but are themselves socially constructed and subject to change over time (Halsey, 1985).

In the context of family obligations, I find the concept of 'public morality' a very useful way of handling these issues. This approach has been developed most influentially by Voysey (1975) in relation to her study of families with a handicapped child, and itself draws upon the idea that rules of conduct are used in social life to construct meanings and to develop accounts of conduct which will be seen by others as both legitimate and plausible. In many life situations social actors are faced with the need to construct accounts of their actions which will offend the least number of people. They therefore rely upon what Douglas (1971) calls the 'least common denominator morality', which Voysey herself refers to as the 'public morality', that which is produced and sustained within the public domain and by official agencies, and is an important part of producing social order (Voysey, 1975, pp. 40–43). It seems to me that this concept of public morality offers a way of locating particular sets of normative rules in relation to social and economic structures, whilst at the same time offering a way of understanding how such beliefs are used by social actors in an active way, rather than seeing them as simply imposed on individuals (as, for example, some of the cruder concepts of 'dominant ideology' would imply).

In relation to the study of family obligations, it means that it is important both to understand what the content of this 'public morality' actually is with respect to responsibilities between relatives, how it is reproduced and reinforced and what sets of interests it represents; but also to understand how individuals make reference to it, and make use of it, in negotiating their own commitments to their kin. Public policies and the actions of public agencies assume a particular importance in these processes, in that they form part of the structure of constraints within which individuals conduct their own negotiations, restricting or expanding the range of alternatives available. Thus, negotiations about giving support to one's elderly parents look rather different in a situation where there is a legal obligation on children financially to maintain their parents, as there was in Britain until 1948 (Anderson, 1977; Wall, 1977), than in a situation where no such legal obligation exists.

The life course perspective on family obligations

Having sketched out the basic framework which I consider to be appropriate for conceptualising family obligations and studying them, I shall now move on to consider how this approach can be informed by a life course perspective.

What is a 'life course perspective'? I take the concept of life course to mean something different from that of life cycle, and to reject the notion of individual progression through a series of fairly fixed and predictable life stages, in favour of a more complex notion of individual progression through a life span which admits more variation in patterns of experience. In relation to studies of the family, it also involves rejecting the very static notion of different stages of the 'family life cycle', in favour of a perspective which attempts to understand individual and family biographies in relation to the specific historical time in which they are occurring (Morgan, 1985, pp. 177-9). A central and influential formulation of this is to be found in Hareven's (1978a) discussion of family time and historical time, which focuses upon transitions within families, and attempts to address questions about the timing of transitions (into marriage, childbearing, retirement and so on) through two different comparisons: first, the alignment of individual time with family time, and the extent to which individual timetables need to be co-ordinated; second, a comparison with those issues of timing in different historical periods, which leads her into an argument about how far economic and social structures determine the flexibility available in the timing of family transitions.

In relation to the study of family obligations, the central idea which I take from this perspective is the importance of time, and the need to inject the perspective of time in a variety of ways into our understanding of how such obligations operate. I shall develop this by looking at the two contrasting elements of my model of obligations – norms and negotiations – and asking how the perspective of time can inform each of these.

NORMS AND THE LIFE COURSE PERSPECTIVE

In this section, I shall suggest three main ways – by no means necessarily exhaustive – in which the concept of time as understood within the life course perspective can refine our understanding of obligations as normative rules.

The first of these is the potentially very fruitful concept of normative timetables, and how they shape both individual time and family time. At the most general level, this is a question about the social meaning of chronological age. Despite the fact that age is frequently treated as an unproblematic 'variable' in social research, we need above all to understand the social context which gives chronological age its meaning and also, as I have argued elsewhere, to see age as marking the progress of individuals through biological and through historical time (Finch, 1986; see also Hareven, 1978a, p. 59). Within this context, the concept of normative timetables refers to cultural definitions of the 'right age' to marry, to leave the parental home, to have children or whatever. As Hareven points out, normative timetables are themselves subject to change and re-definition over historical time, and therefore what counts as a violation of the 'normal' sequence will also vary (Hareven, 1978a, p. 59).

In applying the concept of normative timetables to the issue of family obligations, it seems to me that this suggests one way of understanding why an apparently generalised normative rule may be brought into play in certain circumstances but not in others. Does, for example, the general normative prescription that 'parents should continue to assist their young adult children financially if they can' cease to operate when young people reach a point where the normative timetable suggests that they should be standing on their own two feet by now, whatever their specific needs actually are? If so, is that point defined by chronological age, by biographical events (it can be delayed if the young person is in full-time education, advanced if he or she marries young, and so on) or more individually and idiosyncratically? More generally, the concept of normative timetables may offer one way of understanding how normative rules about obligations to kin are related to biographical events in a patterned and predictable way. One would of course expect these to be gendered in character and to apply differentially to women and men.

A second area in which the life course perspective illuminates the idea of obligations as normative rules is by raising questions about the alignment between individual time and family time. In Hareven's view, in the past there was a much more pressing need to synchronise family timetables than is usually the case now. Most people could not afford to have individual time and family time poorly aligned because the economic well-being and survival of family members depended on the family group being able to deliver effective mutual assistance. Thus decisions such as when an individual would marry or retire from work needed to be synchronised carefully. Only in the relatively recent past, when certain economic and welfare functions have been taken outside the family, has the timing of transitions taken on a voluntary and a more individual character (Hareven, 1978a). Hareven's argument thus suggests some important questions about normative rules about family obligations in contemporary societies. Is there a continuing expectation that individuals will synchronise life decisions with reference to the interests and needs of their kin, and if so, which kin? Or are we in fact living in a period of historical time in which life decisions need not take into account the needs of one's kin, save perhaps those of one's spouse and immature children?

A third area in which the life course perspective illuminates a study of family obligations is by firmly locating the study of normative rules within historical time, by indicating that the character of the normative rules themselves is a product of particular historical circumstances. In a way this point is self-evident but it does highlight the importance of documenting the prevailing normative consensus – if such there be – at a particular point of historical time, before one can understand the way in which normative rules are used by individuals in negotiating their own relationships with kin. Further, one needs to know how far there is a discernible attempt in a given historical period to impose a specific normative structure on a population which may not uniformly find it acceptable, and in what ways individuals handle that in their own negotiations with kin.

NEGOTIATIONS AND THE LIFE COURSE PERSPECTIVE

The concept of negotiations itself introduces a time perspective centrally into the framework which I have outlined for studying family obligations. As I have already indicated, I see negotiations not so much as events which take place in specific circumstances when a decision has to be made, as long-term interactions through which individuals develop commitments to honour certain types of obligation if the circumstances arise. This approach to negotiation implies – and perhaps needs to make explicit – that the circumstances of individual biographies, and the history of specific sets of social relations, are of profound significance in understanding why particular patterns of obligations become 'obvious', in the way in which I illustrated in my hypothetical example at the beginning of this chapter. I shall focus here upon two characteristics of the negotiations of family obligations over the life course, namely that they are both cumulative and reciprocal.

Obligations built up over the life course have to be viewed as cumulative but not in the simple sense that people gather more and more obligations as they go along which can never be shed. Rather the history of particular relationships, along with biographical events, both shape and restrict the range of choices which are open at a given point in time and thus a certain course of action becomes, or is experienced as, unavoidable. It is merely the obvious next step in the circumstances.

I am using the concept of cumulative obligations here in a sense analogous with Becker's (1960) discussion of commitments and how these are built up over time. In both cases, the process is not necessarily conscious or deliberate. Nonetheless over a period of time an individual develops a line of action which has a certain consistency and predictability until a point is reached where, as Becker puts it, it becomes too 'expensive' to withdraw because personal identity and social reputation have been invested in it. A common example in relation to family obligations would be the case of a daughter who initially takes on small tasks for her elderly mother such as occasional shopping or washing, and then gradually gives more and more support until a point is reached when she is giving full-time care without ever having made a conscious decision to do so. To withdraw at that stage, however, would involve a serious disruption of her personal identity as a reliable and caring daughter, built up over many years. In this kind of example, the cumulative consequences of both individual biographies and of patterns of social relations earlier in the life course are central to understanding the exchange of services between kin at a particular point in time (for empirical examples, see for example Evers, 1985).

The second feature of the time perspective which I shall highlight here concerns the operation of the principle of reciprocity. As I indicated earlier, this is usually taken to be a key principle in kin relations, with the idea of mutual aid in many ways defining the distinctive character of the kin group. Here again, the life course perspective, and especially the focus on a pattern of exchanges over time, is important in understanding how reciprocity operates between kin in particular. The main distinction to be drawn here is between reciprocity which operates in a direct way, where the givers are also the receivers within the same relationship, and reciprocity which operates more diffusely, where a 'giver's' anticipation of getting something in return may not be a direct expectation placed on the 'receiver', but applies to a return from another 'giver' in a different time and place. One way of expressing this is the distinction between 'balanced' and 'generalised' reciprocity, where balanced reciprocity implies some fairly immediate and equivalent return, whereas generalised reciprocity is less specific about what should be returned and when, and is capable of tolerating a one-way flow over a long period of time. It is commonly argued that close kin relations are the most likely social relations in which one finds generalised reciprocity (Sahlins, 1965; Lévi-Strauss, 1969).

Understanding reciprocal exchanges between kin may therefore involve a very long time scale, with obligations being honoured in the present as a result of assistance received many years in the past, and perhaps from some different person. The accounting mechanisms through which individuals keep a check on the balance of exchanges are probably very difficult to uncover (Leira, 1984). However these processes may well form the basis for discrimination between different kin in the same genealogical position, in terms of the assistance offered to each, on grounds of their reputation built up over time. It may well be that in some circumstances, the question of how well an individual has fulfilled what was expected of him or her in the past may be crucial in determining whether he or she has a 'right to expect' assistance from relatives in the present. Equally, a particular act of generosity to a third party in the past may entitle that person to expect fairly generous treatment themselves, perhaps especially from the close relatives of that third party.

Finally, in understanding the nature of reciprocal exchanges between kin over time, one needs to know which actions get defined as part of a pattern of exchanges and which do not. There is some evidence that such definitions themselves may change over the life course. In his interesting study of three-generation families in the United States, Hill uncovered a pattern whereby the oldest generation (who on balance were likely to be receiving more than they gave) tended to classify this help as a 'gift', and also to classify any help which they gave as gifts. The middle generation, who gave more to both the older and the younger generation than they received from either, classified themselves as 'givers' when they were offering assistance, but when they were receiving it, they classified this as exchange. The youngest generation (young adults, who scored high on both giving and receiving) defined help both given and received as exchanges not gifts (although sometimes as 'loans') (Hill, 1970, pp. 69–79). One possible underlying theme here is that the normative timetables of exchange between kin take account of how far an individual is likely to be able to reciprocate in the future and can tolerate a one-way flow more readily for an elderly person who cannot be 'expected' to reciprocate, provided that they have done what was expected of them in the past.

However one must never forget that hidden but ultimate counter-gift: inheritance. How significant is the expectation of inheritance in keeping up the flow of services to the end of an individual's life is one important, if sensitive and difficult, area which any study of the negotiation of obligations clearly has to take into account.

CONCLUSION

I have used this chapter to set out the main features of a theoretical framework for the study of family obligations which should, in my view, assist our understanding of underlying social processes, not merely describe patterns of exchange. The central feature of this framework is understanding the relationship between the normative and the negotiated elements of obligations.

In considering how the concept of the life course should be incorporated in this framework, it becomes clear that this injects vital elements which both elaborate and enrich our understanding of how family obligations operate in reality. The concept of the life course, as elaborated especially in the work of Hareven, provides a rich source of ideas and analytical principles with which to approach this topic, principally because it directs our attention to the importance of that classic sociological project which, as Mills put it, entails understanding the relationship between biography and history (Wright Mills, 1959). The study of family obligations is centrally concerned with the biographies of individuals and how they are woven together within the kin group in particular. But equally important is an understanding of the social, political and economic contexts in which obligations are negotiated, honoured or abandoned. This makes the study of family obligations part of the central sociological task of understanding what Abrams has called 'the puzzle of human agency'. As he puts it, we have to find some way of accounting for human experience which acknowledges that at the same time 'history and society are made by constant and more or less purposeful human action and that individual action, however purposeful, is made by history and society' (Abrams, 1982, p. xiii). The importance of this insight is well illustrated by those human experiences to which I have given the label family obligations.

NOTES

1. Findings from this study are not discussed here. I am grateful for the support of the Economic and Social Research Council, who are funding this project under the title 'Family Obligations: Social Construction and Social Policy'. The central purpose of the research is to examine the nature and operation of obligations to provide practical and material assistance between relatives outside the nuclear family, and to compare how these operate in reality with assumptions made about them in social policy. The project is concentrating upon three broad types of obligation: providing personal care; giving or lending money or other substantial forms of material assistance; offering a home on a temporary or permanent basis. The empirical work is in two stages: a large-scale survey and a small-scale qualitative study. Both fieldwork stages are located in Greater Manchester. The project is of four years' duration and began in April 1985.

2. I am using 'family obligations' as a convenient shorthand term, although I recognise that it is imprecise. My particular interest is in obligations between adult kin, but excluding spouses, where I believe that different and additional sets of considerations come into play, based on concepts of the marriage relationship and what it entails. The kind of 'obligations' which I have in mind would include, for example, looking after one's elderly parents, lending money to one's sister or offering one's adult children a roof over their heads.

10 The Effect of Life Cycle on Three Dimensions of Stratification

Angela Dale

INTRODUCTION

Stratification is a key concept of sociology. Traditionally, it has been linked in sociological theory to employment and occupation and, while relationship to the system of production is clearly one of the fundamental forces structuring society, the purpose of this chapter is to consider the effect of the life cycle on three distinct but related dimensions by which society may be stratified.

Previous studies have traced class mobility over several points in men's working lives (Goldthorpe, 1980), and pointed out the importance of recognising the existence of occupational trajectories over time (Stewart *et al.*, 1980), but little attention has been given to the effects of the life cycle stage on a multi-dimensional model of stratification. While the importance of the life cycle has been recognised in the poverty literature since Rowntree (1902, p. 136) identified 'five alternating periods of want and comparative plenty' in his York study (Townsend, 1979; O'Higgins and Bradshaw, 1984), there has been little attempt to carry over this life cycle approach into research on stratification. This chapter sets out to make that attempt.

Life cycle will be represented as the life cycle of the family, involving, for the majority of people, marriage, childbirth, care of children until their independence, and, finally, a period of old-age during which women are likely to outlive their husbands. However, this is not to ignore the fact that not all individuals move through this idealised form of life cycle and that a household may contain two or more families at different life cycle stages.

The three dimensions of stratification considered here are all causally related and often overlapping, but each is independently influenced by life cycle stage. They are: access to the labour market; net disposable household income; and household assets of the kind that can be turned into wealth, time or opportunity. Figure 10.1 shows a flow diagram of the hypothesised relationships between these dimensions. For example, a newly married couple are both likely to be in full-time employment, although if they then have children the total number of hours which they work will probably fall, as will their disposable income; at the same time, the family may feel the need to acquire a car or a washing machine to cope with the extra demands of children. Thus stage of life cycle can directly affect location on each of these three dimensions of stratification.

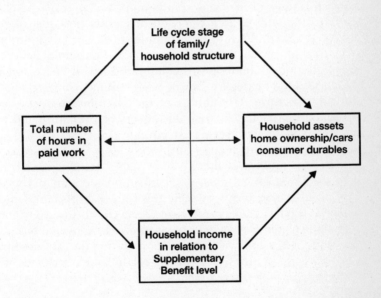

Figure 10.1   Relationship between life cycle, access to paid work, income and household assets

Most households, about 90 per cent, contain only one nuclear family and for these the life cycle stage of the family can be represented by the household; however, a proportion of households contain two or more families who are at different stages of the life cycle – for example an elderly widow may join the household of her married daughter and family. In these circumstances the stratificatory effect of life cycle stage will be mediated by household structure (for example, the elderly widow who lives with her married daughter is likely to be in a household with a far higher level of household income and assets than would be the case if she were living alone).[1] Because the theme of this book is the life cycle, this chapter will be primarily concerned with those households which contain a single family located at a particular life cycle stage. Complex households, containing families which span several generations will, for completeness, be included in the initial categorisation, but are dropped thereafter. An earlier version of this chapter which contains all household categories is available from the author.

Generally, stage of life cycle results in a particular household structure, although variations may occur within the same stage; for instance, one and two parent families are both at the same stage of the life cycle. For this reason the household will be taken as the unit of analysis throughout and it will be assumed that each life cycle category can be represented by a particular household structure. An analysis of the relationships between the productive activity, income and assets of the household is then possible for each life cycle category.

Firstly, a full classification of all households will be presented, followed by a typology of the life cycle stages being used. Then each of the three dimensions of stratification mentioned above will be discussed in terms of their theoretical importance and the way in which they vary with life cycle. Data from the General Household Survey will be used to relate each aspect of stratification to the life cycle categories used. Finally, an attempt will be made to synthesise the inter-relationship between life cycle and each of the three dimensions of stratification.

DATA SOURCE

The data used is the General Household Survey (GHS) for 1979. The GHS is a continuous government survey with a nationally representative achieved sample of about 10 000 households. As its name suggests, it takes the household as its unit of analysis and collects data both at the level of the household – housing tenure, number of cars, consumer durables – and also at the level of the individual – income, employment. In 1979 the GHS contained a detailed section on housing costs, rent and rate rebates, as well as a very extensive income section in which both net and gross income from employment were recorded, and income from all other sources, including investments and property.

THE HOUSEHOLD AS THE UNIT OF ANALYSIS

While it is appropriate to analyse the relationship of the *individual* to the labour market on the basis of occupation (Dale *et al.*, 1985), it is none the less necessary to remember that the labour market power of any individual is either enhanced or restricted by the sexual division of labour within the home. Women who are responsible for the domestic care of children and family enter the labour market with less power than men who are free from such commitments. Thus paid work must be understood in the context of the household. Hareven (1982, p. 204) in her study of Amoskeag at the turn of the century found that 'women who worked outside the home viewed their factory labor and their domestic tasks as complementary, if not interchangeable. It was all part of their collective family enterprise. Their domestic responsibility – the care of the children, the clothing of family members, the feeding of the family and often boarders as well – was itself a form of production.' Recent UK studies have also shown that decisions about employment tend, particularly by women, to be taken in the context of the needs and earning capacity of other household members (Epstein *et al.*, 1986) and have argued for the need to take the household as the unit of production (Hunt, 1980; Yeandle, 1984). The role of the household is well summarised by Mingione (1985, p. 24):

The unit of reproduction (the household) disposes above all of working capacities which, with a limited freedom of choice, conditioned by the historical phases of development and by the socio-cultural background of the unit, it can apply either to working activities that provide a monetary income with which to purchase goods and services for subsistence, or to working activities that directly provide goods and services useful for subsistence (activities for self-consumption or domestic work). Furthermore, the unit may also be able to count on resources from outside, such as assistance from the State or from public bodies (in terms of income or of services and goods).

For these reasons it is appropriate for an analysis which is concerned with the variation in relationship to the systems of both production and consumption at different life cycle stages to take the household as the unit of analysis. Firstly, however, the full categorisation of households will be described, followed by the life cycle categories to be used in the analysis.

A TYPOLOGY OF FAMILY LIFE CYCLE AND HOUSEHOLD STRUCTURE

Table 10.1 shows a categorisation of all households, ordered approximately by age, and gives a brief description of each. The relative size of each household category is given in the middle column. The main groups which do not easily fit into a simple life cycle stage are those which contain two or three generations (G and I).

The categorisation is based on the assumption that the key events in the family cycle are leaving home, getting married, child-bearing and child-rearing, the children leaving home and, finally, old-age and death. Incorporated into this framework are the age-related norms associated with leaving school and entering and leaving the labour market. The age of 35 has been taken as a rather arbitrary point by which to divide couples without dependent children into those who have not yet had any (and may or may not be planning to have any), and those whose children are no longer defined as 'dependent'.[2] The older category will, of course, also contain those who have never had children. For those who are not married, the age of 35 again forms a rough division point between those who have never been married, and those who are separated, widowed or divorced.

Table 10.1   A categorisation of households

Household structure	% all households	Description
A One person household, age <35	2.5	60% male; 80% single
B Two or more non-married adults in household	3.1	Some may be co-habiting couples
C Couple under 35, no children	4.5	These mainly represent couples at a pre-family stage
D Couple with one or more dependent children	25.3	
E One parent – no other adults in the household	2.5	82% are female: the majority aged 23–40; 82% are divorced or separated
F One parent with other adult	1.4	The other adult may be a co-habitee, an adult child or a widowed or divorced mother
G Couple with dependent children + elderly person	0.5	The elderly person is typically the wife's widowed mother
H Couple + dependent children + non-dependent 'children'	6.3	A few 'non-dependent children are other relative' or lodgers
I Non-elderly adults, single or married + elderly person	4.9	Most contain an elderly couple or widow with an adult 'child' living at home
J Couple with non-dependent 'child(ren)'	6.7	A few 'non-dependent children' are other relatives or lodgers
K One person household, 35 and over but not elderly	5.7	Men and women are equally represented; women – 49% are widowed; men – 48% single; 30% divorced or separated
L Couple 35 and over, no children in the household	12.8	Non-elderly couples whose children have left home or who are childless
M Elderly couple	9.4	Includes some elderly not married
N One elderly person	14.5	80% are female; 80% are widowed
Total all households	100.0	(11,486)

Definitions for Table 10.1

Couple The term couple is used for those describing themselves as married.

Parent A parent always has a dependent child.

Elderly Elderly is defined as over 60 for a woman and over 65 for a man. A couple is defined as elderly where the husband is over 65.

Couple 35 and over The age is that of the oldest member of the couples; the couple is not elderly.

Dependent child A dependent child is under 16, or under 19 if still in full-time education.

Household In the GHS 1979 a household consists of those who live at the same address and share at least one meal each day.

However, the same life cycle stage may be found in different forms – one parent families form a parallel stage to couples with dependent children, while lone adults of 35 and over may parallel couples of that age without children at home.

Some categories span more than one generation – for example groups G and I in Table 10.1 combine those of retirement age with younger people. Obviously not all people move through the stages outlined here and the length of time spent in any one stage will vary for different individuals. Many of the categories identified by the cross-sectional data used here will represent transitory states through which families move. As Hareven (1982, p. 154) aptly remarks, households are like a revolving stage, with members appearing and disappearing, either under their own momentum or under the impact of external conditions. Furthermore, families may, over time, break up and be reconstituted (Burgoyne and Clark, 1981); therefore what is shown here is no more than a snap-shot picture of a nationally representative sample of households at one point in time.

Table 10.2 shows those categories that represent fairly discrete life cycle stages; these will form the basis for the rest of the analysis. Although the typology is presented in the form of a cycle, the data used here are cross-sectional and longitudinal inferences *cannot* be made from them. For example, it cannot be inferred that those currently middle-aged will, when they become elderly, hold the characteristics of the elderly groups in this analysis. The data therefore confound life cycle effects with cohort effects.

Table 10.2   A typology of family life cycle

Life cycle stage	No. of households
1. One adult less than 35	291
2. Couple less than 35, no children in the household	516
3. Couple with dependent child(ren)	2908
3a. One parent – no other adults	282
4. Couple with dependent and non-dependent 'child(ren)'	724
5. Couple with non-dependent 'child(ren)'	764
6. Couple, 35 and over, no children in the household	1471
6a. One person 35 or over but not elderly	649
7. Elderly couple	1084
8. One elderly person	1670

These 10 life-cycle categories represent 90% of all households.

ACCESS TO PAID WORK

Access to paid work is not only the means by which most members of society provide for themselves and their families but also has more far-reaching effects. Thus Pahl (1984, p. 334) shows that, in the Isle of Sheppey, 'households with members in employment are most likely to engage in all other forms of work, and the reverse is the case in households where no one is in employment. There is a kind of ratchet effect, so that once households get into a benign spiral upwards their collective efforts keep them there.' He goes on to point out that this can occur only at certain stages of the domestic cycle.

Thus households without any wage-earners may become distanced from those with two or more earners not just on the basis of current income from employment, but over a more wide-ranging basis that incorporates aspects of self-provisioning. These lines of cleavage in the stratificatory system, based upon access to paid work are, as Pahl suggests, directly related to life cycle stage and household structure. While for the individual, age is important in determining access to paid work, at the level of the household the number of members in paid work varies in a more complex way, with life cycle stage. For example, the compulsory state retirement age may be seen as an exclusionary mechanism which restricts the elderly from activities enjoyed by the working population (Midwinter, 1985). In other types of household, for example those of lone parents, access to the labour market will be restricted by the demands of child-care, reinforced by a state philosophy that makes child-care the individual responsibility of women (for example by the very limited provision of day-care). This restricted access to paid work will have repercussions not just on current patterns of income and assets but will also carry through into old age by affecting the amount and availability of an occupational pension.

Whether paid work is inaccessible through age or through unemployment, this effect is likely to influence other household members. Thus wives of unemployed men are less likely to work than wives of employed men (Moylan *et al.*, 1984; Rapoport and Sierakowski, 1982), while over 50 per cent of unemployed men under 25 are in families containing at least one other unemployed person (White, 1985). The young unemployed are likely to have unemployed parents (Jones, 1986) while the wives of men who define themselves as 'early retired' are less likely to be in paid work than the wives of employed men of the same age (Laczko, 1986).

At the older end of the age-spectrum early retirement schemes have meant that a growing proportion of men from 55 onwards are no longer in the labour market (Laczko and Walker, 1985) and, although perhaps nominally having taken voluntary retirement, the pressure upon older workers to leave the way open to the young is an influential factor in determining labour market participation. While retirement is obviously related to stage of life cycle, unemployment is also disproportionately likely to be found at certain points in the life cycle (the single young) and among particular social groups, for example older men who are separated or divorced (Haskey, 1983). Lack of access to paid employment will obviously have effects on both income and household assets; this effect will be mediated by life cycle and household composition.

Although the number of people in the household who are in paid work will vary with life cycle stage, there is also variation in work hours between household members. A substantial proportion of women with dependent children will be working part-time, and some young people may be doing only occasional

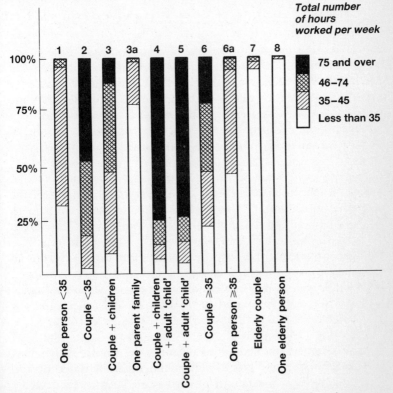

Figure 10.2   Total number of hours worked per week by life cycle stage

or part-time work. To allow these differences to be taken into account household participation in paid work is measured by the total number of hours worked per week by all household members. This is shown in Figure 10.2. The greatest number of hours worked are in households with a couple and an adult 'child'. Couples who are under 35 without children have more hours in paid work than couples with children, who, in turn, have substantially more than one-parent households. The impact of early retirement policies may also be seen among couples over 35 without children.

Clearly, participation in the labour market has considerable influence upon the amount of income which a household has at its disposal. In the following section the importance of household income as a basis for stratification is discussed.

NET DISPOSABLE HOUSEHOLD INCOME

Net disposable income represents the current spending power of the household after taking into account the 'basic needs' of household members – that is, the amount each household would be entitled to claim as Supplementary Benefit. While income generally represents the rewards accruing from a particular relationship to the productive system – either in the form of wages paid for labour, rent gained from property or interest from capital assets, it may also be paid by the state, either acting as the agency for a contributory insurance scheme, as with unemployment benefit, or as a welfare agency, in the case of supplementary benefits. Income from employment accounts for an increasingly small proportion of household resources in Western Europe and North America (Rose, 1985); therefore any measure of income must incorporate that from all sources, not just paid employment.

Although the level of net disposable income within a household will be strongly related to the number of earners and the jobs which they hold, there is also a life cycle effect which is independent of number of earners. By using a standardised form of income that takes into account the number of household members, those households which contain more dependants will have a lower level of disposable income for a given gross income, than households with no dependants.

Income figures will be expressed as current weekly net household income in relation to the long-term DHSS Supplementary Benefit level, and take the form of a percentage, with those households at SB level having a value of 100 per cent, and all those below SB level having values of less than 100 per cent. Conversely, a household at 200 per cent of SB level would have twice the amount of income than it would be entitled to under the SB regulations of 1979. Although the assessment unit used by the DHSS does not necessarily correspond to the household, the entitlement of each assessment unit within the household has been calculated and summed. This form of standardised income therefore controls for the size and composition of the household.

The use of this standardised measure of income is not without its problems. Firstly, it sets arbitrary amounts on the income needs of people of different ages and may underestimate the needs of children by comparison with adults (Berthoud, 1985).[3] It also fails to make any attempt to take into account regional differences in prices, or class based spending customs (Kincaid, 1979). Other problems include the impossibility of taking into account fringe benefits and payment in kind, gifts and personal services (Townsend 1974).

None the less, as a means of making standardised comparisons of the resources available for consumption, across different types of family or household, it is of value and has been very extensively used as a measure of poverty (e.g. Layard, 1978; Bradshaw, 1984). Furthermore, as this standardised form of income is being used as a means of *comparing* the resources available rather than making a judgement about poverty levels, the short-comings outlined above have less importance; it is only where there are systematic differences between sectors of society that these short-comings will cause problems – for example, the resources of white-collar workers may be systematically undervalued *vis-à-vis* manual workers if the former group receive fringe benefits of a greater value than the latter group.

It should be stressed that this measure represents *current* income (although in those cases where this differs from usual income the latter has been used as a more reliable measure). Current income gives no information about earnings over a lifetime; and, although interest on savings and investments can be included, there is no available information on the value of, for example, share-holdings or on investments as paintings and jewellery.

The relationships between life cycle and paid employment and household income are complex. Non-contributory state benefits, such as child benefit, represent a form of income which is related to life cycle but which does not vary with number of earners. Other non-contributory benefits such as supplementary benefit are negatively related to paid employment in the sense that they are only paid in the absence of other earnings, but the level at which they are paid is partially related to stage of life cycle.

Many elderly people, having reached retirement age, are entirely dependent upon the state for income provision. Those who have managed to accumulate money and assets during their working lives or who have an occupational pension that lifts them above a subsistence income are able to carry through into retirement the inequalities of the occupational structure (Walker, 1980). Among the elderly, there are gender-based differences in net disposable household income which again reflect the inequality in access to paid work during a previous life cycle stage.

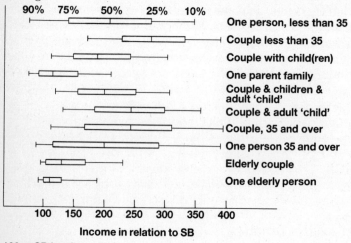

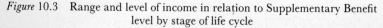

Figure 10.3   Range and level of income in relation to Supplementary Benefit level by stage of life cycle

The use of this household level measure of income makes no assumptions about its distribution *within* the household. It has been well established that there are considerable gender-based inequalities within households (Delphy 1984; Land 1983; Pahl, 1983) which may be manifest either through distribution of income or decisions over expenditure. However, the level and range of disposable income available at different stages of the life cycle sets the parameters within which that income may be distributed and, furthermore, gives an indication of the relative amount of income available for consumption at different life cycle stages.

Figure 10.3 shows the level and distribution of income by life cycle stage. The elderly and one parent families have the lowest median income levels, and also the most restricted range of income. Women predominate among both the lone elderly and lone parents – 80 per cent and 82 per cent respectively are women. These low levels of income result from a lack of access to paid work (or occupational pensions deriving from it) and a consequent reliance upon fixed levels of state benefits. By contrast, the greatest dispersion of income, although not the highest median level, is found among lone adults of 35 and over (where men and women are equally represented), and couples of 35 and over without dependent children. Within both these groups the dispersion results mainly from differences in rewards from paid work although both contain a sizeable proportion of households where no-one is in employment. Highest median income levels are found among couples younger than 35 who have no children, rather than among those households which are most likely to contain three earners. This is explained by the fact that in the former case both members of the couple are likely to be in full-time work, paid at adult rates; however, in the three earners households, both the wife and the adult 'child' may be working for low wages or part-time and therefore contributing less per capita to the total household income. Generally, the stage of life cycle where median income levels are highest are where all adult members are of working age and there are no dependent children.

HOUSEHOLD ASSETS

So far, the household has been considered as the unit within

which a group of people live together within the same accommodation and form both a productive and reproductive unit.
However, the household is also the unit of consumption – in
terms of the household assets used in this analysis. Again, this
does not imply that there is an equality of distribution of resources within the household; for example Land (1983) has
shown that the allocation of space may be very unequal; also,
married women have lower levels of access to cars than married
men (Dale, 1986). None the less, while these important distinctions must be remembered, it is only possible to analyse the
relationship between production, consumption and life cycle at
the level of the family/household. Thus Beechey (1978, p. 194)
refers to the family as the 'primary locus of consumption, which
is essential to the circulation of commodities in the capitalist
mode of production'.

Those household assets used here are all of the kind that may
be converted into some form of wealth or income, time or opportunity. As Figure 10.1 shows, they may directly affect level of
household income and may in some cases (e.g. cars) affect the
number of people in employment in the household. They differ
from aspects of consumption such as holidays, alcohol or
cigarettes which, while reflecting both spending power and
personal preferences, cannot be translated into a means of
wealth accumulation, cannot provide access to increased income or free time, and cannot extend employment opportunities. The assets used here may be acquired over a period of
time and therefore will not necessarily reflect current income.

Home Ownership

The importance of home ownership as a dimension of stratification is primarily related to its role as a source of capital
accumulation; however, it can also act as a focus of self-
provisioning (Pahl, 1984). Murie (1983, p. 168) argues that 'the
potential for accumulation of wealth through individual ownership is a factor maintaining social division'. 'Differences between owners and non-owners of dwellings are not simply
differences in type and value of dwelling in use, but are part of
inequalities in wealth' (Murie, 1983, p. 170). These inequalities
are manifest through inheritance, but also in the accumulation
of a capital asset through a life-time. As Payne and Payne

(1977, p. 132) point out, housing tenure represents an index of achieved life-chances involving 'the disposal of income for the purchase of rights over property'. Those who are living in similar housing conditions in the same tenure category share, in Weberian terms, a common status position and may also share similar life-styles.

Saunders (1984, p. i) has suggested that the division between state and owner-occupied housing may represent 'a long-term transition from a socialised to a privatised "mode of consumption" in Britain (which is) resulting in a major sectoral cleavage between a privileged majority of households who enjoy access to private provision, and an increasingly marginalised and "exploited" minority who remain reliant upon the state'. Saunders suggests that this line of cleavage may not only cut across conventional lines of class cleavage but may be more significant than class in its impact upon political alignments. The extent to which a cleavage along the lines suggested by Saunders coincides with the notion of polarisation based upon access to the labour market, suggested by Pahl is an interesting one which is partly addressed by the work of Sullivan and Murphy (1984). On the basis of data from the Family Formation Survey (FFS) they suggest that although lines of cleavage based upon tenure have, in the past, divided manual from non-manual workers, there is an increasing tendency for skilled manual workers to become owner occupiers, while those unable to achieve this status are most likely to be in low-paid and insecure employment, or to belong to a disadvantaged group with restricted access to the labour market – for example, one parent families.

It will be shown later that the extent of owner-occupation varies with stage of life cycle; however, it is important to remember that there is also likely to be a cohort effect reflecting the increasing availability of owner-occupied accommodation to younger age-groups. The results reported here inevitably conflate the effects of both cohort and life cycle.

Availability of private transport

Access to private transport makes possible a range of facilities and services that are otherwise severely restricted for most people. The unreliability and unavailability of public transport in many areas, and at various times of the day, means that there are considerable differences in opportunity between those with and without a car. Obvious examples include – the ability to visit a supermarket to get a week's shopping; the ability to visit friends, or go to the theatre and return home late at night; the difference in travelling time for the same journey using private and public transport. While the benefits to be gained from use of a car may accrue unevenly within the household, if the household is taken as the unit of analysis, then we are concerned with the total benefits to the household, irrespective of their distribution.

Stanton, Cahill and Howdle (1981) found that those groups with least access to private transport were the young, women, and the unskilled. They suggested that, with the decline in bus services, this would result in less mobility and poorer access to employment opportunities. Thus those households which depend upon members of these groups for their main income, particularly female-headed households, are likely to be particularly disadvantaged. There may therefore be a two-way relationship between income and car ownership (Figure 10.1) and also between numbers in paid work and car ownership.

Consumer durables

Consumer durables such as a freezer and a washing machine may lead to household economies in both time and money. Time freed from domestic work can be used either in paid employment or in leisure activities, thereby widening the gap between those who have such appliances and those who do not. The possession of a freezer allows bulk purchases to be made, resulting in both economies of scale and a decrease in time spent shopping. Central heating adds to the value of an owner-occupied home and also enables living accommodation to be used more effectively because of a comfortable temperature throughout.

All these household assets are not only directly influenced by level of net disposable income, they are also influenced by life cycle stage, past earnings and cohort. At an equivalent level of

	Household has –					
	Washing machine	Colour TV	Car	Central heating	Own house	Freezer
1. One person < 35	----	---	-	-	--	----
2. Couple < 35	+	*	++	+	++	+
3. Couple + child(ren)	++	++	+++	++	++	+++
3a. One parent family	*	-	---	*	---	--
4. Couple + child(ren) + adult 'child'	++	++	++	+++	*	+++
5. Couple + adult 'child'	++	++	++	*	*	+++
6. Couple, 35 and over	+	+	++	*	*	++
6a. One person 35 or over	---	--	--	-	--	---
7. Elderly couple	-	-	--	-	*	--
8. One elderly person	---	---	----	-	--	----

In each category of household, the percentage possessing each item are coded by comparison with the distribution for all households –

Key:
----   household falls into the range of the lowest 11% of all households
---
--
-
*   household falls in median range, between 44.5–55.5% of all households
+
++
+++
++++   household falls in the highest 11% of all households

Figure 10.4   Stage of life cycle by possession of household assets

income, households with young children are more likely to possess a car than are young single people. Similarly, tenure is related to life cycle, with local authority accommodation unlikely to be allocated to the single young, while owner occupation is most likely to be associated with marriage and the advent of children.

Consumer durables also vary with life cycle stage independently of income level, with families with young children being particularly likely to possess labour saving devices such as washing machines and freezers at a given level of net disposable income (Dale, 1985).

Figure 10.4 shows the level of each kind of asset by life cycle stage. It can be seen that possession of assets rises to a peak among couples with dependent children and then falls off again and is lowest amongst the lone elderly. Assets of the kind used here are acquired over a life-time and would not, therefore, be expected to relate directly to current income. None the less, it is noteworthy that the stage of having dependent children is related to a decline in disposable income together with an increase in household assets. Conversely, both the single under 35 and also couples under 35 have higher levels of net disposable income but lower levels of assets than families with children. However, one parent families, despite having the same life cycle requirements as couples with children, have markedly lower levels of assets.

Generally, levels of assets are lowest amongst households which contain only one person, or where the household is 'elderly'; combining these two factors gives the lone elderly the lowest levels of any group. Conversely, those households which contain a non-elderly married couple, particularly if they also have dependent children, have the highest levels of assets. It is likely that the low level of assets amongst the elderly reflects a cohort effect as well as a life cycle effect – for example home-ownership was less common amongst the elderly generation than it is amongst couples setting up home to-day; similarly, fewer consumer durables were available to this generation.

RELATIONSHIP BETWEEN STAGE OF FAMILY LIFE CYCLE, ACCESS TO PAID WORK, INCOME AND ASSETS

It has been argued that the three dimensions of stratification used here are all causally related but that they do not map exactly on to each other. Also, they all vary with stage of family life cycle. Figure 10.5 attempts to bring together all these factors into a single diagram. Each of the three dimensions of stratification has been approximately categorised into four groups – the dividing lines for each are given in the key – shaded from black (high) through to white (low). Each life cycle stage is represented by a section of the pie-chart proportional to the proportion of households represented by that stage.

For most life cycles stages there is no direct mapping of one dimension of stratification on to another. Generally different life cycle stages peak on different dimensions – thus total number of hours in paid work is highest amongst groups 2, 4 and 5, while assets are highest for groups 3 and 4 (both with dependent children). Couples under 35 without dependent children (2) are in the highest category for both income and hours in paid work, although their level of assets is lower than for families with children. One parent families (3a) and the elderly (7 and 8) have low levels on all three dimensions.

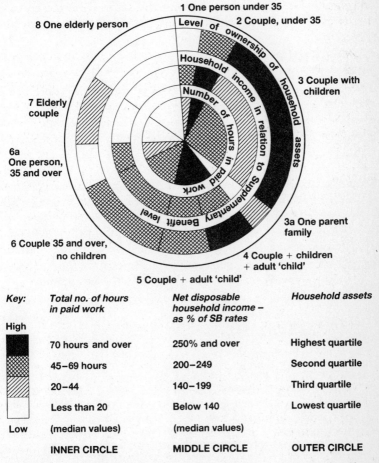

Key:	Total no. of hours in paid work	Net disposable household income – as % of SB rates	Household assets
High			
■	70 hours and over	250% and over	Highest quartile
▨	45–69 hours	200–249	Second quartile
▧	20–44	140–199	Third quartile
□	Less than 20	Below 140	Lowest quartile
Low	(median values)	(median values)	
	INNER CIRCLE	**MIDDLE CIRCLE**	**OUTER CIRCLE**

Figure 10.5   Relationship between family life-cycle, access to paid work income and household assets

It should be pointed out that this diagram is a very crude representation of an extremely complex patterning found within each life cycle stage. The choice of demarcation points are arbitrary and, within any one life cycle group there may be expected to be found considerable diversity.

Among both the lone elderly and one parent families, women are overwhelmingly found as the heads of household and it is these groups which have the lowest levels of income and assets. By comparison with groups at a comparable stage of life cycle but with a husband living in the household, the differences are marked.

CONCLUSION

Households may be stratified in terms of their ability to participate in paid work, their level of net disposable income and the extent to which they possess various household assets. While occupation remains the major influence causing class divisions and cleavages, the analysis presented here shows that, at the level of the household, there are major differences in the extent of access to an occupation, the total net disposable income, and the level of accumulated assets, which are associated with stage of life cycle. Because life cycle stage may also influence occupational position it is not possible to assume that the differences shown here are entirely free from the effects of occupation; none the less, stage of life cycle is an important factor in influencing the level of resources available to the household.

ACKNOWLEDGEMENTS

The research reported in this paper was funded by the ESRC under Grant number G0023139. I would like to thank the Office of Population Censuses and Surveys (OPCS) for allowing the use of the General Household Survey, and the ESRC Data Archive for making the data available. The data files used were prepared in SPSS form at the University of Surrey by Gilbert, O'Byrne, Arber and Dale. The analysis used the Crosslinker Program, written by Nigel Gilbert and available from the ESRC Data Archive.

I would also like to thank members of the Stratification and Employment Group, and also the DHSS Alvey Demonstrator Project at the University of Surrey for comments on an earlier draft of this chapter.

NOTES

1. No assumptions are made about the extent to which either income or household assets are shared by members of the household. The analysis is located at the level of the household and is not able to address the important issue of inequalities within the household.
2. A child is defined as dependent if under 16, or under 19 and still in full-time education.
3. The long-term SB rates used by the DHSS in 1979 gave £31.55 to a married couple. The equivalent rates for the DHSS and a similar rate employed by O'Higgins and Bradshaw are set out below:

DHSS, Scale rates, 1979		O'Higgins and Bradshaw, 1984	
Couple	1.0	Couple	1.0
Single householder	0.63	Adult	0.61
Single adult		Child 12–15	0.45
(non-householder)	0.51	5–11	0.35
Child 16–17 yrs	0.30	less than 5	0.25
13–15	0.25		
11–12	0.21		
5–10	0.17		
0–5	0.14		

The DHSS scale rates were used in the calculations presented in this paper. Others who have used similar methods of standardising income have used slightly different equivalence scales. Those scales which use higher values portray families with children as less well off *vis-à-vis* families without children than is the case using the DHSS scale rates.

11 The Life Cycle and the Labour Market in Hartlepool[1]

Lydia Morris

INTRODUCTION

Most individuals in negotiating a path through their biological and social development will enter into varied states of cooperation with, and incur numerous obligations towards, a number of other individuals, principally parents, mate(s) and children. The implications carried by specific events for the social groupings which emerge will vary with different types of decisions and problems characterising particular stages of life cycle development.

Thus, a sociological approach to the life cycle, domestic cycle or family cycle has traditionally and reasonably started from the assumption that at each stage of life the individual, family, and domestic group will be faced with different sorts of demands, and will be in a position to marshall different kinds of resources to confront them.

Pahl (1984) set out to document the 'work strategies' of households on the Isle of Sheppey asking: what *sorts* of labour do household members perform, and what *sources* of labour do they call upon? He makes the point that the household is a constantly changing social unit, and quickly reaches the conclusion that his preliminary thinking underestimated the importance of household composition and domestic cycle in the construction of a 'work strategy'. Hence he argues, the work provided by, and supplied to, different households is mediated by the intervening variable of stage in the domestic cycle:

In terms of patterns of work and sources of labour, household structure, especially as reflecting number of earners and domestic cycle, is more significant than social class. (Pahl, 1984, p. 23)

Writers have long acknowledged the importance of stage in the domestic cycle for labour market participation, manifest both through orientation to employment and availability for employment. Thus, the kind of job a 'family man' will require is different from that which he accepted as a youth; a woman with young children will be in a different labour market position from a childless young wife; etc.[2]

It is paid employment for women which has been most discussed in relation to the domestic cycle, stage in the cycle being used to account for movement in and out of work, and between full-time and part-time jobs. Whilst clearly not fully determining, it is an important factor affecting employment decisions, opportunities and prospects, although a wealth of historical material shows how financial need can override the constraints of the domestic cycle on women's participation in the labour market.[3]

Fagin's (1984) work on *un*employment has also applied a life cycle perspective, as a means of considering the ways in which family life may be affected by job loss. Specifically focusing on the difficulties faced in the nuclear family household, he argues that the impact of unemployment will be different at different stages in the life cycle. He also suggests that problems will be greatest and experienced most frequently in transitional phases of development.[4]

What each of these uses of 'domestic cycle' and 'family cycle' implies is a stable model of progression within which changes in economic and social life are accommodated and through which they are mediated. Whilst I would not wish to disagree with the substance of such work, I shall advocate a rather more flexible approach to the relationship between the domestic and family cycle and the labour market; one which focuses less exclusively on the internal dynamic or 'requirements' of family or household development, and looks rather at the external constraints imposed by economic decline on the very nature of that development.

Using material collected in Hartlepool in the north east of England, I shall suggest that established patterns and expectations of inter and intra-generational progression have been disrupted by changes in opportunities for employment; and that at different stages of development households will be facing different labour market conditions, with different prospects of employment, and occupying different positions in the housing market.[5]

I shall also argue that the way members of different households perceive and respond to their situation will differ according to position in the family cycle and domestic cycle, not simply because of the constraints peculiar to that *position* but also because of the changing attitudes towards work and gender roles engendered by different experiences in the labour market.

The term 'domestic cycle' is taken to refer to the development of a particular household through different stages in structure and composition. 'Family cycle' is used to refer to a wider conception of generational change which may involve more than one household and can therefore encompass the formation of new households.

BACKGROUND TO HARTLEPOOL

Hartlepool is a town with a population of about 98 000, located on the north east coast of England, just north of the mouth of the Tees, and some distance south of the Tyne. Its strategic coastal location to the south of the Durham coalfield meant that by the middle of the 1800s the town had become established as a busy port, and soon developed a prosperous shipyard.

A local steel industry grew up in association with these activities, and Hartlepool came to be characterised by a male workforce skilled in construction, engineering and metal manufacture, supported by the domestic services of mothers and wives, and spawning a rigid division of labour between the sexes.

Decline began in the 1950s with the rundown and eventual disappearance of shipbuilding, and by the late 1970s the town's steel industry had also ceased production. Although there was some respite provided by an oil and gas linked construction boom, high levels of public employment in the 1960s, and the attraction of some new manufacturing industry, unemployment began a steady climb in 1975. By June 1986 it stood at

22.4 per cent; 27.0 per cent for men and 15.5 per cent for women.

ACCESS TO EMPLOYMENT

It is now well established that long-term unemployment is most likely to occur at the beginning and end of working life and there are a number of commonsense explanations for this pattern. For example, those too young to have entered employment prior to recession are clearly in a weaker position than those who still hold jobs acquired in times of relative prosperity. But not only has there been a *reduction* of employment opportunities as a result of economic decline, there is less movement of employees between secure jobs, which will also mean fewer vacancies. It is also the case that recession in Hartlepool, as well as reducing the number of jobs available, has led to a change in the structure of employment and the *shape* of a career.[6]

In post-war Hartlepool, jobs in engineering, construction and maintenance work meant that apart from secure employment in heavy industry, it was possible to fashion a career in permanent employment through a series of short-term contracts. Such employment opportunities still exist, and it seems likely that the shift towards sub-contracting for an increasing number of services will mean a rise in the *proportion* of the total number of jobs made up of short-term contract work.

Thus, despite a reduction in opportunities for secure employment an area of extremely high turnover still exists, and at least *proportionally* may be expanding. Competition for such jobs, however, has increased, and access to them is not equally available to all potential workers; they are not allocated on the 'open market'. What, then, are the implications for the employment prospects of those *currently* at different stages in the life and family cycle, and how do such changed conditions act back upon the 'clustering' of events throughout the life course?[7]

The easiest approach to an understanding of the nature and effects of particularistic recruitment to short-term work, change across generations, and the implications for the family cycle is perhaps through a series of case studies.

Mr Johnson, rigger-erector of Hartlepool, aged 55, unemployed

Mr Johnson left school at 15, though unofficially some time before that, and began work immediately on his uncle's fishing boat. As soon as he was old enough he applied for work with the merchant navy:

> You just called at the shipping office and if there was a ship sailing, well they'd send you to it . . . the shipping industry has collapsed now of course . . . Well I got married and carried on with the Merchant for a couple of years until the wife had had enough of me going to sea. So I packed that in, but my father got me on at the shipyards laying deckplates . . . eventually I left there and did a bit of driving, the money was better, then some years on I took a job on the Cleveland Bridge as a steel erector. I'd done rigging in the Merchant, and rigging and erecting will always cross paths, you almost need one for the other . . . I got on this job because my mate was a foreman, and you worked your way from job to job, mostly chasing the money, because as a job came to an end the tonnage fell and so did the money, so you kept on the move. That kind of work was like a grapevine. All the work-men would be on the lookout as a job came to an end, and you'd hear where the next site was. Well I carried on like that for a good 10 years and more. Never out of work to speak of, and you could always fall back on the steel works for a daft spell if nothing came up. Anyway, eventually, I was taken on as a foreman with an engineering firm . . . oh yes, it was all contract stuff, but I was permanent staff by then; I got the team together if you like. I was in there about 15 years before they finally folded.
>
> You see how it happens then, I was in through my father at the start, and when the time came my son had a good few jobs with me. Couldn't make it reliable of course, things had got a bit sticky by then, but he'd get 6 months on a contract, then be out of work for a bit and so on. Actually he hasn't worked since the last thing I set him up with – that would be a good 3 years ago and he's 23 now, married with a couple of kids. He's a good worker, and he can turn his hand to any mortal thing, but not strictly speaking skilled. He gets the

odd fiddle on the side, but you'd have to ask him about that. To be honest with you, his and my prospects now are just about zero.

There are a number of basic points which may be usefully extracted from this case study:

1. A man who entered the labour market in the late 1940s or 1950s was in a position to secure work fairly easily in any one of a number of related areas of employment, acquiring construction skills and work-based contacts which would lead to a relatively uninterrupted career in temporary contract work.
2. Such a man is currently unlikely to be in employment or to have any real prospects of finding work in his customary field, because of his age.
3. Cross-generational contacts and influence operated as part of the father–son relationship and provided a means by which the father could transmit his own position of privileged access to work to his son.
4. It is no longer the case that a young man recently arrived on the labour market can necessarily look to his father to pave the way into employment.
5. The stages and routes by which men arrive at a condition of long-term unemployment will vary with age of entry into the labour market, and consequently with stage in the life cycle, and there will be related consequences for the development of the domestic and family cycle.

How then are younger men faring, what does a contract career look like today, and what are the means of entry? Again a case study can illustrate the way in which men seek and gain access to employment.

Mr Geoffreys, welder-fabricator of Hartlepool, aged 30, in temporary employment

Mr Geoffreys began work at 16, apprenticed at Tees Marine:

My uncle heard of the opening and spoke for me, so I suppose he got me in. I was paid off half way through but the Training Board fixed me up somewhere else where I qualified . . . plating and welding were the trades to be in, anything to do with, construction really, and that's what nearly all the mates I had were trying to get into.

Anyway, I qualified and stayed for a few years, then I heard of a new job through a friend, and so I moved on. It was supposed to be permanent but it only lasted a year until they went bust. Then I went off on spec with the brother-in-law to do an offshore survival course, up in Aberdeen, but a couple of weeks later a friend was packing in his job and tipped me off so I moved in there.

I hadn't been there long when I bumped into my old foreman on the street. He lived down the road from my mother and I'd been pestering him, well he gave me a start the next day. It was only for three weeks but at £200 a week you'll take the chance. I'd only been finished there a week or so when some mates got me a start at M and M oil for six weeks. That took me up to August, and by October I was back on the same site with another company – the first lot made a few recommendations to the site manager, he rang me up, and there you are.

The history continues in this vein, with local contracts in construction work in Hartlepool, interspersed with occasional spells offshore from Aberdeen, and never more than two months at a stretch out of work.

As you go around the different jobs you get to know people and there's always someone you get on well with. So when you're not working you keep in touch and it's easier to find out what's going. But it depends on your trade of course. The big call for plating was in the steel works and shipyards, and there was the boom in the 70s, oil and gas. But I was too young to be in on that. The rigs are picking up a bit now, and there's still some off shore work around, if you're on the right communications line. But you've got to be able to start tomorrow, and you can't live without a phone in this line.

I've been lucky, and I'm about the right age just now; late 20's to mid 30's is your best time. Off-shore work is definitely only for the under 40's; older than that they don't want to know. I've been on jobs where its been 14 twelve hour night shifts in a row. There's a limit to who you'll take on for work like that, and a limit to how long you can do it.

What this particular case indicates is again an example of entry into employment through the influence of an older male relative, at a time when apprenticeships were harder to come by than for the previous generation. This opportunity has had a number of implications:

1. Mr Geoffreys has acquired a skill which is still a ticket to certain kinds of employment, albeit much less certainly than in the past.
2. He is of an age which maximises his chances of employment, but aware that his prospects remain good only for the next ten years, and that is on the assumption that *some* level of demand in his area of work continues.
3. His access to such opportunities as may arise is now dependent not on older male relatives, but on a wider network of friends in the same age group and line of work, who consciously operate as a mutually supportive system of information and influence.
4. Membership of this system is both *age* related and *work* related; it was bred of time of entry onto the labour market, and developed through work-based contacts established whilst in employment.
5. The jobs which made up such a career structure are unlikely to increase, the training which produced the relevant skills has almost disappeared, and the same pattern of opportunities and access is unlikely to be available to the next generation.

A concentration of long-term unemployment among young workers has already been noted. It would seem that they are at a *particular* disadvantage in those areas of work where vacancies arise most regularly, i.e. short-term employment. Jobs of this kind, as the above case demonstrates, tend to be distributed through informal mechanisms, and access is usually by means of contacts established and maintained in the world of work. Where such contacts never developed, or have atrophied, the prospects of relieving unemployment even with temporary work seem slight. Those at the beginning of their career and at the age when household formation is likely to occur, are effectively excluded from the recruitment mechanisms. Mr James, at 23 years old, has been out of work for the last five years, and has only ever had employment on government schemes. His feeling was: 'To get that kind of job round here, even on the fiddle, you've got to be in the know. Your face has got to fit, it's like a closed shop, a little group all looking after each other.'

The processes implied by the cases of Mr Johnson and Mr Geoffreys do not necessarily operate only for skill specific employment. Contacts, influence and experience count for much in most areas of employment in the town, and with closures, early retirement and a general preference for younger but experienced labour, the concentrations of long-term unemployment among new entrants to the labour market, and older workers, seems set to continue. Thus men currently at different stages of life cycle and family cycle have been born into different labour market conditions and the associated break in tradition in some ways challenges the nature of the relationship between the generations, as one man, aged 24, unemployed for two years, explained:

> If we're stuck over a bill I'll go to my parents. My dad's retired now, and I don't like to have to ask him. I should be helping him out. All his kids are on the dole, and in a way he's worried by it more than we are. My dad's worked all his life and he thinks we should have a chance to do the same ... I've always thought of my dad as working. I wasn't proud of it at the time but when I look back I am. He worked hard to bring me up, and what am I doing? Living off the state. And my kids can only look at me and their memory will be of me sitting about the house all day in an armchair like an old man, and they'll know the state's brought them up, not me.

GENDER AND GENERATION

What is implicit in the statement above is both a notion of duty to one's children, the obligation to provide for them through one's own labour, and an image of gender identity. This was made explicit by a number of men, who remarked on feelings of frustration at being out of work: 'I suppose I do feel guilty really. We're brought up to believe in work. That's what a man does. I'm not ashamed or anything, I mean it's not my fault, but I know I should be working.' But could it be that for the young unemployed, in the absence of any past experience of employment, the challenge to male gender identity will mean a weakening of adherence to traditional gender roles?

There are a number of possible ways of approaching this question, and three related issues will be briefly examined: (i) women's employment cycle; (ii) sources of gender identity; (iii) parenthood and gender roles.

(i) Women's employment cycle

Women's introduction to employment seems in many cases to have been similar to that of men. A growth in new manufacturing industry in the sixties meant plentiful factory jobs for women. Many now in their thirties recall either turning up at a factory where a mother or aunt was employed, or being taken along by them, and so embarking upon their first job: 'You can get whole families at the same factory or in the same trade. The devil you know sort of thing. If you know someone in the family and have no bother off them, you probably think it works right through.' Although there have been drastic reductions in manufacturing employment, the relatively high turnover of *women* workers means there has been some recruitment even in times of contraction, and this has seemed even more likely to occur 'through the family'. Work based contacts can also be critical, and many women told of old employers seeking them out for spells of temporary work.

Expansion of public spending in the sixties meant increases in service sector opportunities for women, which have now been substantially reduced. The common career path in the past was to begin in employment on leaving school and to continue until the birth of the first child. There would then be a break, or the assumption of a part-time job which accommodated both the working hours of the husband and child care needs. Some women would plan to return to full-time employment when the children were older, others would assume part-time employment fairly quickly, and yet others would hope for part-time work later in life.

Unemployment for women has been rising in step with men's since 1982, although there has been consistent *growth* in women's part-time employment since 1971. Interestingly, these changes in employment opportunities seem likely to produce a pattern not unlike that for men: some older women workers will retain pre-recession employment, whilst those with young children will have taken on the increasingly available part-time or intermittent employment, probably to supplement the income of an employed spouse.

Just at that stage in the domestic cycle in which household duties are lightest, however, and when a young, childless wife might previously have expected to be in full-time employment, women are having much the same sorts of difficulties as men. Benefit regulations discourage young women with unemployed spouses from taking part-time work and so the employment prospects for young couples amongst whom male unemployment is concentrated, are fairly bleak. This is particularly significant for the question of renegotiating gender roles since it is only a full-time job which would *financially* warrant a woman taking employment if her husband was claiming benefit.[8]

The period of marriage before the birth of children is when the potential for flexibility in gender roles seems greatest but coincides with minimal probability of *either* husband or wife finding full-time employment. The reaction seems to be a feeling of guilt and inadequacy on the part of the man over his inability to find work, and withdrawal on the part of the woman into the domestic role, and notably motherhood, as providing the most secure base for identity.

However, even if the woman cannot easily assume the role of main earner, there remains the possibility that the younger generation will show greater flexibility in their *attitudes* towards gender roles, which we might expect to be reflected in the organisation of domestic tasks.

(ii) Sources of gender identity

This is a complex issue to address from the point of view of generational change and perhaps should be prefaced by a general statement about attitudes to gender identity in Hartlepool. Across an age band spanning from 18 to 60, and across a wide variety of occupations – though all working class – I found a remarkable adherence to ideas about gender identity characteristic of the area. As I noted in the background discussion of the town the development of the local economy has been such as to encourage a rigid division of labour between the sexes. A supporting ideology seems to have grown up alongside this division, and indeed to have survived the decline of the economy upon which it was based.

Ideas about the man as 'natural' provider, and about his employment having priority over the woman's, are still strong across all age ranges and for *both* sexes. It is also the case, however, that the division of domestic labour between husband and wife is remarkably *more* flexible amongst young couples than amongst older couples. The notable instances are:

(a) when both husband and wife are themselves employed full-time. In such cases the notion of justice which is used in support of a sexual division of labour is also called upon to explain male participation in domestic tasks due to the wife's commitment to earning.

(b) when the couple is young and *childless*, and the man unemployed. Although the traditional *ideas* about male and female responsibility remain, there is also a fairly high level of male participation in domestic tasks, notably washing dishes, cooking and cleaning through the house on a fairly regular basis. Changes appear to set in, however, once there are children present.

(iii) Parenthood and gender roles

There are strong feelings in the local culture about the nature and value of motherhood. Consequently, the woman's identity and her obligations take on added dimensions and become both more demanding and rewarding on the birth of a child. This seems to lead to a less companionate marriage and to encourage male withdrawal from the domestic sphere. Thus although long periods of male unemployment early in the domestic cycle do seem to loosen ideas about domestic roles, there will be a shift towards a more traditional division on the birth of children. For the woman the birth of a child represents a strengthening of her gender identity. For an unemployed *man* it is perhaps something of a threat, which breaks up the earlier tone of companionship in marriage and leaves him feeling isolated and without a specific role.

FAMILY AND HOUSEHOLD FORMATION

There is another issue to be addressed, however, concerning the connection between the domestic cycle and labour market conditions. Given the weakened position of both male and female entrants to the labour market, how and why do young people ever embark upon setting up their own home, and at what stage do they contemplate producing children?

When discussing these questions, it should be borne in mind that entry into the housing market and home formation could happen in a variety of ways in times of full employment. The options were as follows:

(a) To start out in private rented accommodation and wait for rehousing by the local authority, either with compulsory purchase or overcrowding.

(b) To begin married life with the parents of one of the couple, and even produce a first child before being rehoused by the council on grounds of overcrowding.

(c) To save for a deposit and start married life as owner occupiers.

(d) To start marriage in the parental home, using the opportunity to save, and moving on later to house purchase.

In cases of long-term unemployment for both members of a couple owner occupation is out of the question. With the other options available, the birth of children assumes greater significance because it means a higher priority rating for local authority accommodation. There are other senses in which the birth of children assumes importance for the unemployed young couple.

In the absence of employment, marriage, and more especially the birth of children, becomes the only means available of marking entry into adult life. Even though it can mean a reduction in joint benefit, this is something that couples seem eventually prepared to concede for the sake of their 'own place'. It is also the case that for those resigned to long-term unemployment the only way to secure an increase in their income is through the birth of children. Some couples have pointed out that taking this step will mean the chances of finding appropriate employment are more remote because earnings would have to be higher to compete with benefit levels. They are thus aware of the danger of locking themselves into unemployment through raising children.

One result will be that the demand for and dependence upon public housing is growing at a time when stock has been depleted by council house sales, and when many of the families currently renting are unlikely to move on to owner occupation as they might have done in a more secure economic climate. The implications for the young and for local authorities are obvious: growing demand at a time of falling turnover and reduced stock. Progression through the established domestic cycle for many of the present generation of adolescents will inevitably be disrupted.

CONCLUSION

I have argued in this paper that during a period of rapid economic decline the developmental cycle of the individual, the domestic group and the family, and the relationship of each with opportunities for employment cannot be understood in terms of a stable model of progression. The stages through which one generation passed will not be repeated by the next, since sections of the population separated by as little as ten years or less are born into very different labour market conditions.

Although one might expect young couples with little prospect of employment to shrink from marriage it would seem that the formation of an independent household is now their obvious means of asserting adult status, and access to council housing is strengthened by the birth of children. The problems posed by shrinking stock and growing demand from a young benefit dependent population have yet to be faced, however, and may pose greater problems for progression through the domestic and family cycles than have yet been confronted.

NOTES

1. Research for this paper was completed in my capacity as New Blood lecturer, in the Department of Sociology and Social Policy, University of Durham.
2. For a discussion of women's position in the labour market see Dex (1985).
3. See for example Hareven (1982); Tilly and Scott (1978).
4. He uses a seven stage model adapted from Carter and McGoldrick (1980).

5. Forty married couples, half with an unemployed husband/father, and half with a husband/father in work, were randomly selected from the electoral register. The rate of co-operation was 83 per cent.
6. See Morris (1986).
7. See C. C. Harris in the present volume.
8. For a discussion of this complex of factors see Morris (1985a).

12 The Impact of Mortgage Arrears on the Housing Careers of Home Owners

Lawrence Took and Janet Ford

INTRODUCTION

Common to many prevailing notions about the structure and functioning of the housing market is the idea of a housing career. According to this model the actions of individuals and households collectively with regard to the purchase and maintenance of owner occupation can be located within a structure intended in some way to explain their current needs and predict the future course of their lives as home owners. The housing career is usually understood as following certain clear and common sense pathways that are linked with their passage through the life cycle. The following comments made by the Nationwide Building Society in 1976 (quoted in Jones, 1978, p. 552) illustrate this approach.

> It is well known that people tend to move up the housing ladder. Most young people buy their first home in their 20s (about 70 per cent of first-time buyers are under 30) usually after a short period of living with in-laws or in rented accommodation. Considerably less than a quarter of first-time buyers purchase a new property and well over a quarter purchase property built before 1919. First-time buyers tend to trade up to a better and usually larger house in their mid-30s . . .

Such careers have typically been supported by rising property values, and the 'reverse monopoly syndrome'[1] Underlying this understanding of a housing career, however, are a number of

207

assumptions, the most crucial being that the home owner will enjoy an uninterrupted capability to maintain regular payments of their mortgage. Recent research sponsored by the Economic and Social Research Council (ESRC)[2] has examined in detail the current incidence of mortgage default and the circumstances of forty cases of home owners in difficulty followed over a period of nine months. The research indicates along with other work conducted in this field, that given recent social trends and the government thrust toward owner occupation, that our current understanding of a housing career must be reviewed.

FILTERING THEORY

The traditional concept of a housing career as outlined above rests on a number of assumptions that when brought together are often referred to as filtering theory, an account of the housing market that stresses 'vacancies filtering down the income/social scale, and households filtering up the housing scale' (Boddy and Gray, 1979, p. 41). With regard to the household, filtering theory assumes that home owners purchase as a matter of 'free choice', that buyers pursue a strategy of rational investment and see home ownership as a means to accumulate wealth, and that the buyer is male, married and part of a stable household where all participating individuals share the same goals. Further, the home owner is perceived as 'thrifty', able to have saved a deposit by an early age, and located within a framework of secure and rising income that permits the households to trade up the housing ladder, but with sufficient disposable income to protect and enhance the investment by carrying out repairs, improvements and maintenance.

Seen in this light home owners' actions in relation to the housing market are safely located on a ladder of escalating opportunities. This body of opinion not only informs the approach of numerous individual building societies, as was demonstrated by the quote included in the introduction to this chapter, but indeed the Building Societies Association (BSA) as a whole and the context of government policy within which it operates. These ideas support a continuing thrust of government housing policy that focuses upon ways of easing entry to owner occupation, such as option mortgages and low start schemes (Forest and Murie, 1984) and minimises efforts to ensure the maintenance of households within owner occupation. Overall, filtering theory is, as Thorns (1980) has summed it up, based on a free market interpretation of housing allocative structures. The approach is thus individual, voluntaristic and consumer or demand based. It makes no examination of the supply of housing or the beliefs or practices characteristic of those organisations that control the allocation of housing. Filtering theory thus:

> derives from a clear political and ideological position which translation into policy in turn supports. At the specific level of housing policy it legitimates the persistence of gross inequalities in housing provision, and of substandard housing, and justifies allocation of resources and subsidies to those already well off and well housed, directing support away from those in greater need. (Boddy and Gray, 1979, pp. 50–51)

Each of the assumptions that underpin filtering theory can and has been questioned (for example Boddy and Gray, 1979). Increasingly it is possible to offer evidence to support the suggestions that the assumptions are particularly inappropriate with regard to certain parts of the owner occupier market. That is, that the universal applicability of ideas such as 'trading up' or of a 'typical' housing career may in practice be frameworks that apply only to some owner occupiers, and that the market is more heterogeneous and segmented than often portrayed. In particular it has been argued that low income owner occupation increasingly forms a separate segment (Karn *et al.*, 1986). Some of the grounds for questioning the assumptions outlined above are offered below.

UNWARRANTED ASSUMPTIONS?

The notion of buying out of 'free choice' takes on a rarified meaning in a market where the availability of alternatives in the form of good private rented accommodation has been steadily declining (Bovaird *et al.*, 1985). The increasing lack of investment in public housing, the sale of council property at discounted prices and a government policy that has encouraged an 'ideology of tenures' (Harloe, 1985, p. xxiv) which endows the freeholder with particular virtues in comparison with those who rent, have conspired to lead many who might otherwise have rented their home to buy one instead. Furthermore, many households can no longer be described as persisting stable units. Not only do current rates of separation and divorce contribute to this, but also the employment policies of the 1980s that cause some to migrate in search of work. Similarly, as evidence from the debt counselling agencies suggests, not every household member may share similar goals with regard to the financial priorities and management of the household.

The lending criteria typically used by the building societies in relation to home loans have until recently confined owner occupation to those able to provide a reasonable deposit for the property. Thus the assumption that intending home owners 'save' has been largely borne out. The discipline of saving for a deposit has been regarded by the building societies as evidence of reliability, sound financial management and 'thrift'. However, since the inter-war years the mortgage guarantee introduced by the building societies has permitted larger and larger proportions of the purchase price to be advanced. As lenders have sought to extend the demand for owner occupation by moving 'down market' there has been an increase in the number of 100 per cent mortgages. Of the advances made in 1984, 20 per cent of loans to first-time buyers were 100 per cent loans, while 3 per cent of former owner-occupiers took 100 per cent loans (BSA, 1985a). As a result, whereas in the past entry into owner occupation required a preparatory period of several years, today it may take only a few hours. Thus the assumption that only the thrifty, with some proven ability to save and manage money with ease, enter owner occupation is increasingly difficult to maintain.

'Trading up' is a notion that is central to ideas about the 'housing ladder', where the trading up of older households to bigger and better property releases the smaller cheaper property for purchase by first time buyers. A study conducted in Northern Ireland, however, published in the same year as the comments made by the Nationwide Building Society quoted at the beginning of this paper, noted that new housing was disproportionately used by new households. In fact, 26 per cent of new dwellings were occupied directly by new households without further moves being generated (Murie *et al.*, 1976). Kemeny (1980) too notes that 'there is some evidence that trading up may be less common than is sometimes assumed and may be restricted to higher income groups'. Trading up is also often presented as the mechanism whereby home owners can accumulate wealth and as something that is rationally pursued. The extent to which home ownership acts as a means to accumulate wealth is still under debate, and has been discussed by, for example, Forest (1983) and Saunders (1984).

Currently, it cannot be assumed that in every household there will be sufficient disposable income to meet the need for repairs and maintenance. Attention has already been drawn to the fact that increasing numbers of home owners enter owner occupation with little or no savings. This not only points to a slender capital backing for the move into owner occupation, but also to the increasing numbers of home owners who have high outgoings in relation to their income (Walker, 1986, p. 15). This, coupled with the fact that, as preceding comments have shown, owner occupation has ceased to be the preserve of the professional middle classes, but has come to incorporate an increasing number of low income groups, buying smaller older property (Fleming and Nellis, 1985), the opportunities amongst many home owners for 'spare' income has decreased. Boddy and Gray (1979, p. 47) drew attention to the fact that amongst these 'a significant proportion . . . having bought cheaper, older property, are unable to afford repairs and maintenance necessary to maintain the value of the property and are, in effect, disinvesting as the property deteriorates'. Such observations cast further doubts on the ability of many households to trade up.

Perhaps however, the fundamental assumption underpinning filtering theory is the notion of long-term income stability, if not increasing income for households. The pattern of social and economic change over the last decade is such as to throw doubt on the certainty of income stability, and both lending and borrowing, with regard to house purchase, are becoming more risky. For the building societies this has resulted in an increasing number of possessions. Using BSA figures, in 1979 only 2530 homes were possessed or 0.84 per thousand of building society mortgage loans. By 1984 the figure was 1.72 per thousand. Among the borrowers it has resulted in an increased incidence of mortgage arrears. In 1985 there were 58 000 building society borrowers six to twelve months in arrears. The BSA statistics are however inadequate as a guide to the number of households in default to them as typically they refer only to those who owe six or more months payments. A recent survey of building societies indicates that in March 1985 154 600 borrowers owed three or more months payments, with a further 140 800 owing two months payments (Ford and Took, 1985).

MORTGAGE ARREARS: AN EMPIRICAL STUDY

In 1984 the ESRC provided support for a qualitative study of building society mortgage holders who were experiencing problems with mortgage repayments. In contrast to the major emphasis in the literature, which is on possessions, the focus has been upon those owing under six months back-payments and the project was designed to explore the borrower's perception of the emergence, experience and management of arrears. A cohort of forty borrowers was established and followed over a period of nine months. Establishing the cohort was a lengthy and time consuming process. Rock (1973, p. 264) has commented upon the invisibility of those in debt, their lack of external symbols and absence of meeting places. Strategies to obtain respondents by advertising carry their own disadvantages, and this project opted to approach arrears cases via the building societies who remain the only comprehensive source of knowledge of such people. Four societies co-operated.[3] To maintain confidentiality between lender and borrower, and researcher and respondent, a strategy was evolved whereby the societies contacted all those cases owing three months' payments in selected parts of the East and West Midlands, requesting them to help in the project, and enclosing a letter from us. Those who were interested replied directly to us. Thus we have no idea who was contacted but declined to be involved, and the societies have no idea who replied to us. Approximately 600 contacts were made by the societies, in order to establish a cohort of 40 borrowers. The first interview took place in April 1985, a second in October and a third in January 1986.

In the context of this chapter, and the concern with the idea of a housing career, material from the project will be presented in order to examine two issues. First the extent to which borrowers have internalised the beliefs and assumptions about owner occupation and their likely housing careers and have entered owner occupation with a sense that owner occupation is for example 'chosen', 'non-problematic', 'advantageous' and superior to renting in economic, social and environmental terms. Second, the ways in which such expectations and careers are threatened and disrupted by the development of mortgage arrears.

STEPPING ONTO THE LADDER

Not all the respondents had just stepped on to the ladder. Twenty-five were first time buyers (usually recent) while the remainder were living in their second or third home, although sometimes ownership had been interspersed with periods of renting. All respondents were asked about the reasons that lay behind their initial entry to owner occupation, and where appropriate the reasons that lay behind their continuation in the sector. The responses suggest that the ideology of owner occupation is very powerful in terms of motivating entry and movement in the market. For example many perceived entry as a natural progression, clearly linked to certain life cycle changes, most notably marriage or childbirth:

We lived in a flat and I was expecting a baby and it was upstairs and there was nowhere to hang up your washing or anything. We wanted a house eventually anyway.

It's the first thing that everybody does.

Other respondents stressed the environmental and social hazards of living in public housing, and endorsed the view expressed by the Inquiry into British Housing (1985) that renting is a second class tenure where tenants become stigmatised as second class citizens who have somehow failed. Mrs S., previously a council tenant, when asked why she had wanted to buy her own home said:

It was new when we went down there, new estate and everybody that was down there was all nice, you know, kept it all nice and then come about 3 years of being down there they started sending all the rough ones down from all the other rough estates. And now it's got as bad a name as them other rough estates have got.

She went on to talk about the noise and of rat infested houses in the same street as her own. Similarly Mr T. had decided to buy rather than rent in an effort to find a better social environment:

It's the quality of fellow people I'm afraid. We were living on a council estate, there was loads of trouble in the evening . . . vandals all over the place . . . we just wanted to get away from the racket and the row.

Yet another respondent spoke of the stigma attached to living on an estate referred to by the rest of the community as 'Colditz'.

Our interviews also brought to light various cases where individuals expressed a belief that it was as cheap to buy as it was to rent. The equation of rent and mortgage is apparently a common one. A recent observation by Shelter held that 'people who move from renting to buying are often surprised to find that the mortgage does not cover local authority rates, insurance and maintenance – and that it can fluctuate wildly with interest rates' (Harris, 1985, p. 362). The following comments were common and were often followed by an admission that other costs had not been taken into account: 'Well basically what you pay out in rent these days is more or less the same as what you are paying out on the mortgage.' 'It's cheaper than the council.' These comments not only reveal the vulnerability of a great number of first-time buyers but also call into question how adequately they were counselled by their building societies when they took the mortgage out. Further the way in which mortgages are often advertised does little to prevent such confusion. An advertisement that regularly appears in the 'Houses to Let' column of the *Leicester Mercury* reads 'Why rent when you can afford a mortgage?'

These beliefs and expectations are further reinforced by the ease of entry into owner occupation that contemporary home buyers enjoy. In this respect builders' packages have increasingly become a feature of the modern housing market. Often offering cash incentives for quick completions, providing facilities for removals, contract exchange and even in some cases buying up your old home if you have one, these packages permit one to buy a house much as one would any other consumer item. Indeed it could be argued that in many cases it is easier to get a mortgage through these arrangements than it would be to get a personal loan from a bank. Such facilities of course allow the decision about buying a home to be made very quickly, taking away the months of financial preparation formerly required to enter owner occupation. The following comments were made by a couple who put down a hundred pounds and traded up from their two-up two-down terraced house to a new semi-detached house on a modern estate.

> Yes, it was so easy. At the time we had a house in E., . . . Literally, how it happened that we had this house. I was walking around finding something to do for the boring last few weeks waiting for the baby to come. Had a drive round, thought I'll go and look at those show houses, and I said to him 'Oh, you should see that house . . .'
>
> We came down and got talking to the lady, and she was saying they would have the old house off us, and before we knew, in a matter of weeks we were moved in. It was so quick.

In summary the data indicate that the prevailing beliefs and expectations about owner occupation are internalised by borrowers. Whatever the subsequent divergence between these expectations and the reality (which is pronounced in some cases) cohort members started owner occupation optimistically, believing it to be advantageous and unproblematic. In practice, as we have already indicated, for a growing number of people the reality of owner occupation is different. The next section in this chapter examines the factors that are argued to threaten and/or disrupt the home owner's career, and presents some data from the empirical study. Although we do not intend in this chapter to discuss the economic data about size of loans/repayments, arrears, etc., these data are summarised in Appendix 1 in order to provide readers with some sense of the scale of the problem for households.

THE DEVELOPMENT OF ARREARS

The marriage relationship and mortgage payments

The BSA in their recent report on Mortgage Repayment Difficulties (BSA, 1985b) draw attention to the fact that recently there have been an average of 160 000 divorces a year, a figure that does not include those marriages where individuals may separate but not divorce. The BSA go on to assert that 'the single most important cause of mortgage arrears is matrimonial problems' and attribute some 40 per cent of repossessions to this 'cause'. How they arrive at this figure is, however, not open to inspection, but is not based on systematic data analysis. Tunnard (1976), on the other hand, used evidence from the National Child Development Study and pointed out that when the housing position of families with children aged seven was compared to their position four years later, among families in which both parents were present throughout, 95 per cent of those who owned their own home when their children were seven did so four years later. But among families that were fatherless through marital breakdown the figure was only 67 per cent. Whilst her study did not establish whether the marital breakdown preceded or followed the move out of owner occupation (and both Tunnard and the BSA point out that it is often uncertain whether it is marital dispute that causes arrears or arrears that cause marital dispute), it nevertheless pointed to an association between the exit from owner occupation and marital breakdown. Evidence from the 1976 Family Formation Survey has recently been discussed by Sullivan (1986). She examines the position of women who remained in the owner-occupied marital home on breakdown, but subsequently moved. Amongst this group, those women that remarry (or cohabit) tend to move to another owner-occupied house. For women who remain divorced, separated or widowed, the proportion staying within owner occupation at the next move drops (from 32 per cent to 19 per cent of all women considered) suggesting that:

> many of the housing movements represented (in this table) were 'forced' moves out of unshared owner-occupancy into local authority tenure by women who were unable to maintain mortgage repayments. (Sullivan, 1986, p. 40)

Among our sample of forty home owners in difficulty with their mortgage eight respondents were separated, six women and two men, all of whom remained in the marital home after separation. Seven of these were drawing supplementary benefit payments, the remaining one living off revenue from rented property.

A detailed analysis of these eight cases reaffirms the previous suggestion that the direction of causality is unclear, but also indicates the diversity of circumstances accommodated under the terms marital 'dispute' and 'breakdown'. In some cases arrears emerged before separation. In other cases arrears emerged after separation had been effected, sometimes because marital dispute persisted, and sometimes because separation reduced the income available to the person paying the mortgage. The eight included two respondents, one male, one female, who had initially left the marital home. Upon their return (when their partners promptly left) they discovered that their spouses had neglected to pay the mortgage during their absence. The respondents then found themselves in the position of having to clear the debt that they perceived the other partner had incurred. A further case was that of a woman who after her husband left had claimed social security but due to a misunderstanding thought that the Department of Health and Social Security (DHSS) would pay the mortgage interest direct to the building society when in fact it was of course being included in the weekly benefit payment made to her. She received a shock when after three months her building society wrote to her to inform her that her account was almost four hundred pounds in arrears. She had no means to pay this off. The money given her had gone to pay other bills and because she had already been awarded DHSS payments she could not claim for any back payments to clear the arrears. Further cases included a man, separated from his common law wife who, because of the emotional turmoil this had created in his life had simply decided to stop paying; cases of women who found that they simply could not make ends meet on the regular payments they received, and women in receipt of maintenance that was variable or paid irregularly.

Observations made by debt counsellors suggest that there is a strong link between financial problems that a couple may face and a lack of communication or understanding of each partner's respective priorities or practices. Our own study has highlighted that divorce or separation are not the only circumstances that might jeopardise a couple's ability to remain owner occupiers. The following comments were made by one couple regarding not only the mortgage but bills in general. They indicate a substantial discrepancy in attitudes to creditors and a fertile ground for tension and misunderstanding.

Woman: 'Well, I like to have them paid, I don't like anything hanging around me at all. I don't like nagging bills at all, I like to get them done and out of the way. So as soon as the money comes in the bills are paid and that's it.'

Man: 'It doesn't worry me at all. As far as I'm concerned if I haven't got it I can't pay it. They wait. I mean I'm having to go without, I've got no car anymore, I've got nothing so if I've got to go without, they have to wait.'

So great was the discrepancy between these two partners that during a later interview when the man was not present, the woman described how even money she set aside for the mortgage would 'disappear' from her purse because he felt that 'he should have money in his pocket'.

Another women also found that her husband made it difficult to keep up regular payments.

Interviewer: And so the money goes into a bank account?
Woman: Unless he stops it, because he can.
Interviewer: And did he do that?
Woman: Yes, he stopped it.
Interviewer: And where does he send his money to when he stops it?
Woman: He fetches it, collects it (from work) on a Friday morning.
Interviewer: So at that point you've no access to the money at all?
Woman: No, I haven't now. I've had nothing off him for 3 weeks . . . I've tried to keep payment when I can, but it's hard you know.

Similarly two husbands expressed ways in which their financial strategies differed from those of their wives:

> The wife's always been a spendthrift. She couldn't save any money . . . I'm more 'let's stop and think' first, but the wife spends and regrets it later.

> Although I'd had unemployment, sporadically, I'd managed to pay the mortgage because that was the first payment . . . But then my wife took over and I think women tend to think another way, they think well, the first thing I want is for the kiddies and food.

The first of the above respondents admitted that he and his wife often argued over money and that he had many times 'taken a walk around the block' to cool off when his wife arrived home after shopping. The second only discovered his wife's different views on how to spend the household money when callers arrived to ask why he was eight hundred pounds in arrears with his mortgage. His wife, unbeknown to him, had not paid it for eleven months.

Unemployment and mortgage arrears

> While marital break-up is clearly a very major continuing cause of default, the steep trend in arrears and possessions since 1979 cannot be attributed to any similar rapid increase in marital break-up. What has increased is of course unemployment. (Doling, Karn and Stafford, 1985b, p. 3)

Thirty-seven of the cohort members had stable incomes from employment when they entered owner occupation. Although many were in low income occupations only one case provides any evidence of an excessive loan in relation to income (in terms of the lender's conventions). Twenty-six of the forty cases examined lost income as a result of unemployment, short time working, or loss of overtime. In a number of cases the borrowers found re-employment over the period of the study, but typically at a lower wage than previously. This is not to say that unemployment (or other labour market changes) alone were a cause of the arrears in every case; intervening variables such as budgeting practice and decisions about priorities were also important factors, but evidence from the study does show the way in which unemployment and other labour market changes act as a context for these decisions and can be seen to precipitate a crisis for those households concerned, by cutting or jeopard-ising their access to stable and rising incomes.

The Building Societies Association (BSA, 1985b), despite con-firming that according to building society records, a regional relationship between unemployment and levels of arrears has been observed, go on to argue that unemployment in Britain has not had the effect on arrears that might be expected. They point out that the unemployed are entitled to Supplementary Benefit which includes a 'generous' payment toward housing costs that can cushion the impact of unemployment on the mortgage. Although Supplementary Benefit claims do include money toward mortgage interest the cushioning effects of this benefit are restricted by two factors. Doling, Karn and Stafford (1985b) point to not only the limitation of eligibility for such payments, for these payments are not a safety net for those who suffer a drop in income as a result of short-time working, change of job or loss of overtime, or the loss of a second income in the household, but also the declining value of benefits in general making it harder for those in receipt of benefit to reserve a sum entirely for their mortgage payment when faced with the immediate need to eat, keep warm and clothe oneself. The number of mortgagors in receipt of regular weekly pay-ments of Supplementary Benefit (counted during one week of either November and December of those years shown) has risen from 75 000 in 1967, through 98 000 in 1979 to 242 000 in 1983 according to DHSS Social Security Statistics. Nationally, the number of mortgagors with reduced income, but no eligibility for supplementary benefit is unknown. Of the forty cohort respondents, sixteen were claiming and receiving supplementary benefit with mortgage interest relief. In a further seven cases benefits had been claimed in the past, but changed circumstances (such as finding work) had removed the eligibility even though arrears had not been cleared.

The interviews show that in a number of the eligible cases the use of the benefit system is delayed so that mortgage arrears develop even when support is available. The delay is most usually associated with a lack of understanding by the borrower, and lack of clear guidance from the lender. This paper has already drawn attention to one home owner who failed to correctly understand the mechanisms of benefit payment, to her cost. Another respondent was similarly baffled and did not go and make a claim because she thought that it was 'automatic' upon being made redundant. Consequently before discovering the true facts she lost three months' benefit.

> I went straight to see the building society and they said 'don't worry, it's all taken care of by the DHSS'. So I thought that to mean they were paying it, and then after four payments had been missed I got this snotty letter from the building society saying we owed all that money.

A number of respondents indicated their lack of ease over DHSS claims, in particular the extent to which they felt stigmatised by the questioning. In two cases, respondents who were eligible for mortgage interest relief (and knew they were) simply refused to claim.

> But I think we went once to the Social Security office and that was it. We didn't even wait . . . I mean I've never had anything like that. We've always paid our own way. I just couldn't see myself sitting there at all. I just didn't want to do it.

The data very much reflect a recent comment made by Doling, Karn and Stafford (1985a, p. 93):

> Within the ideology that most home owners share, they are supposed to be independent, to stand on their own two feet and certainly not to 'scrounge' off the state. Many have no or minimal experience of the welfare system. So some owner occupiers who get into financial difficulties have no predilection to turn to the State for help, nor if they do so, much knowledge of how to deal with its welfare agencies.

There is also evidence that payments from DHSS for interest relief become diverted, knowingly to pay other bills, perceived as more pressing, or unknowingly due to a failure to understand the make up of the DHSS giro cheque and an assumption that the building society is paid direct. Both circumstances are likely to result in arrears increasing. Mortgage interest payments may be diverted to pay fuel, and rates bills, or be absorbed in the general domestic expenditure.

Property conditions and mortgage arrears

The ideology of home ownership stresses the no-risk nature of the investment. Thus, there is a sense in which it might be expected that those who find themselves in difficulties will, if all else fails, be able to sell their property, pay their debts and have a little to start again. One reason for this is the assumed increase in property values. In a recent article Doling, Stafford, and Karn (1986) have indicated that property may in fact deteriorate if home owners find their income stretched due to unemployment, etc. because 'owners may neglect repairs and maintenance as a means of minimising housing expenditure'. Surveys such as the English House Condition Survey (DOE 1982) and the Inquiry into British Housing (National Federation of Housing Associations 1985) have noted the prevalence of such problems in the owner-occupied sector.

Our interviews suggest that in many cases repairs and maintenance are neglected, but significantly in four cases the condition of the property purchased was so poor that arrears can be said to have been caused or exacerbated by the diversion of mortgage payments to essential repairs. Further these four cases raise doubts about whether the owners could sell and leave owner occupation with their debts and arrears cleared. All four respondents are currently unemployed.

The first case is that of a single man who had purchased a terraced house for £17 000 with a 100 per cent mortgage. His problems began the day he moved in and were made worse when after three months he lost his job:

> The day I moved in, to switch on the stairs light, you had to switch on the kitchen light, and to switch off the stairs and the landing light, you had to switch off from the living room. Then in the kitchen there was a fitted kitchen . . . when it started to rain . . . about two days after that slugs and insects attacked the kitchen . . . and I found that they hadn't plastered the walls at the bottom or put in any skirting board.

The third problem was a lot of damp came in the bedroom. Water started coming in through the walls and the windows ... The immersion heater blew up ... All the money that I've received as unemployment benefit has gone to get this lot repaired.

On the day of his interview he received a letter from his building society's solicitors requiring him to pay arrears of £1100 or face eviction in seven days. Six months later the house was empty and derelict. As Walker (1986, p. 34) points out: 'There is a tendency for poor households to buy older, cheaper property, which is, inevitably, prone to require substantial repairs.' He also notes that lack of access to alternative tenures may trap owner occupiers in dwellings without basic amenities and that whilst some local authority grants are mandatory, the authority concerned has considerable discretion in the proportion of costs to meet, in fact between 50 and 90 per cent. Given the enormous cut back in public expenditure on housing already mentioned earlier in this chapter, currently many local authorities cannot find funds for the awarding of generous grants. It is a situation such as this that created problems for another of our respondents. Mr G. came from London and bought a terraced house in the East Midlands in 1976.

Originally it cost me – it was advertised at £7600 in 1976 ... now we paid £6000 because the house was in such appalling condition, it was totally botched about and unmodernised and when I first got into this house I thought I would get a proper grant.

Unfortunately Mr G's hopes were not realised and his local council only felt able to offer £1600 toward a total cost of £4300 to complete the work necessary to modernise the property. Mr G. turned down the offer on the grounds that he would have to borrow the remainder. 'It would have meant going into debt for years and years.' Unfortunately this is still exactly what happened. Mr G. damaged his back in an accident and was unable to find work thereafter. He used considerable amounts of his benefit to carry out repairs and maintenance on the house. They were consequently unable to afford clothes except those found at jumble sales and drank water rather than tea, so saving 40 pence a week. Mr G. was however in a better position than two further respondents in another old terraced house in the West Midlands. Mr G. could at least realise £8000 of equity from the sale of his property, but in this further case selling up to escape the misery and poverty of owner occupation on the dole was not even possible. The property, bought originally for £15 000, was now worth less. It required new floors and a new roof. The owners, both unemployed, were not only in debt to the building society but also to finance companies for second mortgages taken out to cover the costs of other repairs. The fourth and final case concerned a couple, also both unemployed, for whom the burdens of repairs and maintenance had come to completely alter their perceptions about home ownership:

Interviewer: So you feel you've had to alter the way you live?

Respondent: Yes.

Interviewer: What do you feel about that?

Respondent: Well, if you'd have told me what would have happened – we won't bother buying another house.

Interviewer: Why not?

Respondent: Because we never realised at the time, when we was both at work – we never realised that if we needed any repairs or anything we've got to pay for them ourselves. We never took into account that we might be out of work . . . if you're a tenant you have more freedom, you've got no repair bills, no water rates, no nothing to find. If you're an owner you've got to pay the repair bills.

Interviewer: What then do you think of the present government's policy of extending owner occupation; extending the chance for people to buy their own homes?

Respondent: A load of bullshit.

CONCLUSION

The housing market must be seen as a ladder. People join at

the bottom end; they move gradually upwards until they reach old age when they may move down again (BSA, 1976, p. 11)

While those responsible for the provision of owner occupation may continue to argue this way, in reality there are a growing number of home owners, whose climb up the housing ladder is not always as smooth and sweet as they had expected. Unsupported by freedom to choose between tenures, unsupported by government grants and investment in housing, undermined by marriage difficulties and an economic recession, for these people their experience of the housing market resembles not so much a climb on the ladder of escalating opportunity as a game of snakes and ladders, with many going up, many coming down and some falling off. At the start of the project the forty cohort members were all experiencing mortgage repayment difficulties. Nine months later only nine had cleared their arrears in a manner that enabled them to remain as owner occupiers. Five had either left owner occupation, or were still trying to sell in order to clear their problems, and these five were unlikely to re-enter owner occupation at least in the short term. Twenty-two were still in arrears, and the circumstances of four households were unknown. Thus, not only are a growing number of building society mortgage holders experiencing repayment difficulties but the cohort data suggest that many families take a long time to clear, if this can in fact be achieved. Obviously, one of the reasons that the debt period is prolonged is the limited capacity of low income families to increase their monthly repayments in order to clear arrears. Eventually, persisting arrears may lead to repossession proceedings, but the cohort data show that before then a number of families 'voluntarily' sell and leave owner occupation in order to clear the debts. The data presented support the idea that in terms of experience, housing conditions and outcome the housing market is becoming segmented and increasingly polarised into home owners who 'succeed' and those who 'fail', between those whose housing careers take them on the up and up, and those whose experience of home ownership is a precarious one that often leads them into debt, and sometimes persisting debt that in turn forces a proportion of them out of the owner-occupied sector and either back to the public rented sector that they perceived as stigmatised, and bought to escape from, or into homelessness. There are a number of interesting questions that follow from this, not least the extent to which those who fail to maintain owner occupation reassess their ideological commitment to owning that initially was so strong and positive. Equally while the data reported here add support to the contention that it is low income owner occupation that is particularly problematic, there is an indication that those traditionally regarded as more secure, for example, older, established second and third time buyers, those towards the end of a mortgage, etc., may be increasingly vulnerable as unemployment, increasing housing costs and matrimonial breakdown prove no respecter of class and status groupings.

NOTES

1. This term was introduced by Martin Pawley in an article in the *Guardian* in 1985. It provided the theme of a television programme in 1986.
2. The support of the ESRC is gratefully acknowledged.
3. We wish to acknowledge the interest shown and help provided by The Abbey National, The Nottingham, The Melton Mowbray and The Loughborough Permanent Building Societies.

APPENDIX 1 COHORT MEMBERS: MORTGAGE AND ARREARS DATA

Case number	Age of mortgage	Size of loan £	Approximate monthly repayment at first interview[1] (excluding any arrears repayments) £	Arrears at first interview £	Arrears at second interview £	Arrears at third interview £
1	1983	17000*	136	700	700 (selling)	Sold
2	1979	9000	130	300	Decreased	Decreased
3	1975	6500	75	200	Cleared	N/A
4	1983	15900	134	300	250/300	Increased
5	1984	16800*	142	1150	Selling	Selling – left property
6	1983	12500	115	800	800	Decreased
7	1981	19000	200	700	Cleared	N/A
8	–	–	105	400	Selling	Sold
9	1984	19000	165	575e	N/A	N/A
10	1982	17500*	167	700	100	Decreased
11	1977	5100	38	100	Cleared	N/A
12	1981	25000	235	1300	Cleared	N/A
13	1983	12000	92	240	340	Increased
14	1983	10500	80	100	D/K	D/K
15	1982	11450	78	240	D/K	D/K
16	1981	3300*	34	135	Selling	Selling
17	1983	10500	95	200	Increased	Constant
18	1983	21400*	162	700	Decreased	Decreased
19	1984	10500*	100	300	Decreased	Decreased
20	1982	15000*	127	180	500	Decreased

APPENDIX 1 *continued*

Case number	Age of mortgage	Size of loan £	Approximate monthly repayment at first interview[1] (excluding any arrears repayments) £	Arrears at first interview £	Arrears at second interview £	Arrears at third interview £
21	1983	27350*	270	1700	1700	Decreased
22	1983	11000*	90	200	Decreased	Decreased
23	1982	13500*	104	300	Cleared	N/A
24	1970	2000	30	150E	Cleared	N/A
25	1980	3000	40	120+E	120+E	D/K
26	1980	5000	48	600e	N/A	N/A
27	1979	7000	70	300	300	Increased
28	1976	7500	90	370	Decreased	Decreased
29	1978	6500	95	900	Decreased	Still in arrears £ uncertain
30	1981	14500	177	500E	Decreased	Decreased
31	1981	3000	37	190	260	Increased
32	1978	10500	100	200	300	Increased
33	1982	19000	157	700	1200 (Selling)	Sold
34	1982	16500	150	600	500	350/400
35	1979	10500	100	700	500	Decreased
36	1982	17000	150	450E	D/K	D/K
37	1979	11000	110	Nk	30	30
38	1972	4000	30	40	10	Cleared
39	1982	60000	643	2000	2000	2000
40	1976	4000	30	800	500	Still in arrears

Notes

1 – For any specific loan size, the monthly repayments for different borrowers can vary, depending upon, for example, type of mortgage (endowment, option, repayment) and length of repayment period (15–25 years within the cohort)

* – Indicates a 100% mortgage

e – Borrower cleared arrears just prior to first interview

E – Estimate

N/A – Dropped from cohort as arrears were cleared

Nk – Respondent unable to supply information

D/K – Non-response on request for second or third interview

Bibliography

ABRAMS, P. (1982) *Historical Sociology* (London: Open Books).

ALDOUS, J. (1978) *Family Careers: Developmental Change in Families* (New York: John Wiley & Sons).

ALLAN, G. (1979) *A Sociology of Friendship and Kinship* (London: Allen & Unwin).

ALLAN, G. (1983) 'Informal networks of care: issues raised by Barclay', *British Journal of Social Work*, 13, 417–33.

AMOSS, P. T. and HARRELL, S. (eds) (1981) *Other Ways of Growing Old* (Stanford, California: Stanford University).

ANDERSON, D. (1985) 'Ripe for a moral majority', *The Times*, 5.10.85, 7.

ANDERSON, M. (1971) *Family Structure in Nineteen Century Lancashire* (Cambridge: Cambridge University Press).

ANDERSON, M. (1977) 'The impact on the family relationships of the elderly of changes since Victorian times in governmental income-maintenance provisions' in E. Shanas and M. B. Sussman (eds), *Family, Bureaucracy and the Elderly* (Durham, N.C.: Duke University Press).

ANDERSON, M. (1983) 'What is new about the modern family: an historical perspective' in *The Family*, Paper 31 (London: Office of Population, Censuses and Surveys) pp. 1–16.

ANDERSON, M. (1985) 'The emergence of the modern family life cycle in Britain', *Social History*, 10, 69–87.

ARENSBERG, C. M. and KIMBALL, S. T. (1968) *Family and Community in Ireland*, 2nd edn (Cambridge: Harvard University Press).

ARIES, P. (1973) *Centuries of Childhood* (Harmondsworth: Penguin Books).

ARIES, P. (1974) *Western Attitudes Toward Death* (London: Johns Hopkins University Press).

ARIES, P. (1983) *The Hour of Our Death* (Harmondsworth: Penguin Books).

ARMSTRONG, D. (forthcoming) 'The invention of infantile mortality', *Sociology of Health and Illness*.

BALTES, P. and BRIM, O. G. (1980) *Life-span and Behaviour* (New York: Academic Press).

BALTES, P. and SCHAIE, K. W. (1973) *Life-span Developmental Psychology* (New York: Academic Press).

BEACH, C. (1981) *Distribution of Income and Wealth in Ontario* (Toronto: University of Toronto Press).

BECKER, H. S. (1960) 'Notes on the concept of commitment', *American*

Journal of Sociology, 66, 32–40.

BEECHEY, V. (1978) 'Women and production: a critical analysis of some sociological theories of women's work' in A. Kuhn and A. Wolpe (eds), *Feminism and Materialism* (London: Routledge and Kegan Paul).

BELL, C., McKEE, L. and PRIESTLEY, K. (1983) *Fathers, Childbirth and Work* (Manchester: Equal Opportunities Commission).

BELLABY, P. (1984a) 'What is a *genuine* sickness?', British Sociological Association, Medical Sociology Group, Conference (Sheffield University, mimeo).

BELLABY, P. (1984b) 'The relation between work organisation and sickness absence in the pottery industry', End of Grant Report, F0925 0001 (London: Economic and Social Research Council).

BELLABY, P. (1985) 'Experiments in changing work organisation at Staffordshire Potteries Ltd., End of Grant Report, F0925 0036 (London: Economic and Social Research Council).

BELLABY, P. (1986) 'Please boss, can I leave the line? A sociological alternative to stress and coping discourse in explaining going sick at work', *International Journal of Sociology and Social Policy*, 6.

BELLABY, P. and SIDAWAY, J. E. (1985) 'Sexual joking in a potbank', Association of Social Anthropologists, Conference (Keele University, mimeo).

BENGSTON, V. L. and CUTLER, N. F. (1976) 'Generations and intergenerational relations' in R. H. Binstock and E. Shanas (q.v.).

BERGER, B. M. (1961) 'How long is a generation?', *British Journal of Sociology*, 11.

BERNARDES, J. (1985) ' "Family ideology": identification and exploration', *The Sociological Review*, 33, 275–97.

BERNARDES, J. (1986) 'Multidimensional developmental pathways: a proposal to facilitate the conceptualisation of "Family Diversity" ', *The Sociological Review*, 34, 590–610.

BERTAUX, D. (1981) *Biography and Society: the Life History Approach in the Social Sciences* (London: Sage).

BERTAUX, D. (1982) 'The life course approach as a challenge to the social sciences' in T. Hareven and L. J. Adams (q.v.).

BERTHOUD, R. (1985) *The Examination of Social Security* (London: Policy Studies Institute).

BIESELE, M. and HOWELL, N. (1981) ' "The old people give you life": ageing among !Kung hunter-gatherers' in P. T. Amoss and S. Harrell (q.v.).

BIGELOW, H. F. (1942), Chapter 17 in H. Becker and R. Hill (eds), *Marriage and the Family* (Boston: D.C. Heath).

BINSTOCK, R. H. and SHANAS, E. (eds) (1976) *Handbook of Ageing and the Social Sciences* (New York: Van Nostrand Rheinhold).

BLACKBURN, R. M. and MANN, M. (1979) *The Working Class in the Labour Market* (London: Macmillan).

BLOCH, E. (1986) *The Principle of Hope*, vols I–III (Oxford: Basil Blackwell).

BLOCH, M. (1973) 'The long term and the short term: the economic and political significance of the morality of kinship' in J. Goody (ed.), *The Character of Kinship* (Cambridge: Cambridge University Press).

BLOCH, M. (1982) 'Death, women and power' in M. Bloch and J. Parry (eds), *Death and the Regeneration of Life* (Cambridge: Cambridge University Press).

BLOOR, D. (1976) *Knowledge and Social Imagery* (London: Routledge and Kegan Paul).

BLUEBOND-LANGER, M. (1978) *The Private Worlds of Dying Children* (Princetown, New Jersey: Princetown University Press).

BODDY, M. and GRAY, F. (1979) 'Filtering theory and the legitimation of inequality', *Policy and Politics*, 7, 39–54.

BOLTANSKI, L. (1969) *Prime Education et Morale de Classe* (Paris: Mouton).

BOVAIRD, A., HARLOE, M. and WHITEHEAD, C. E. M. (1985) 'Private rented housing: its current role', *Journal of Social Policy*, 14, 1–23.

BRADSHAW, J. (1984) 'Families sharing poverty: an analysis of the living standards of single and multi-unit households', Social Security Workshop (London: Economic and Social Research Council).

BRANCA, P. (1975) *Silent Sisterhood* (London: Croom Helm).

BRISTOL, M. D. (1985) *Carnival and Theatre* (London: Methuen).

BROWN, M. (ed.) (1983) *The Structure of Disadvantage* (London: Heinemann).

BROWN, R. (1976) 'Women as employees: some comments on research in industrial sociology' in D. L. Barker and S. Allen (eds), *Dependence and Exploitation in Work and Marriage* (London: Longman).

BROWNING, H. and HERBERGER, L. (1978) 'The normative life cycle of the nuclear family' in *Health and the Family* (Geneva: World Health Organisation), pp. 13–20.

BUILDING SOCIETIES ASSOCIATION (1976) 'Evidence submitted to the Housing Finance Review' (London: Building Societies Association).

BUILDING SOCIETIES ASSOCIATION (1985a) *Bulletin*, 42.

BUILDING SOCIETIES ASSOCIATION (1985b) 'Mortgage Repayment Difficulties' (London: Building Societies Association).

BURCHILL, F. and ROSS, R. (1977) *A History of the Potters' Union* (Stoke-on-Trent: Ceramic and Allied Trades Union).

BURGOYNE, J. (1985a) 'Cohabitation and contemporary family life', End of Grant Report (London: Economic and Social Research Council).

BURGOYNE, J. (1985b) 'Unemployment and married life', *Unemployment Unit Bulletin*, November, 7–10.

BURGOYNE, J. (1985c) 'Marriage on the dole', *The Listener*, 13 June, 113.2913, 12–13.

BURGOYNE, J. and CLARK, D. (1981) 'Reconstituted families' in R. N. Rapoport, M. P. Fogarty and R. Rapoport (q.v.).

BURGOYNE, J. and CLARK, D. (1983) 'You are what you eat; food and family reconstitution' in A. Murcott (ed.), *The Sociology of Food and Eating* (London: Gower Press).

BURGOYNE, J. and CLARK, D. (1984) *Making a go of it: a Study of Stepfamilies in Sheffield* (London: Routledge and Kegan Paul).

BURGOYNE, J., ORMROD, R. and RICHARDS, M. (1987) *Divorce Matters* (Harmondsworth: Penguin).

BURR, W. (1973) *Theory Construction and the Sociology of the Family* (New York: Wiley).

CALHOUN, R. B. (1978) *In Search of the New Old: Redefining Old Age in America 1945–1970* (New York: Elsevier).

CARTER, E. A. and McGOLDRICK, M. (eds) (1980) *The Family Life Cycle* (New York: Gardner Press).

CENTRAL STATISTICAL OFFICE(1986) *Social Trends 16* (London: Her Majesty's Stationery Office).

CHEAL, D. (1983) 'Intergenerational transfers', *Journal of Marriage and the Family*, 45, 805–13.

CHEAL, D. (1985) 'The system of transfers to and from households in Canada', *Western Economic Review*, 4, 35–40.

CHEAL, D. (forthcoming, a) 'The social dimension of gift behaviour', *Journal of Social and Personal Relationships*.

CHEAL, D. (forthcoming, b) 'The family and the state of theory', in K. Ishwaran (ed.), *The Modern Family* (Toronto: Oxford University Press).

CHEAL, D. (forthcoming, c) 'Theories of serial flow in intergenerational transfers', *International Journal of Ageing and Human Development*.

CHEN, Y.-P. (1985) 'Economic status of the aging' in R. Binstock and E. Shanas (eds), *Handbook of Aging and the Social Sciences*, 2nd edn (New York: Van Nostrand Reinhold).

CHEN, Y.-P. and CHU, K.-W. (1982) 'Household Expenditure Patterns', *Journal of Family Issues*, 3, 233–50.

CHESTER, R. (1985) 'The rise of the neo-conventional family', *New Society*, 72, 185–8.

CHRISTENSEN, H. T. (ed.) (1964) *Handbook of Marriage and the Family* (Chicago: Rand McNally).

CLARK, D., McCANN, K., MORRICE, K. and TAYLOR, R. (1985) 'Work and marriage in the off-shore oil industry', *International Journal of Social Economics*, 12.

CLARK, R., MADDOX, G., SCHRIMPER, R. and SUMNER, D. (1984) *Inflation and the Economic Well-Being of the Elderly* (Baltimore: Johns Hopkins University Press).

CLARK, R. and SPENGLER, J. (1980) *The Economics of Individual and Population Aging* (Cambridge: Cambridge University Press).

COLLVER, A. (1963) 'The family life cycle in India and the United States', *American Sociological Review*, 28, 86–96.

CONCEPCION, M. B. and LANDA-JOCANO, F. (1974) 'Demographic factors influencing the family life cycle' in *The Population Debate: Dimensions and Perspectives*, World Population Conference, Bucharest (New York: United Nations) pp. 252–62.

CONSULTATIVE COMMITTEE on School Attendance of Children below the age of Five (1908) *Report* (London: Her Majesty's Stationery Office).

COOLIDGE, E. L. (1905) *The Mother's Manual* (London: Hutchinson).

CORNWELL, J. (1984) *Hard-Earned Lives* (London: Tavistock).

COURGEAU, D. (1985) 'Interaction between spatial mobility, family and career life-cycle: a French survey', *European Sociological Review*, 1, 139–62.

CUISENIER, J. (ed.) (1977) *Le Cycle de la Vie Familiale dans les Sociétés Européenes* (Paris: Mouton).

CUNNINGHAM-BURLEY, S. (1985) 'Constructing grandparenthood: anticipating appropriate action', *Sociology*, 19, 421–36.

DALE, A. (1985) 'Family poverty in Great Britain', End of Grant Report (London: Economic and Social Research Council).

DALE, A. (1986) 'A note on differences in car usage by married men and married women', *Sociology*, 20, 91–2.

DALE, A., GILBERT, G. N. and ARBER, S. (1985) 'Integrating women into class theory', *Sociology*, 19, 384–408.

DATAN, N. and GINSBERG, L. (eds) (1975) *Life-span Developmental Psychology: Normative Life Crises* (New York: Academic Press).

DAVIN, A. (1978) 'Imperialism and motherhood', *History Workshop*, 5, 9–65.

DAVIS, J. A. (1985) *The Logic of Causal Order* (Beverly Hills: Sage).

DAYUS, K. (1985) *Where There's Life* (London: Virago).

DELPHY, C. (1984) *Close to Home* (London: Hutchinson).

DENNIS, N., HENRIQUES, F. and SLAUGHTER, C. (1969) *Coal is Our Life*, 2nd edn (London: Eyre and Spottiswoode).

DEPARTMENT OF THE ENVIRONMENT (1977) *Housing Policy*, Tech. Vol. Pt. II (London: Her Majesty's Stationery Office).

DEPARTMENT OF THE ENVIRONMENT (1983) *English Housing Condition Survey*, Pt. II (London: Her Majesty's Stationery Office).

DEX, S. (1985) *The Sexual Division of Work* (Sussex: Wheatsheaf Books).

DINGWALL, R. and HEATH, C. (eds) (1977) *Health Care and Health Knowledge* (London: Croom Helm).

DOLING, J., KARN, V. and STAFFORD, B. (1985a) 'An Englishman's home under siege', *Housing Review*, 34, 92–5.

DOLING, J., KARN, V. and STAFFORD, B. (1985b) 'Unemployment and mortgage arrears', *Unemployment Unit Bulletin*, 18, 3–5.

DOLING, J., KARN, V. and STAFFORD, B. (1986) 'The impact of unemployment on home ownership', *Housing Studies*, 1, 49–59.

DONZELOT, J. (1979), *The Policing of Families* (London: Hutchinson).

DOUGLAS, J. (1971) *American Social Order: Social Rules in a Pluralistic Society* (New York: Free Press).

DOUGLAS, M. (1966) *Purity and Danger: An Analysis of Concepts of Pollution and Taboo* (London: Routledge and Kegan Paul).

DOUGLAS, M. (1970) *Natural Symbols: Explorations in Cosmology* (London: Barrie and Rockliff).

DUNCAN, G. J. and MORGAN, J. N. (1985) 'The panel study of income dynamics', in G. H. Elder (ed.), *Life Course Dynamics: Trajectories and Transitions, 1968–80* (Ithaca: Cornell University Press).

DUPREE, M. (1981) 'Family structure in North Staffordshire, 1840 to 1880', D.Phil (Oxford: Oxford University).

DURKHEIM, E. (1952) *Suicide* (London: Routledge and Kegan Paul).

DUVALL, E. M. (1977) *Marriage and Family Development*, 5th edn (Philadelphia: J. B. Lippincott).

DYHOUSE, C. (1981) 'Working-class mothers and infantile mortality in England, 1896–1914' in C. Webster (ed.), *Biology, Medicine and Society 1840–1940* (Cambridge, Cambridge University Press).

ELDER, G. H. (1977) 'Family history and the life course', *Journal of Family History*, 2, 279–304.

ELDER, G. H. (1981) 'History and the family: the discovery of complexity', *Journal of Marriage and the Family* 43, 489–519.

ELDER, G. H. (1984) 'Families, kin and the life course' in R. Parke (ed.), *Review of Child Development Research*, vol. 7, (Chicago: University of Chicago Press).

ELIAS, N. (1985) *The Loneliness of Dying* (Oxford: Basil Blackwell).

EPSTEIN, S. T., CREHAN, K., GRERZER, A. and SASS, J. (1986) *Women, Work and the Family in Britain and Germany* (London: Croom Helm).

ESTES, C. L. (1979) *The Aging Enterprise* (San Francisco: Jossey-Bass).

EVANS, P. and BARTOLOME, F. (1970) *Must Success Cost So Much?* (London: Grant McIntyre).

EVERS, H. (1985) 'The frail elderly woman: emerging questions in ageing and women's health' in E. Lewis and V. Olesen (eds), *Women, Health and Healing: Towards a New Perspective* (London: Tavistock).

FAGIN, L. (1984) *The Forsaken Families* (Harmondsworth: Penguin Books).

FEUERBACH, L. (1980) *Thoughts on Death and Immortality* (Berkeley, University of California Press).

FINCH, J. (1984) 'Community care: developing non-sexist alternatives', *Critical Social Policy*, 10, 6–18.

FINCH, J. (1986) 'Age as a variable' in Burgess R. G. (ed.), *Key Variables in Social Investigation* (London: Routledge and Kegan Paul).

FIRTH, R. (1956) *Two Studies of Kinship in London*, Monographs on Social Anthropology No. 15 (London: Athlone Press).

FIRTH, R., HUBERT, J. and FORGE, A. (1969) *Families and Their Relatives* (London: Routledge and Kegan Paul).

FLANDRIN, J. L. (1979) *Families in Former Times* (Cambridge: Cambridge University Press).

FLEMING, M. and NELLIS, J. (1985) 'Socio-economic aspects of the housing market in the UK and the expansion of home ownership: a study of new entrants in 1983', International Conference on Housing Research and Policy Issues in an Era of Fiscal Austerity (Amsterdam, 1985).

FLETCHER, R. (1971) *The Family and Marriage in Britain* (Harmondsworth: Penguin).

FONER, A. (1974) 'Age stratification and conflict in political life', *American Sociological Review*, 39, 187–96.

FONER, P. S. (1973) *When Marx Died* (New York: International Publishers).

FONTANA, A. (1977) *The Last Frontier* (London: Sage).

FORD, J. and TOOK, L. (1985) 'Owner occupation and mortgage arrears', Working Paper No. 1 (Loughborough: Loughborough University).

FOREST, R. (1983) 'The meaning of home ownership', *Environment and Planning D: Society and Space*, 205–16.

FOREST, R. and MURIE, A. (1980) 'Wealth, inheritance and housing policy', *Policy and Politics*, 8, 1–19.

FOREST, R. and MURIE, A. (1984) 'A foot on the ladder? An evaluation of low cost home ownership initiatives' (Bristol: School of Advanced Urban Studies).

FORSTER, N. (1987) 'Economic and social change in the 1980s: a study of the effects of redundancy on a group of South Yorkshire steelworkers and their families', Ph.D. thesis (Sheffield: Sheffield City Polytechnic).

FORTES, M. (1958) 'Introduction' in J. Goody (ed.) *The Developmental Cycle in Domestic Groups* (Cambridge: Cambridge University Press), pp. 1–14.

FOUCAULT, M. (1970) *Madness and Civilisation: A History of Insanity in the Age of Reason* (London: Tavistock).

FOUCAULT, M. (1976) *The Birth of the Clinic* (London: Tavistock).

FOUCAULT, M. (1979) *The History of Sexuality* (London: Allen Lane).

FRANKENBERG, R. (1966) *Communities in Britain* (Harmondsworth: Penguin Books).

FRANKENBERG, R. (1980) 'Medical anthropology and development: a theoretical perspective', *Social Science and Medicine*, 14B, 197–207.

FRANKENBERG, R. (1986) 'Malattia come festa: sickness as celebration and socialisation: children's accounts of sickness episodes in a Tuscan community' (unpublished).

FREIDSON, E. (1970) *Profession of Medicine* (New York: Dodd Mead).

GAULLIER X. (1982) 'Economic crisis and old age policies in France', *Ageing and Society*, 2, 165–82.

GEERTZ, C. (1973) *The Interpretation of Cultures* (New York: Basic Books).

VAN GENNEP, A. (1960) *The Rites of Passage*, translated by M. K. Vizedom and G. L. Caffee (London: Routledge and Kegan Paul).

GERSHUNY, J. (1985) 'Economic development and change in the mode of provision of services' in N. Redclift and E. Mingione (q.v.).

GERTH, N. and WRIGHT MILLS, C. (1954) *Character and Social Structure* (London: Routledge and Kegan Paul).

GIDDENS, A. (1984) *The Constitution of Society* (London: Polity Press).

GILBERT, B. B. (1966) *The Evolution of National Insurance in Great Britain: the Origin of the Welfare State* (London: Michael Joseph).

GIOVANNINI, F. (1983) *La Morte Rossa: I Marxisti e La Morte* (Milan: Edizione Dedalo).

GLASER, B. G. and STRAUSS, A. L. (1965) *Awareness of Dying* (London: Weidenfeld and Nicholson).

GLASER, B. G. and STRAUSS, A. L. (1971) *Status Passage* (London: Routledge and Kegan Paul).

GLICK, P. C. (1947) 'The family life cycle', *American Sociological Review*, 12, 164–74.

GLICK, P. C. (1977) 'Updating the life cycle of the family', *Journal of Marriage and the Family*, 39, 5–13.

GLICK, P. C. and PARKE, R. (1965) 'New approaches in studying the life cycle of the family', *Demography*, 2, 187–202.

GOLDTHORPE, J. (1980) *Social Mobility and Class Structure in Modern Britain* (Oxford: Clarendon Press).

GOULDNER, A. (1971) *The Coming Crisis of Western Sociology* (London: Heinemann).

GOVERNMENT OF THE UNITED STATES (1985) *Economic Report of the President* (Washington, D.C.: United States Government Printing Office).

GRASSIC GIBBON, L. (1973) *A Scots Quair* (London: Pan Books).

GREEN, M. (1984) *Marriage* (London: Fontana).

GREGORY, D. and URRY, J. (1985) *Social Relations and Spatial Structures* (London: Macmillan).

GUILLEMAND, A. M. (1983) *Old Age and the Welfare State* (London: Sage).

HABERMAS, J. (1969) 'Technology and society as "Ideology" ' in J. Habermas (ed.), *Toward a Rational Society* (London: Heinemann).

HAINES, M. (1985) 'The life cycle, savings and demographic adaptation' in A. Rossi (ed.), *Gender and the Life Course* (New York: Aldine).

HALL, C. (1979) 'The early formation of Victorian domestic ideology' in S. Burman (ed.), *Fit Work for Women* (London: Croom Helm).

HALSEY, A. H. (1985) 'On methods and morals' in M. Abrams, D. Gerard and N. Timms (eds), *Values and Social Change in Britain* (London: Macmillan).

HAMMOND, S. B. (1954) 'General orientation' in O. A. Oeser and S. B. Hammond (eds), *Social Structure and Personality in a City* (London: Routledge and Kegan Paul) pp. 3–10.

HAREVEN, T. K. (1975) 'Family time and industrial time', *Journal of Urban History*, 1.

HAREVEN, T. K. (1978a) 'Family time and historical time' in A. S. Rossi, J. Kagan and T. K. Hareven (q.v.).

HAREVEN, T. K. (1978b) 'Introduction: the historical study of the life course' in T. K. Hareven (ed.) *Transitions: the Family and the Life Course in Historical Perspective* (New York: Academic Press).

HAREVEN, T. K. (1982) *Family Time and Industrial Time* (Cambridge: Cambridge University Press).

HAREVEN, T. K. and ADAMS, L. J. (eds) (1982) *Ageing and Life Course Transitions* (London: Tavistock).

HARLOE, M. (1985) *Private Rented Housing in the United States and Europe* (London: Croom Helm).

HARRIS, C. C. (1983) *The Family and Industrial Society* (London: Allen and Unwin).

HARRIS L. and ASSOCIATES, INC. (1981) *Aging in the Eighties* (Washington D.C.: The National Council on the Aging).

HARRIS, M. (1985) 'Re-possessed', *New Society* (November), 361–2.

HASKEY, J. (1983) 'Children of divorcing couples', *Population Trends*, 31, 20–6.

HAVIGHURST, R. (1973) 'History of development psychology' in P. Baltes and K. W. Schaie (q.v.).

HEIDEGGER, M. (1962) *Being and Time* (London: SCM Press).

HENRETTA, J. and CAMPBELL, R. (1978) 'Net worth as an aspect of status', *American Journal of Sociology*, 83, 1204–23.

HIEBERT, P. G. (1981) 'Old age in a South Indian village' in P. T. Amoss and S. Harrell (q.v.).

HILL, R. (1958) 'Sociology of marriage and family behaviour, 1945–56', *Current Sociology*, 7, 1–33.

HILL, R. (1970) *Family Development in Three Generations* (Cambridge, Mass.: Schenkman).

HILL, R. and METTESSICH, P. (1979) 'Family development theory and life-span development' in P. Baltes and O. Brim (eds), *Life-span Development and Behavior*, vol. 2 (New York: Academic Press).

HILL, R. and RODGERS, R. (1964) 'The developmental approach' in H. T. Christensen (q.v.) pp. 171–211.

HOBCRAFT, J. and MURPHY, M. (1986) 'Demographic event history analysis: a selective review', *Population Index*, 52, 3–27.

HOBSBAWM, E. J. and RANGER, T. (eds) (1983) *The Invention of Tradition* (Cambridge: Cambridge University Press).

HOCHSCHILD, A. (1973) *The Unexpected Community: Portrait of an Old Age Subculture* (Berkeley: University of California Press).

HOCHSCHILD, A. (1975) 'Disengagement theory: a critique and proposal', *American Sociological Review*, 40, 553–69.

HOGAN, D. P. (1978) 'The variable order of events in the life course', *American Sociological Review*, 43, 573–86.

HOGAN, D. P. (1980) 'The transition to adulthood as a career contingency', *American Sociological Review*, 45, 261–76.

HOHN, C. (1983) 'The family life cycle – on the necessity to enlarge the concept', Workshop on Family Demography Methods and Applications (New York: Committee on Family Demography and the Life Cycle of the International Union for the Scientific Study of Population, and the Population Council).

HOOD, E. (1916) *Fighting Dirt* (London: Harrap).

HUNT, P. (1980) *Gender and Class Consciousness* (London: Macmillan).

HUNTER, R. (1904) *Poverty* (New York: Macmillan).

HUXLEY, A. (1964) *Island* (Harmondsworth: Penguin Books, 1964).

INTERNATIONAL CONGRESS FOR THE WELFARE AND PROTECTION OF CHILDREN (1902) *Report of the Proceedings of the Third International Congress* (London: P. S. King and Son).

JEWSON, N. D. (1976) 'The disappearance of the sick man from the medical cosmology 1770–1870', *Sociology*, 10, 225–44.

JOHNSON, T. J. (1972) *Professions and Power* (London: Macmillan).

JONES, C. (1978) 'Household movements, filtering and trading up within the owner occupied sector', *Regional Studies*, 12, 551–61.

JONES, G. (1986) 'Youth in the social structure: class and gender stratification in the transitions from adolescence to adulthood', Ph.D. thesis (Guildford: University of Surrey).

JOWELL, R. and WITHERSPOON, S. (1985) *British Social Attitudes: the 1985 Report* (London: Gower Press).

KAPP, Y. (1972) *Eleanor Marx, Vol I: Family Life, 1855–1883* (London: Lawrence and Wishart).

KARN, V., KEMENY, J. and WILLIAMS, P. (1986) *Home Ownership in the Inner City: Salvation or Despair* (Aldershot: Gower).

KEITH-ROSS, J. (1977) *Old People, New Lives: Community Creation in a Retirement Residence* (Chicago: University of Chicago Press).

KELLAHER, A. (1984) 'Are we a "death-denying" society?, *Social Science and Medicine*, 18, 713–23.

KEMENY, J. (1980) 'Home ownership and the family life cycle', Working Paper No. 70 (Birmingham: Centre for Urban and Regional Studies).

KIERNAN, K. (1983) 'The structure of families today: continuity or change?' in British Society for Population Studies, Occasional Paper 31 (London: Office of Population, Censuses and Surveys).

KIERNAN, K. (1986) 'Teenage marriage and marital breakdown: a longitudinal study', *Population Studies*, 40, 35–54.

KINCAID, J. C. (1979) 'Poverty in the welfare state' in J. Irving, I. Miles and J. Evans (eds) *Demystifying Social Statistics* (London: Pluto Press).

KIRKPATRICK, E. L. *et al.*, (1934) 'The life cycle of family experience', Agricultural Experiment Station Research Bulletin, No. 121 (Madison: University of Wisconsin).

KLEIN, D. M. and ALDOUS, J. (1979) 'Three blind mice: misleading criticisms of the "family life cycle" concept', *Journal of Marriage and the Family*, 41, 689–91.

KLEINMAN, A. (1980) *Patients and Healers in the Context of Culture: an Exploration of the Borderland between Anthropology, Medicine and Psychiatry* (Berkeley: University of California Press).

KOHLI, M., ROSENOW, J. and WOLF, J. (1983) 'The social construction of ageing through work', *Ageing and Society*, 3.

KUHN, T. (1962) *The Structure of Scientific Revolutions* (Chicago: University of Chicago Press).

LACZKO, F. and WALKER, A. (1985) 'Excluding older workers from the labour force: early retirement policies in Britain, France and Sweden' in *The Yearbook of Social Policy, 1984–5* (London: Routledge and Kegan Paul).

LACZKO, F. (1986) 'The social impact of early retirement', British Sociological Association, Conference (Loughborough).

LAND, H. (1983) 'Poverty and gender: the distribution of resources within the family' in M. Brown (q.v.).

LANSING, J. B. and KISH, L. (1957) 'Family life cycle as an independent variable', *American Sociological Review*, 22, 512–9.

LANSING, J. B. and MORGAN, J. N. (1955) 'Consumer finances over the life cycle' in L. H. Clark (ed.), *Consumer Behaviour, Vol II: the Life Cycle and Consumer Behaviour* (New York: New York University Press).

LASH, N. (1981) *A Matter of Hope: A Theologian's Reflections on the Thought of Karl Marx* (London: Darton, Longman and Todd).

LASLETT, P. (1971) *The World We Have Lost* (London: Methuen).

LASLETT, P. (1983) *The World We Have Lost – Further Explored* (London: Methuen).

LAYARD, R., PIACHAUD, D. and STEWART, M. (1978) *The Causes of Poverty*, Royal Commission on the Distribution of Income and Wealth (London: Her Majesty's Stationery Office).

LAZONICK, W. (1979) 'Industrial relations and technical change: the case of the self-acting mule', *Cambridge Journal of Economics*, 3, 231–62.

LEIRA, A. (1984) 'Women's work strategies: an analysis of the organisation of everyday life in an urban neighbourhood' in A. Leira (ed.), *Work and Womanhood: Norwegian Studies* (Oslo: Institute for Social Research).

LEONARD, D. (1981) *Sex and Generation* (London: Tavistock).

LEVINE, D. C. (1977) *Family Formation in the Age of Nascent Capitalism* (New York: Academic Press).

LEVI-STRAUSS, C. (1968) *Structural Anthropology* (Harmondsworth: Penguin Books).

LEVI-STRAUSS, C. (1969) *The Elementary Structures of Kinship* (Boston: Beacon Press).

LEWIS, J. (1980) *The Politics of Motherhood: Child and Maternal Welfare in England, 1900–1939* (London: Croom Helm).

LITTLER, C. R. (1982) *The Development of the Labour Process in Capitalist Societies* (London: Heinemann).

LOCAL GOVERNMENT BOARD, Maternity and Child Welfare (1914) 'A Memorandum on Health Visiting' (London: Her Majesty's Stationery Office).

LOCK, M. (ed.) (1986) *Culture, Medicine and Psychiatry*, Special Issue: Cultural Variation and the Menopause.

LONSDALE, M. (1885) *The Care and Nursing of Children* (London: Hatchards).

LOOMIS, C. P. and HAMILTON, C. H. (1936) 'Family life cycle analysis', *Social Forces*, 15, 225–31.

McCONNEL, C. and DELJAVAN, F. (1983) 'Consumption patterns of the retired household', *Journal of Gerontology*, 38, 480–90.

MACINTYRE, S. (1977) 'Old age as a social problem' in R. Dingwall and C. Heath (q.v.).

McKENDRICK, N. (1961) 'Josiah Wedgwood and factory discipline', *Historical Journal*, 4, 30–55.

MAHON, J. (1976) *Harry Pollitt: A Biography* (London: Lawrence and Wishart).

MANNHEIM, K. (1952) 'The problem of generations' in K. Mannheim and D. Kecskemeti, *Essays on the Sociology of Knowledge* (London: Routledge and Kegan Paul).

MANNHEIM, K. (1959) *Essays on the Sociology of Knowledge* (London: Routledge and Kegan Paul).

MANSFIELD, P. (1985) *Young People and Marriage*, Occasional Paper No. 1 (Edinburgh: Scottish Marriage Guidance Council).

MARSHALL, V. (1986) 'Dominant and emerging paradigms in the social psychology of aging' in V. Marshall (ed.), *Later Life* (Beverly Hills: Sage).

MARTIN, J. and ROBERTS, C. (1984) *Women and Employment: a Lifetime Perspective* (London: Her Majesty's Stationery Office).

MARTINEAU, H. (1859) 'Breast feeding' *Medical Times and Gazette* (10 September).

MARX, K. (1959) *Economic and Philosophical Manuscripts of 1844* (London: Lawrence and Wishart).

MARX, K. and ENGELS, F. (1973) 'Manifesto of the Communist Party, English Edition, 1888' in D. Fernbach (ed.), *The Revolution of 1848* (London: Pelican Marx Library).

MATTHEWS, S. H. (1979) *The Social World of Old Women* (London: Sage).

MAUSS, M. (1954) *The Gift* (Glencoe: Free Press).

MAYNARD, E. L. (1906) *Baby: Useful Hints for Mothers* (Bristol: Wright).

MEANS, R. and SMITH, R. (1983) 'From public assistance institutions to sunshine hotels: changing state perceptions about residential care for elderly people, 1939–1948', *Ageing and Society*, 3, 157–81.

MIDWINTER, E. (1985) *The Wage of Retirement: the Case for a New Pensions Policy* (London: Centre for Policy on Ageing).

MINGIONE, E. (1985) 'Social reproduction and the surplus labour force' in N. Redclift and E. Mingione (q.v.).

MIRER, T. (1979) 'The wealth-age relation among the aged', *American Economic Review*, 69, 435–43.

MIRER, T. (1980) 'The dissaving behavior of the retired aged', *Southern Economic Journal*, 46, 1197–205.

MITTERAUER, M. and SIEDER, R. (1982) *The European Family* (Oxford: Basil Blackwell).

MODELL, J. and HAREVEN, T. K. (1973) 'Urbanization and the malleable household: an examination of boarding and lodging in American families', *Journal of Marriage and the Family*, 35, 467–79.

MOEN, P., KAIN, E. and ELDER, G. H. (1983) 'Economic conditions and family life' in R. Nelson and F. Skidmore (eds), *American Families and the Economy* (Washington D.C.: National Academy Press).

MORIOKA, K. (1967) 'Life cycle patterns in Japan, China, and the United States', *Journal of Marriage and the Family*, 29, 595–606.

MORGAN, D. H. J. (1975) *Social Theory and the Family* (London: Routledge and Kegan Paul).

MORGAN, D. H. J. (1985) *The Family, Politics and Social Theory* (London: Routledge and Kegan Paul).

MORRIS, L. D. (1985a) 'Renegotiation of the domestic division of labour' in B. Roberts, R. Finnegan and D. Gallie (eds), *New Approaches to Economic Life* (Manchester: Manchester University Press).

MORRIS, L. D. (1985b) 'Responses to redundancy: labour market experience, domestic organisation and male social networks', *International Journal of Social Economics*, 12, 5–16.

MORRIS, L. D. (1986) 'The changing social structure of Hartlepool' in P. Cooke (ed.), *Global Restructuring: Local Response* (London: Economic and Social Research Council, Imprint).

A MOTHER (1884) *A Few Suggestions to Mothers* (London: Churchill).

MOYLAN, S., MILLER, J. and DAVIES, R. (1984) *For Richer, For Poorer? Department of Health and Social Security Cohort Study of Unemployed Men* (London: Her Majesty's Stationery Office).

MURIE, A. *et al.* (1976) 'New building and housing need', *Progress in Planning*, 6, 85–186.

MURIE, A. (1983) *Housing Inequality and Deprivation* (London: Heinemann).

MURPHY, M. J. (1983) 'The life course of individuals in the family: describing static and dynamic aspects of the contemporary family' in British Society for Population Studies, Occasional Paper 31 (London: Office of Population, Censuses and Surveys) pp. 50–70.

MURPHY, M. J. (1984) 'The influence of fertility, early housing career and socio-economic factors on tenure determination in contemporary Britain', *Environment and Planning*, A, 16, 1301–18.

MURPHY, M. J. (1985) 'Demographic and socio-economic influences on recent British marital breakdown patterns', *Population Studies*, 39, 441–60.

MYLES, J. (1980) 'The aged, the state and the structure of inequality' in J. Harp and J. Hofley (eds), *Structured Inequality in Canada* (Scarborough, Ontario: Prentice-Hall).

NAG, M. (1974) 'Socio-cultural patterns, family cycle and fertility' in *The Population Debate: Dimensions and Perspectives*, World Population Conference, Bucharest (New York: United Nations) pp. 289–312.

NATIONAL COUNCIL OF WELFARE (1984) *Sixty-Five and Older* (Ottawa: Minister of Supply and Services, Canada).

NATIONAL COUNCIL OF WELFARE (1985) *Poverty Profile 1985* (Ottawa: Minister of Supply and Services, Canada).

NATIONAL FEDERATION OF HOUSING ASSOCIATIONS (1985) *Inquiry into British Housing* (London: National Federation of Housing Associations).

NEUGARTEN, B. (1964) *Personality in Middle and Later Life* (New York: Atherton Press).

NEUGARTEN, B. (1968) *Middle Age and Ageing* (Chicago: Chicago University Press).

NEWSHOLME, A. (1935) *Fifty Years in Public Health* (London: Allen & Unwin).

NOCK, S. L. (1979) 'The family life cycle: empirical or conceptual tool?' *Journal of Marriage and the Family*, 41, 15–26.

NORTON, A. J. (1980) 'The influence of divorce on traditional life cycle measures', *Journal of Marriage and the Family*, 42, 63–9.

NORTON, A. J. (1983) 'Family life cycle: 1980', *Journal of Marriage and the Family*, 45, 267–75.

OAKLEY, A. (1974) *The Sociology of Housework* (Oxford: Martin Robertson).

OFFICE FOR ECONOMIC AND CULTURAL DEVELOPMENT (1979) *Child and Family: Demographic Developments in the OECD Countries* (Paris, Office for Economic and Cultural Development).

O'BRIEN, E. (1963) *The Country Girls* (Harmondsworth: Penguin Books).

O'HIGGINS, M. and BRADSHAW, J. (1984) 'Life cycle income inequality' (unpublished paper).

OPPENHEIMER, V. (1974) 'The life-cycle squeeze', *Demography*, 11, 227–45.

OPPENHEIMER, V. (1981) 'The changing nature of life-cycle squeezes' in R. Fogel, E. Hatfield, S. Kiesler and E. Shanas (eds), *Aging: Stability and Change in the Family* (New York: Academic Press).

OPPENHEIMER, V. (1982) *Work and the Family* (New York: Academic Press).

PAHL, J. (1983) 'The allocation of money and the structuring of inequality within marriage', *The Sociological Review*, 31, 237–62.

PAHL, R. E. and PAHL, J. (1971) *Managers and their Wives* (Harmondsworth: Penguin).

PAHL, R. E. (1984) *Divisions of Labour* (Oxford: Basil Blackwell).

PAHL, R. E. and WALLACE, C. (1985) 'Household work strategies in economic recession' in N. Redclift and E. Mingione (q.v.).

PALMORE, E. (1981) *Social Patterns in Normal Aging* (Durham N.C.: Duke University Press).

PAMPEL, F. (1981) *Social Change and the Aged* (Lexington: D. C. Heath).

PAYNE, J. and PAYNE, G. (1977) 'Housing pathways and stratification: a study of life-chances in the housing market', *Journal of Social Policy*, 6, 129–56.

PHILLIPSON, C. (1982) *Capitalism and the Construction of Old Age* (London: Macmillan).

A PHYSICIAN (1894) *Infant Care and Sterilized Milk* (London: Sampson and Low).

PILCHER, W. W. (1972) *The Portland Longshoremen* (New York: Holt Rinehart and Winston).

PLATT, J. (1976) *Social Research in Bethnal Green* (London: Tavistock).

PLATT, J. (1981) 'The social construction of "Positivism" and its significance in British sociology 1950–80' in P. Abrams, R. Deem, J. Finch and P. Rock, (eds), *Practice and Progress: British Sociology 1950–1980* (London: Allen & Unwin).

PLOT (1686) *The Natural History of Staffordshire.*

PLUMMER, K. (1975) *Sexual Stigma: an Interactional Account* (London: Routledge and Kegan Paul).

PLUMMER, K. (1983) *Documents of Life* (London: Allen & Unwin).

POLLERT, A. (1981) *Girls, Wives and Factory Lives* (London: Macmillan).

PORTER, C. (1900) 'Suggestions as to the feeding and care of infants' (Stockport: Thompson).

PRESTON, S. H. (1976) 'Family sizes of children and family sizes of women', *Demography*, 13, 105–14.

RAPOPORT, R. (1963) 'Normal crises, family structure and mental health', *Family Process*, 2, 68–80.

RAPOPORT, R. N., FOGARTY, M. P. and RAPOPORT, R. (1981) *Families in Britain* (London: Routledge and Kegan Paul).

RAPOPORT, R. and SIERAKOWSKI, M. (1982) *Recent Trends in Family and Work in Britain* (London: Policy Studies Institute).

RAYMOND, J. (1985) 'Science in the service of medicine: germ theory, bacteriology and English public health, 1860–1914', Conference on Science in Modern Medicine, Manchester.

REDCLIFT, N. and MINGIONE, E. (eds) (1985) *Beyond Employment* (London: Basil Blackwell).

RICHMAN, J. (1982) 'Men's experience of pregnancy and childbirth' in L. McKee and M. O'Brien (eds), *The Father Figure* (London: Tavistock).

RIDDLE, S. M. (1984) 'Age, obsolescence and unemployment', *Ageing and Society*, 4.

RILEY, M. W., JOHNSON, M. and FONER, A. (1972) *Ageing and Society: a Sociology of Age Stratification*, vol. 3 (New York: Sage).

ROBERTS, R. (1971) *The Classic Slum* (Harmondsworth: Penguin).

ROCK, P. (1973) *Making People Pay* (London: Routledge and Kegan Paul).

ROSE, A. M. and PETERSON, W. A. (1965) *Older People and their Social World* (Philadelphia: Davis).

ROSE, H. (1981) 'Re-reading Titmus: the sexual division of welfare', *Journal of Social Policy*, 10, 477–50.

ROSE, R. (1985) *Public Employment in Western Nations* (Cambridge: Cambridge University Press).

ROSOW, I. (1967) *Social Integration of the Aged* (New York: Free Press).

ROSSER, C. and HARRIS, C. C. (1965) *The Family and Social Change* (London: Routledge and Kegan Paul).

ROSSI, A. S., KAGAN, J. and HAREVEN, T. (eds) (1978) *The Family* (New York: Norton).

ROSSI, P. H. (1980) *Why Families Move*, 2nd edn (Beverly Hills: Sage).

ROTH, J. A. (1962) 'The treatment of tuberculosis as a bargaining process' in A. M. Rose (ed.), *Human Behaviour and Social Processes* (London: Routledge and Kegan Paul).

ROWNTREE, B. S. (1902) *Poverty: a Study of Town Life* (London: Macmillan).

ROWNTREE, B. S. (1941) *Poverty and Progress* (London: Longmans).

RUSSELL, C. (1981) *The Ageing Experience* (Sydney: Allen & Unwin).

RYDER, N. B. (1965) 'The cohort as a concept in the study of social change', *American Sociological Review*, 30, 843–61.

SAHLINS, M. (1965) 'On the sociology of primitive exchange' in M. Banton (ed.), *The Relevance of Models in Social Anthropology* (London: Tavistock).

SARSBY, J. (1985) 'Sexual segregation in the pottery industry', *Feminist Review*, 21, 67–93.

SARTRE, J.-P. (1956) *Being and Nothingness* (New York: Philosophical Library).

SAUNDERS, P. (1984) 'Beyond housing classes: the sociological significance of private property rights in the means of consumption', *International Journal of Urban and Regional Research*, 8, 202–27.

SCHON, D. A. (1979) 'Generative metaphor: a perspective on problem-setting in social policy' in A. Ortony (ed.), *Metaphor and Thought* (Cambridge: Cambridge University Press).

SEARLE, G. R. (1971) *The Quest for National Efficiency* (Oxford: Oxford University Press).

SEGAL, L. (1981) *What is to be done about the Family?* (Harmondsworth: Penguin).

SEMMELL, B. (1960) *Imperialism and Social Reform* (London: Allen & Unwin).

SMELSER, N. (1959) *Social Change in the Industrial Revolution* (London: Routledge and Kegan Paul).

SMITH, C. and SIMMS, M. (1982) 'Young fathers: attitudes to marriage and family life' in L. McKee and M. O'Brien (eds), *The Father Figure* (London: Tavistock).

SMITH, F. B. (1979) *The People's Health 1830–1910* (London: Croom Helm).

SMITH, R. M. (1984) 'The structural dependence of the elderly in the Middle Ages and thereafter', *Ageing and Society*, 4, 409–28.

SNELL, K. D. M. (1985) *Annals of the Labouring Poor* (Cambridge: Cambridge University Press).

SONTAG, S. (1978) *Illness as Metaphor* (New York: Farrar, Strauss and Giroux).

SOROKIN, P. A., ZIMMERMAN, C. C. and GALPIN, C. J. (eds) (1930–32) *A Systematic Source Book in Rural Sociology* (Minneapolis: University of Minnesota Press, three vols).

SPANIER, G. B., SAUER, W. and LARZELERE, R. (1979) 'An empirical evaluation of the family life cycle', *Journal of Marriage and the Family*, 41, 27–38.

SPANIER, G. B. and GLICK, P. C. (1980) 'The life cycle of American families: an expanded analysis', *Journal of Family History*, 5, 97–111.

SPEARE, A. (1970) 'Home ownership, life cycle stage, and residential mobility', *Demography*, 7, 449–58.

STACEY, M. (1969) 'Family and household' in M. Stacey (ed.), *Comparability in Social Research*, British Sociological Association/Social Science Research Council (London: Heinemann) pp. 32–55.

STACEY, M. (1981) 'The division of labour revisited or overcoming the two Adams' in P. Abrams, R. Deem, J. Finch and P. Rock (eds), *Practice and Progress: British Sociology 1950–80* (London: Allen & Unwin).

STANTON, D., CAHILL, M. and HOWDLE, M. (1981) 'Mobility within local labour-markets', Research Paper No. 24 (London: Department of Employment, 1981).

STEDMAN JONES, G. (1971) *Outcast London: a Study of the Relationship between Classes in Victorian England* (Oxford: Oxford University Press).

STEWART, A., PRANDY, K. and BLACKBURN, R. (1980) *Social Stratification and Occupations* (London: Macmillan).

STRAUSS, A. (1978) *Negotiations: Varieties, Contexts, Processes and Social Order* (San Francisco: Jossey-Bass).

STRAUSS, A., FAGERHAUGH, S., SUCZEK, B. and WIENER, C. (1985) *Social Organisation of Medical Work* (Chicago: University of Chicago Press).

SULLIVAN, O. (1986) 'Housing movements of the divorced and separated', *Housing Studies*, 1, 35–48.

SULLIVAN, O. and MURPHY, M. (1984) 'Housing pathways and stratification: some evidence from a British national survey', *Journal of Social Policy*, 13, 147–65.

SUSSMAN, M. (1965) 'Relationships of adult children with their parents in the United States' in E. Shanas and G. Streib (eds), *Social Structure and the Family* (Englewood Cliffs: Prentice-Hall).

SWEET, J. A. (1977) 'Demography and the family', *Annual Review of Sociology*, 3, 363–405.

THOMAS, G. (1953) *A Frost on my Frolic* (London: Gollancz).

THOMAS, W. I. and ZNANIECKI, F. (1918–20) *The Polish Peasant in Europe and America*, 2 vols (Boston: W. B. Badger).

THOMPSON, E. (1963) *The Making of the English Working Class* (London: Gollancz).

THOMSON, D. (1984) 'The decline of social welfare: falling state support for the elderly since Victorian times', *Ageing and Society*, 4, 451–82.

THORNS, D. (1980) 'The role of the family life cycle in residential mobility', Working Paper No. 69 (Birmingham: Centre for Urban and Regional Studies).

TILLY, L. A. and SCOTT, J. W. (1978) *Women's Work and Family in 19th Century Europe* (New York: Holt, Rinehart and Winston).

TOWNSEND, P. (1957) *The Family Life of Old People* (London: Routledge and Kegan Paul).

TOWNSEND, P. (1974) 'Poverty as relative deprivation: resources and style of living' in D. Wedderburn (ed.), *Poverty, Inequality and Class Structure* (Cambridge: Cambridge University Press), pp. 15–42.

TOWNSEND, P. (1979) *Poverty in the United Kingdom* (Harmondsworth: Penguin).

TROST, J. (1977) 'The family life cycle: a problematic concept' in J. Cuisenier (q.v.).

TUMA, N. B., HANNAN, M. T. and GROENEVELD, L. P. (1979) 'Dynamic analysis of event histories', *American Journal of Sociology*, 84, 820–54.

TUMA, N. B. and HANNAN, M. T. (1984) *Social Dynamics: Models and Methods* (Orlando, Florida: Academic Press).

TUNNARD, J. (1976) 'Marriage breakdown and the loss of the owner occupied home', *Roof*, (March), 40–3.

TUNSTALL, J. (1962) *The Fishermen* (London: McGibbon and Kee).

TURNER, C. (1969) *Family and Kinship in Modern Britain* (London: Routledge and Kegan Paul).

TURNER, V. (1974) *Dramas, Fields and Metaphors* (Ithaca: Cornell University Press).

TURNER, V. (1982) *From Ritual to Theatre: the Human Seriousness of Play* (London: Performing Arts Journal Publications).

TURNER, V. and TURNER, E. (1978) *Image and Pilgrimage in Christian Culture* (Oxford: Basil Blackwell).

UHLENBERG, P. (1974) 'Cohort variations in family life cycle experiences of US females', *Journal of Marriage and the Family*, 36, 284–92.

VOYSEY, M. (1975) *A Constant Burden: the Reconstruction of Family Life* (London: Routledge and Kegan Paul).

WADDINGTON I. (1977) 'General practitioners and consultants in early 19th Century England: the sociology of intra-professional conflict' in J. Woodward and D. Richards (eds), *Health Care and Popular Medicine in 19th Century England* (London: Croom Helm).

WALDO, F. J. (1900) 'Summer diarrhoea' (The Milroy Lectures to the Royal College of Physicians), *Lancet*, 1340–4, 1426–30, 1494–8.

WALKER, A. (1982) 'Dependency and old age', *Social Policy and Administration*, 16, 115–35.

WALKER, A. (1986) 'Owner occupation and the reform of housing finance', Occasional Paper No. 8 (London: Catholic Housing Aid Society).

WALL, R. (1977) 'The responsibilities of kin', *Local Population Studies*, 19, 55–60.

WARBURTON, W. H. (1939) *The History of Trade Union Organization in the North Staffordshire Potteries* (London: Allen & Unwin).

WARNER, J. H. (1985) 'Science in the historiography of American medicine' in S. G. Kohstedt and M. Rossiter (eds), *Historical Writing on Science in American Society* (New York: Osiris).

WEEKS, J. (1981) *Sex, Politics and Society* (London: Longman).

WEISBROD, B. and HANSEN, W. L. (1968) 'An income-net worth approach to measuring economic welfare', *American Economic Review*, 58, 1315–29.

WELLS, R. V. (1971) 'Demographic change and the life cycle of American families', *Journal of Interdisciplinary History*, 2, 273–82.

WELLS, W. C. and GUBAR, G. (1966) 'Life cycle concepts in marketing research', *Journal of Marketing Research*, 3, 355–63.

WHIPP, R. (1983) *Potbank and Union*, unpublished PhD thesis (University of Warwick).

WHITE, M. (1985) *Long-term Unemployment and Labour Markets* (London: Policy Studies Institute).

WIEDER, D. L. (1974a) 'Telling the code' in R. Turner (ed.), *Ethnomethodology* (Harmondsworth: Penguin).

WIEDER, D. L. (1974b) *Language and Social Reality: the Case of Telling the Convict Code* (The Hague: Monton).

WILLEKENS, F. J., SHAH, I., SHAH, J. M. and RAMACHANDRAN, P. (1982) 'Multi-state analysis of marital state life tables: theory and application', *Population Studies*, 36, 129–44.

WILSON, C. (1985) *The Dictionary of Demography* (Oxford: Basil Blackwell).

WILSON, C. S. and LUPTON, T. (1959) 'The social background and connections of "top decision-makers" ', *The Manchester School*, 27, 30–51.

WILSON, E. (1980) *Halfway to Paradise* (London: Tavistock).

WOOD, S. (1985) 'Recruitment and the recession', *British Journal of Industrial Relations*, 23, 103–20.

WORLD HEALTH ORGANISATION (1978) *Health and the Family* (Geneva: World Health Organisation).

WRIGHT, P. W. G. (1978) 'Child care, science and imperialism', *Bulletin of the Society for the Social History of Medicine*, 23, 13–17.

WRIGHT, P. W. G. and TREACHER, A. (eds) (1982) *The Problem of Medical Knowledge: Examining the Social Construction of Medicine* (Edinburgh: Edinburgh University Press).

WRIGHT MILLS, C. (1940) 'Situated actions and vocabularies of motive', *American Sociological Review*, 5, 904–13.

WRIGHT MILLS, C. (1959) *The Sociological Imagination* (London: Allen & Unwin).

WRIGLEY, E. A. and SCHOFIELD, R. S. (1981) *The Population History of England: a Reconstruction* (London: Edward Arnold).

YEANDLE, S. (1984) *Women's Working Lives* (London: Tavistock).

YOUNG, A. (1982) 'The anthropologies of illness and sickness', *Annual Review of Anthropology* (Annual Reviews Inc.).

YOUNG, C. (1977) 'The family life cycle. Literature review and studies of families in Melbourne Australia', Australian Family Formation Project Monograph No. 6 (Canberra: The Australian National University Press).

YOUNG, M. and WILLMOTT, P. (1957) *Family and Kinship in East London* (London: Routledge and Kegan Paul).

YOUNG, M. and WILLMOTT, P. (1973) *The Symmetrical Family* (London: Rout-ledge and Kegan Paul).

ZBOROWSKI, M. (1969) *People in Pain* (San Francisco: Jossey-Bass).

Name Index

Abrams, P., 168
Aldous, J., 32, 38, 42, 144
Allan, G., 157–8
Amoss, P. T., 89
Anderson, D., 85, 133
Anderson, M., 2–3, 36, 71, 158, 162
Arensberg, C. M., 127
Ariès, P., 103, 135–6
Armstrong, D., 108–9, 120

Baltes, P., 23
Bartolome, F., 83
Beach, C., 149, 153
Becker, H. C., 165–6
Beechey, V., 184
Bell, C., 82
Bellaby, P., 6, *53–71*, 56, 61, 63
Bengston, V. L., 90
Berger, B.M., 28
Bernardes, J., 127
Bertaux, D., 21
Berthoud, R., 181
Biesele, M., 89
Bigelow, H. F., 34
Blackburn, R. M., 6
Bloch, E., 138
Bloch, M., 123, 125, 158
Bloor, D., 121
Bluebond-Langer, M., 122
Boddy, M., 208–9, 211
Boltanski, L., 116
Bovaird, A., 209
Bradshaw, J., 170, 181, 191
Branca, P., 79
Brim, D. G., 23
Bristol, M. D., 135

Brown, R., 1
Browning, H., 38
Bunyan, J., 132
Burchill, F., 67
Burgoyne, J., 7, *72–87*, 76, 78–80, 87, 176
Burr, W., 145

Cahill, M., 186
Calhoun, R. B., 90
Campbell, R., 147
Carter, E. A., 205
Chaucer, B., 132
Cheal, D., 10, 13, *141–54*, 141, 145–7, 149, 151
Chen, Y.-P., 141, 148
Chester, R., 84–5
Chu, K.-W., 141
Clark, D., 76, 78, 83, 87, 176
Clark, R., 147–8, 151
Collver, A., 39
Concepcion, M. B., 39
Coolidge, E. L., 117
Cornwell, J., 157
Courgeau, D., 49
Cuisenier, J., 33
Cunningham–Burley, S., 160
Cutler, N. F., 90

Dale, A., 11, 13, *170–91*, 173, 184, 187
Datan, N., 144
Davin, A., 109–11, 119–20
Davis, J. A., 2
Dayus, K., 80
Deljavan, F., 141
Delphy, C., 183

248

Dennis, N., 70, 83, 136
Dex, S., 205
Doling, J., 219–22
Donne, J., 125
Donzelet, J., 116
Douglas, J., 160–1
Douglas, M., 117–18
Duncan, G. J., 45
Dupree, M., 65
Durham, Bishop of, 133
Durkheim, E., 123–4, 131
Duvall, E. M., 33–5, 39, 144
Dyhouse, C., 110, 114, 116, 120

Elder, G. H., 2–3, 33, 35, 40, 45, 147, 149, 154
Elias, N., 135, 138
Engels, F., 69, 124, 136
Epstein, S. T., 173
Estes, C. L., 90
Evans, P., 83
Evers, H., 166

Fagin, L., 193
Feuerbach, L., 125, 131
Finch, J., 10–11, 13, *155–69*, 161, 163
Firth, R., 62, 157–9
Flandrin, J. L., 71
Fleming, M., 211
Fletcher, R., 74
Foner, A., 102
Foner, P. S., 124
Fontana, A., 88–9
Ford, J., 12, 13, *207–29*, 212
Forest, R., 209, 211
Forge, A., 157–9
Forster, N., 78
Fortes, M., 32
Foucault, M., 103, 109
Franco, 133
Frankenberg, R., 9, 71, *122–38*, 134, 136
Freidson, E., 103
Freud, A., 122

Gaullier, X., 90
Geertz, C., 104
Gennep, A. van, 54, 134

Gershuny, J., 71
Gerth, N., 160
Giddens, A., 20, 28
Gilbert, B. B., 109
Ginsberg, L., 144
Giovannini, F., 125
Glaser, B. G., 129, 138
Glick, P. C., 31–2, 35–6, 43
Goldthorpe, J., 170
Gouldner, A., 84
Gramsci, A., 125
Grassic Gibbon, L., 101
Gray, F., 208–9, 211
Green, M., 75
Gregory, D., 20
Gubar, G., 34
Guillemard, A. M., 90

Habermas, J., 116
Haines, M., 151
Hall, C., 79
Halsey, A. H., 161
Hamilton, C. H., 43
Hammond, S. B., 32
Hannan, M. T., 49
Hansen, W. L., 151
Hareven, T. K., 2–3, 12, 26, 37, 162–4, 168, 173, 176, 205
Harloe, M., 210
Harrell, S., 89
Harris, C. C., 3, *17–29*, 74, 159, 206
Harris, L., 147, 153
Harris, M., 214
Haskey, J., 77, 179
Havighurst, R., 144
Heidegger, M., 123
Henretta, J., 147
Henriques, F., 70
Herberger, L., 38
Hiebert, P. G., 89
Hill, R., 32, 35, 45, 76, 144–5, 167
Hobcraft, J., 48
Hobsbawm, E. J., 63
Hochschild, A., 88–90
Hogan, D. P., 2–3
Hohn, C., 42
Hood, E., 118–19
Howdle, M., 186
Howell, N., 89

Hubert, J., 157–9
Hunt, P., 173
Hunter, R., 143
Huxley, A., 136

Jewson, N. D., 103
Johnson, T. J., 103
Jones, C., 207
Jones, G., 178
Jowell, R., 76

Kain, E., 149
Kapp, Y., 124
Karn, V., 219–22
Keith-Ross, J., 89–90, 102
Kellaher, A., 123
Kemeny, J., 211
Kiernan, K., 48, 87
Kimball, S. T., 127
Kincaid, J. C., 181
Kirkpatrick, E. L., 34
Kish, L., 39
Klein, D. M., 42
Kleinman, A., 103
Koch, R., 118
Kohli, M., 26
Koltsov, M., 124
Kuhn, T., 103

Laczko, F., 178
Land, H., 183–4
Landa-Jocano, F., 39
Lansing, J. B., 34, 39
Lash, N., 124
Laslett, P., 37, 71
Layard, R., 181
Lazonick, W., 65
Leira, A., 167
Leonard, D., 78
Levine, D. C., 64
Lévi-Strauss, C., 55, 167
Lewis, J., 120
Lister, J., 118
Littler, C. R., 68
Llewellyn Davies, M., 71
Lock, M., 71
Lonsdale, M., 111
Loomis, C. P., 43
Lupton, T., 76

McConnel, C., 141
McGoldrick, M., 205
Macintyre, S., 90
McKendrick, N., 65
Mahon, J., 125
Mallory, Sir T., 123
Mann, M., 6
Mannheim, K., 28, 90, 101
Mansfield, P., 77
Marshall, V., 149
Martin, J., 77
Martineau, H., 107
Marx, K., 9, 69, 123–5, 136
Matthews, S. H., 88
Mauss, M., 149
Maynard, E. L., 117
Means, R., 90
Mettessich, P., 144
Midwinter, E., 178
Mills, C. Wright, *see* Wright Mills
Mingione, E., 173
Mirer, T., 153
Mitterauer, M., 147
Modell, J., 37
Moen, P., 149
Morgan, D. H. J., 3, 73–4, 157, 162
Morgan, J. N., 34, 45
Morioka, K., 39
Morris, L. D., 12, 13, 80, *192–206*, 206
Moylan, S., 178
Murie, A., 184, 209, 211
Murphy, M. J., 4, 11, 13, *30–50*, 37, 47–9, 185
Myles, J., 154

Nag, M., 39
Nellis, J., 211
Neugarten, B., 23
Newsholme, A., 110, 113
Nock, S. L., 40, 42
Norton, A. J., 36, 38, 46

Oakley, A., 81
O'Brien, E., 127
O'Higgins, M., 170, 191
Oppenheimer, V., 149–51
Ormrod, R., 76

Pahl, J., 71, 83, 183
Pahl, R. E., 69–71, 83, 127–8, 131, 135, 147, 177–8, 184–5, 192–3
Paine, T., 132
Palmore, E., 151
Pampel, F., 147
Parke, R., 43
Parsons, T., 17, 21
Pasteur, L., 118
Pawley, M., 226
Payne, G., 184
Payne, J., 184
Paynter, W., 136
Phillipson, C., 89–90, 124
Pilcher, W. W., 62
Platt, J., 73–4
Plot, 64
Plummer, K., 21, 75
Pollert, A., 60
Porter, C., 117
Powell, E., 133
Preston, S. H., 46

Ranger, T., 63
Rapoport, R., 74, 85, 144, 178
Rapoport, R. N., 74, 85
Raymond, J., 113
Richards, M., 76
Richman, J. L., 82
Riddle, S. M., 26
Riley, M. W., 99
Roberts, C., 77
Roberts, R., 80
Rock, P., 212
Rodgers, R., 32, 35, 144
Rose, A. M., 89
Rose, H., 161
Rose, R., 180
Rosow, I., 89
Ross, R., 67
Rosser, C., 74
Rossi, P. H., 50
Roth, J. A., 103
Rowntree, B. S., 4, 31–2, 142–4, 146, 148, 170
Russell, C., 88
Ryder, N. B., 32

Sahlins, M., 167

St Augustine, 30
Sarsby, J., 67
Sartre, J.–P., 133
Saunders, P., 185, 211
Schaie, K. W., 23
Schofield, R. S., 43
Schon, D. A., 8, 107, 120
Scott, J. W., 71, 205
Searle, G. R., 109–10
Segal, L., 84
Semmell, B., 109
Semmelweis, I. P., 118
Shakespeare, W., 4, 30, 101
Sidaway, J. E., 53, 61, 63
Sieder, R., 147
Sierakowski, M., 178
Simms, M., 82
Slaughter, C., 70
Smelser, N., 65
Smith, C., 82
Smith, F. B., 114
Smith, R., 90
Smith, R. M., 88
Snell, K. D. M., 64, 66
Sontag, S., 117
Soper, D., 133
Sorokin, P. A., 4, 31
Spanier, G. B., 40–3
Speare, A., 50
Spengler, J., 151
Stacey, M., 35, 161
Stafford, B., 219–22
Stanton, D., 186
Stedman Jones, G., 109
Stewart, A., 170
Strauss, A. L., 9, 128–31, 133, 135, 138, 156, 160
Sullivan, O., 50, 185, 216
Sussman, M. B., 143
Sweet, J. A., 39

Terman, L. M., 45
Thomas, G., 136
Thomas, W. I., 43
Thompson, E., 132
Thomson, D., 102
Thorns, D., 209
Tilly, L. A., 71, 205
Took, L., 12–13, *207–29*, 212

Torres, C., 133
Townsend, P., 143–4, 147–8, 170, 181
Treacher, A., 104
Trost, J., 36, 38, 45
Trotsky, L., 125
Tuma, N. B., 49
Tunnard, J., 216
Tunstall, J., 83
Turner, C., 37
Turner, E., 132
Turner, V., 54, 126, 132–4

Uhlenberg, P., 37
Urry, J., 20

Voysey, M., 79, 161

Waddington, I., 103
Waldo, F. J., 113
Walker, A., 154, 178, 182, 211, 223
Wall, R., 162
Wallace, C., 71
Warburton, W. H., 67
Warner, J. H., 121
Weber, M., 104
Weeks, J., 72

Weisbrod, B., 151
Wells, R. V., 37
Wells, W. C., 34
Whipp, R., 66
White, M., 178
Wieder, D. L., 55, 160
Wild, P., 87
Willekens, F. J., 48
Williams, R., 7–8, *88–102*
Willmott, P., 74, 76, 122, 132
Wilson, C., 30
Wilson, C. S., 76
Wilson, E., 79
Witherspoon, S., 76
Wood, S., 59
Wright, P. W. G., 8, *103–21*, 104, 109
Wright Mills, C., 11, 72, 160, 168
Wrigley, E. A., 43

Yeandle, S., 173
Young, A., 71
Young, C., 33, 35
Young, M., 74, 76, 122, 132

Zborowski, M., 103
Znaniecki, F., 43

Subject Index

absenteeism, 53. 54–5, 56–7
age, 4, 17–19, 23–5, 26, 53, 88, 91–102,
    143, 146, 147, 149, 153, 163–4,
    178
ageing, *see* age

babyhood, 8, 104–5, 107

childcare, 7, 54, 58, 73, 81–2, 83, 116,
    128, 201–2
cohort analysis, 25, 41, 43–50, 147,
    188, 212
consumer durables, 186–8

death, 9, 36–7, 47, 122–6, 130–1, 134,
    135–7
    see also infant mortality
dependency, 154
division of labour, household, 1, 7, 69–
    70, 73, 78, 80, 81–3, 127, 173, 183,
    192, 202–3
divorce, *see* marital breakdown

education of children, 150, 152
elderly, *see* old age
employment of women, 7, 149, 150–1,
    152, 161, 179–80, 193, 201–2
employment patterns, changes in,
    72–3, 149–50, 195–200, 201, 220

family, analysis of change in, 7, 37–50,
    72–86, 149, 150
family obligations, 10–11, 54, 56, 142,
    152, 154, 155–68, 192
feminism, 79, 84, 123
functionalism, 74, 144–5, 146

gender relations, 6, 11, 12, 41–2, 54,
    56, 60–2, 65, 69, 75, 77, 79–80,
    161, 164, 194, 200–3
General Household Survey (GHS),
    172–3
generation, 5, 8, 12, 28, 88, 90, 92,
    100–2, 141, 143–5, 148, 194, 202,
    205
gift giving, 146–7, 149, 167
government policy and intervention,
    10, 12, 75, 90, 108, 109, 115, 141,
    148, 149, 150, 208, 210, 220–1,
    223

health, 44, 53, 54–5, 56–7, 60, 61, 103,
    105, 129
home ownership, 12, 40, 44–5, 48,
    147–8, 184–5, 194, 204, 207–26
household assets, 171, 179, 183–90
household income, 171, 179, 180–3,
    184, 188–90, 204
housing, *see* home ownership
housing career, concept of, 207–12,
    213, 215, 224

illness, *see* health
industrialisation, *see* modernisation
infant mortality, 106–8, 110, 112–14,
    117–18
infant rearing, 106, 111–13, 115, 120
Institute of Community Studies, 74
interactionism, 131, 133, 149, 156, 160

job search, 6, 59, 63, 65–6, 195,
    197–200, 201
joking relationships, 61–2

kinship, 26, 55, 57–60, 62, 63, 65–7, 69, 157–8, 166–7

labour market, access to, 11–12, 58, 171, 177–8, 183, 185, 194, 195–9
leisure, 44, 186
life course, compared with life cycle, 2–4, 12, 13, 21–28, 33, 42, 49, 53, 155, 162–4, 166, 168
life cycle
  as everyday construct, 5–6, 8–9, 12, 54–5, 57, 59–60, 62–3, 86
  as ideology, 5–6, 8, 9, 13, 63
  as metaphor, 53, 126–37 (*see also* pilgrimage, life cycle as)
  as normative sequence, 2, 3, 11, 13, 18, 24–5, 33, 36–42, 49–50, 54–5, 84, 144, 150, 152, 154, 162, 163, 192–3
  definitions, 2, 30
life cycle stages, classifications of, 4, 9, 11, 30–5, 38–9, 54, 130, 142, 172, 174–6
  criticisms of, 35–50, 86, 126, 142–3, 145, 153–4, 162

management–worker relations, 61–2, 63
marital breakdown, 13, 36–9, 44–7, 49–50, 76–8, 81–2, 85, 210, 216–19, 225, 226
Marxian analysis, 124–6
medical knowledge, 103–5, 109, 117, 118–19, 120–1, 131
methodological issues, 21, 28, 30, 32–3, 40–50, 53, 55–6, 63–4, 73, 78–9, 80, 81, 132, 153, 176, 185, 212
modernisation, 17, 64–6, 69, 127, 134
mortgage arrears, 12–13, 208, 212–26

National Child Development Study (NCDS), 44–5, 216
negotiated commitments, 155, 158–68
normative rules, 155, 157–8, 159–68

Office of Population Censuses and Surveys (OPCS), 43–4

old age, 7–8, 23–5, 88–102, 141, 143, 146–7, 148, 150, 151, 152, 154, 156, 167, 175–6, 178, 182, 183, 188, 189–90

parenthood, 81–3, 203
personal savings, 151, 152–3, 181, 208, 210–11
personal time and historical time, 2–4, 11, 12, 19, 21–8, 35, 162–4
  see also physical location and historical time
physical location and historical time, 19–21, 25, 26
pilgrimage, life cycle as, 9, 123, 132–7
power relations, 160–1
professional practitioners, 106, 109, 111, 115, 116, 120, 123

recession, 1, 8, 12, 59, 68, 85, 102, 193, 194, 195, 205
recruitment strategies, 6, 59–60, 63, 66, 68
resources, distribution of, 10, 11, 13, 40, 54, 55, 76, 143, 151, 184
resources, transfer of, 10, 13, 54, 55, 141, 143, 144–50, 152, 167–8
responsibility, concept of, 155
retirement, 54, 80, 89–102, 150, 151, 179–80, 182, 200
return to work, married women, 68

sexual behaviour, 46, 54, 61, 81
sickness, *see* health
single-parent families, 37–8, 44, 85, 148, 172, 176, 179, 180, 183, 185, 188, 189–90
social class, *see* social stratification
social constructivism, 103–5, 120–1, 160, 161
social stratification, 11, 13, 85, 100, 102, 143, 146, 148, 170–90, 226
stigma, 89, 99, 100–101, 213–4, 225
symmetrical marital partnership, 74, 76–82, 85

trade unions, 61, 67
trajectories, 9, 20, 24, 26–7, 43–5, 123, 128–31, 133